MW00973645

MORE PRAISE FOR JOYCE MARCEL'S COLUMNS...

"Joyce Marcel's musings are miraculous at capturing the intimacy, foibles and challenges in the often-overlooked moments of our daily lives. She'll take your breath away in recounting the magic and mystery of mother-daughter relationships. She relishes womanhood's hard-fought battles for equality and the lingering issues of inequality. She knows what it takes to live a full life and she gladly shares that with us. You'll recognize your own struggles and triumphs in these columns and more likely than not, you'll be recalling her words long after you've finished reading."

Sabina Haskell, editor of the *Brattleboro Reformer*

"Joyce Marcel's work has enlightened our pages for eight years now, and I have to consider her the very best writer among the 350 or so who have contributed to *The American Reporter*. Her work achieves a grace and simplicity that is elegant, warm, compassionate and highly readable. A lot of writers on the Left could learn by reading her; it is writing that is never tendentious, repetitive or anything but easy, graceful and free, and yet it packs a powerful, powerful punch. Like a fine wild mare racing across the Great Plains, hers is a voice that is quintessentially American, and also one that is vanishing in the welter of ugly and meaningless corporate prose that now dominates so much of the press."

Joe Shea, the founder and editor of *The American Reporter*
the Internet's first and oldest original daily newspaper
(american-reporter.com)

A Thousand Words or Less

Favorite Columns 1996 - 2005

by Joyce Marcel

The Owl Publishing Project

AUTHOR: Joyce Marcel

COVER DESIGN: Jessica Butterfield

COVER PHOTO: Randolph T. Holhut

LAYOUT: H. Donald Kroitzsh

Published by:
The Owl Publishing Project
443 Spaulding Hill Road
East Dummerston, Vermont 05346

Telephone: (802) 254-4784

Prepared by:
Five Corners Press
Plymouth, Vermont 05056

Printed and bound in the United States of America

A Thousand Words or Less — Favorite Columns 1996 - 2005

ISBN-10: 0-9778062-0-0   us$14.⁹⁵
ISBN-13: 978-0-9778062-0-1

ACKNOWLEDGMENTS

First I want to thank the members of the Academy... Oh sorry, wrong speech.

First and foremost, I want to thank my husband, Randy Holhut, who has always been my first reader, first editor, idea-generator, researcher and systems manager. Without his love, support and patience, this project would not be possible.

I want to thank Lynn Barrett for being an invaluable provider of marketing and moral support, Phyllis Isaacson for being the queen of the red pencil, Sharon Myers for her culinary expertise and emotional support, and all three women for the warmth of their friendship.

I want to thank Don Kroitzsh of Five Corners Press for gracefully designing this beautiful book and demystifying self-publishing.

I want to thank Jessica Butterfield for designing the cover.

I want to thank my family and friends for letting me write about them. I especially want to thank my mother, Rose Kagan, and the members of the Lauderdale West Theater Club in Florida for making me feel so welcome at their rehearsals and shows. I'll always be their biggest fan.

I want to thank all my editors, past and present. In particular, I'd like to thank Norman Runnion for allowing me to be a columnist, Eric Ebeling for lifting my column out of the entertainment ghetto and putting it on the editorial page, Sabina Haskell for being so supportive, Joe Shea for publishing me on-line and for keeping The American Reporter going for so long at such a sacrifice, and the people at CommonDreams.Org for giving me access to such an enlightened and responsive readership.

And I want to thank the people of Windham County for putting up with me for all these years.

Thank you all.

DEDICATION

To My Mother and Randy, of course.

Foreword

A Thousand Words Or Less

First of all, about the title.

When I first started writing newspaper columns in 1989, the accepted limit was 1,000 words. Since then, it's been shrunk to about 700 on the assumption that readers, due to television, have shorter attention spans. For the most part, I have tried to ignore that limitation because a) if I am responsible for providing you with a good read, it might occasionally demand more than 700 words, and b) I have faith in your intelligence.

Over the years, however, I seem to have internalized the limitation.

This column has had several incarnations. It started in the Brattleboro (Vt.) Reformer as a music column that couldn't keep its hands off political and social issues.

Then it became "Culture Shock" and led the entertainment section of the much larger Springfield (Mass.) Sunday Republican. (At one point, my smiling face was advertised on every newsbox in Western Massachusetts.) After about a year, though, the editors pulled the column because I was, in their words, "too opinionated."

The column then migrated to the Internet, where it eventually found a home at The American Reporter (american-reporter.com), the first and now the oldest original-content daily newspaper on the Web. It still appears there every Thursday.

My exile in the entertainment pages ended in 2000, when I made it onto the Op-Ed pages of Thursday's Reformer. Since then, I have also been honored now and then to be a contributor to Common Dreams (commondreams.org), one of the best and most popular progressive news and commentary sites on the Web. Through the vast reach of the Internet, my column has also popped up in print in publications as diverse as The Progressive Populist and The Arab News.

The Reformer, however, a feisty daily in a feisty town, has always been my true home.

It was there, while I was working as a metro reporter, that I met Randolph T. Holhut. Back then, Randy (he claims the "T" stands for "The") was the new sports guy. We became roommates on Sept. 1, 1990, became lovers six months later, bought our house in Dummerston in 1994, and got married on the deck there on Sept. 1, 1999.

Randy is a widely-respected political columnist on the Web. He's the editor of "The George Seldes Reader." He is currently one of the Reformer's night editors, and writes the paper's editorials. He won best-in-show for editorial writing from the Vermont Press Association in 2005. Even though he has imposed a gag order on me about writing about him — it's always dangerous to live with a writer — he often appears in my columns.

My mother, Rose Kagan, has become a chapter by herself. When she visits, people tell her that she's famous in Brattleboro. If you read the columns, you'll see why.

Apart from the column, I have been supporting myself as a journalist for 17 years. By the time I left full-time work at the Reformer, in 1994, I was already a music critic for the Union-News and had started contributing stories to Vermont Business Magazine — I won the American Association of Business Publications Gold Award for Best Reporter in 2000.

After I became a full-time freelancer, I also started contributing to The Boston Globe, and, ultimately, the Globe's Sunday Magazine. For a while, I was also writing travel stories that appeared in many of the larger newspapers on the East Coast. I also taught travel writing in the adult education program at the University of Massachusetts.

Things were going well until 2000, when The New York Times (which owns the Globe) ordered all freelancers to sign a contract giving away their copyrights on-line, in print and "throughout the universe," as many contracts, including the one from the Union-News, put it. Print had discovered the Web, and the Globe wanted to sell stories to its readers on-line and to other on-line data bases — without sharing the profit. Most other newspapers and magazines issued these kinds of contracts, too. They were — and still are — a violation of the 1976 U.S. Copyright Act. Writers groups — I was a member of two — went to court to protect their rights. Even though we won at the U.S. Supreme Court level (Tasini v. New York Times), we still lost if we didn't sign the contracts.

I was just ornery enough to be offended at being pushed around by The New York Times. I refused to sign. Overnight, I lost my two biggest clients, the Springfield Newspapers and The Boston Globe, and with them 80 percent of my yearly income.

I'm still glad I didn't sign.

So I scaled down my life and started again from scratch. I now write for Vermont Business Magazine and several other Vermont publications, but my real focus has turned out to be these columns. Into them I pour my heart, my soul, the best of my writing skills, and, at the very least, whatever is happening to me each week when I sit down at the computer.

Over the years, I have been moved when someone tells me they like a particular column. The pieces I write about my mother — who is still dancing at 88 — are the ones that people remember best. Others remember pieces about President George W. Bush and the Afghanistan and Iraq wars.

I have divided this book into sections: Columns about myself; about my family; about the gospel cross-cultural exchange between Brattleboro, the central market town in my area and an endless source of interesting stories, and Newark, N.J.; Brattleboro and Dummerston, my home town; politics and wars; September 11; and obituaries. The last is the unfortunate result of writing for so long — mourning in print the passing of too many close friends, family members and cultural icons.

In putting together this book, I have tweaked and edited a few of the pieces, but nothing critical has been changed.

It's been a honor to find, through these columns, a voice and an audience.

And look, even this foreword is just over 1,000 words!

A Thousand Words or Less

INTRODUCTION

READERS BITE: I HAD NO IDEA

People who like my work send me notecards, letters and emails. Sometimes they call. People who hate my work write to the Brattleboro Reformer, which prints their letters. This means I am frequently slagged in print, but hardly ever praised.

Since I started appearing on-line, however, my in-box has been flooded with mail, both pro and con.

That's the way it goes when you write a column.

When I started, I wanted to tell people about the great blues music I was finding in Brattleboro.

I had no idea what I was getting into.

Over the years, I've been accused — in print — of many things. Being "filled with malice." "Helping perpetuate the denial of sex abuse." I've been called a "sensationalist" and "a total and complete jerk." One woman delicately said my writing style "is prosaic at best, and you often appear to miss the point altogether... There must be a paucity of competitors indeed for you to maintain such a delicate position with such indelicacy."

Another one said, "Marcel's almost mystical lack of logic or consistency makes her writing so weirdly compelling."

Sometimes you can't win for losing. There was the time I spent an enchanted evening hanging out with Willie Nelson in his tour bus. I wrote ecstatically about it, including something about the fumes of his excellent marijuana. The next day the Reformer printed: "Ms. Marcel was clearly thrilled to be in King Willie's Court, but I doubt that his tour bus got 50 miles down the interstate the moment Sgt. Drago read the opening lines of her review... I know some neighborhoods where a person thus fingered for a bust would send around a couple of friends later to rearrange the relative proportions of the fink's mouth and brains."

Many readers' complaints have enlightened me. A long time ago, for example, I wrote that all the young girls wanted to sleep with the

Beatles. A woman wrote to say that it might be true for heterosexual young girls, but it wasn't true for all of them. Point well taken.

I'll be the first to admit that when I started writing a column for the Brattleboro Reformer, I was long on opinions and short on craft. Looking back on it now, I can almost agree with the woman who wrote to the Reformer, "Ms. Marcel's provincialism lowers our standards...It's hard to imagine how a person can routinely make pronouncements on subjects she doesn't seem to know anything about."

I was also a little dense about the relationship that writers have with readers, especially in a small town. This was brought home early, after my second music column trashed the bubble-gum pop music played on our local radio stations. The paper received many positive remarks about my comments, and I was still pleased with myself when I went to cover a selectman's meeting and found myself sitting between the owner of one station and the lead reporter of the other. They teased me unmercifully all night long. We ended up being good friends, but it was a strong reminder of something I later found out had a name: the Afghanistan principle. It says that the further you are from something, the more freedom you have to write about it. Attack a selectman and you can count on meeting her in the supermarket the next day. Write about Afghanistan and no one there will know or care.

I think the editor of the Reformer when I started, the great Norman Runnion, enjoyed the fact that I could cause a ruckus. In 1991 I was at the center of a controversy over whether I had my head up my ass in a postmodern or pre-postmodern way. (In 1991, by the way, I couldn't use the word "ass." I wrote that someone "played his ass off" and got a snippy note from the editor who took over when Runnion left.)

Back to the controversy. One man called my work "a preventable disaster," and said, in an analytical way, that I was "misreading the culture." Another, knowledgeable about arts criticism, pointed out that I was "ideological" and "cheap." A third, Richard Ewald, defending me (I think), said, "When Joyce sits down to write her column, she steps on board the critic's craft, unties from the dock, unfurls every sail, grabs the wheel and sets off. She hasn't checked the wind, the charts or the forecast. Wheee! Is it any wonder she winds up so often on the rocks?" He said that instead of preventable disasters, my columns were "a relief, sometimes comic or tragic, from the resolutely dull voyages in the rest of the paper."

These exchanges had an unexpected effect. Suddenly, everyone in Windham County knew my name. Readers apparently love to see someone trashed, the fiercer the better. Everywhere I went people said, "Oh, so you're the one everyone hates." It made me famous in Windham County.

All that happened before I jumped from the entertainment pages to the Op-Ed section of the paper. Since then, I've been slammed for my "leftist" viewpoints from the right and my "insufficently leftist" viewpoints from the left.

One man wrote to ask me if my name should really be spelled "Marxel." Another said, "If everyone in Vermont is as without a clue as you are, then we should throw Vermont out of the country. You don't deserve to be in this great nation. America has its problems (mostly ignorant people like you) but it is certainly better that any other nation I can think of. Maybe you need to go live in a communist or Muslim country for awhile... I wonder how you will feel after the terrorists hit us again. They may even manage to kill you or your loved ones. If that happens, I really don't want to hear you or any other idiot complain!"

This last letter points up something about my hate mail that bewilders me. Many angry people have offered to buy me one-way tickets out of America, but their chosen destination is always someplace like North Korea or Saudi Arabia or Iran. How about a ticket to France, Spain or anywhere in southern Italy, folks?

There's a bottom line to all this — the amazing amount of support I receive for this work. Talking about it would be immodest and embarrassing, but know that I am extremely grateful.

For a writer, having readers is a gift. Having readers who respond? Well, that's an honor, and I want to thank you all.

Wheeee!

A Thousand Words or Less

CONTENTS

A Thousand Words or Less

ONE:
SOME COLUMNS FROM MY LIFE

January 4, 1996

ONE LEGACY OF A GOOD TEACHER: DONALD MCKAYLE

The music starts and seven men, torsos naked, long, pale, tights-clad legs, come on stage holding hands. They are silhouetted by the light. They are matched in height and musculature and the curves of their closely-shaved skulls match the curves of the muscles in their forearms, torsos and legs. They are a chain gang, a taut, powerful and imposing line of men writhing in pain. As they move downstage into the light, a man's voice sings an old folk song. "Well it's ear-ly in the morning, huh, when I rise, wellah..."

It's a cliché that a good teacher can have a lifelong effect on a child. This is the story of a very good teacher and how I came — very late — to an understanding of how profound his effect had been.

I was about seven years old and as gawky and geeky as a girl-child can be when my mother started taking me into the city on Saturday mornings for dance lessons at a professional dance school called the New Dance Group. She was a dancer and a student there, too, and she loved it so much that she wanted me to have dance in my life.

Donald McKayle, a soft-spoken African-American man who wore large round glasses, was my teacher. I remember the floor work, the barres, bounces, pointed and flexed feet, brushes, leg lifts and stumbles across the floor, but I have stronger memories of his quiet voice and his great gentleness. He made me feel safe.

"He used to tell such beautiful stories in the children's class," my mother remembered. "They weren't dance, but motion stories. There was one about a woman combing her long hair. The children did it in pantomime. I was enchanted by his stories."

At first, after the classes, Mom and I would have lunch at Reuben's Delicatessen, where the Reuben sandwich was invented. Then my mother decided it was cheaper to have picnics in Central Park. The day usually

I

ended with a trip to F.A.O. Schwartz, so I could lust after the six-foot stuffed lions. Then back home to Brooklyn on the subway.

In 1959, McKayle's ballet, "Rainbow 'Round My Shoulder," premiered, and I was in the audience. *"Well it's early in the morning, huh, when I rise, wellah..."*

The men move downstage into the light and work at breaking rocks, while unseen guards whip their bodies. "Got a rainbow, rainbow 'round my shoulder..."

They curl up to sleep, and they dream. A slender woman comes out to dance with them. She is all the women they have known, the stern mother, the flirtatious girlfriend — "Oh, I'm goin' downtown, gonna get me a jug of brandy, gonna give it all to Nancy, keep her good and drunk and goosey all the time, time, time, time, keep her good and drunk and goosey all the time," the loving wife — "I have a woman, long and tall, and she moves her body like a cannonball...,"

The woman disappears, one dreamer cries out, the whips snap, something in the men snaps — "Take this hammer, carry it to the captain, tell him I'm gone, boy, tell him I'm gone." Two of the men try to escape. They are shot. They die. They are carried off the stage — "Another man done gone, they killed another man..."

When the dance ended, back then in 1959, I was left with sheer beauty and the searing rage of injustice. I was left with something else, too, but I didn't know it then.

I never became a dancer, although my mother, now close to 80, is still choreographing and leading a dance troupe. Instead, I write about music, especially world-beat music, folk, blues and jazz. If you had asked me, last month, about my earliest influences, the deepest songs in me, I would have sung the ones I've quoted from the ballet. They were the songs I sang to keep the loneliness away when I was on the road, the ones that led me to the Weavers and later to Bob Dylan, the ones that brought me to the doorstep of the blues and dumped me there forever.

But a month ago, I wouldn't have known why I chose those songs.

Then I read that the glorious Alvin Ailey Dance company was reviving "Rainbow 'Round My Shoulder." I took the train from Vermont into the city and bought myself a ticket. There was a huge snowstorm that night, so I didn't plan a picnic in the park. From the first notes and the first steps, I was again overwhelmed by the strength and beauty of the men, the suppleness of the woman, the strong emotions of the dance. I watched with my mouth open and my heart inside it. And I was astonished by the score. All the folk songs I have loved all my life, they came from this one dance! Collected by John and Alan Lomax, arranged by Rober de Cormier and Milton Okun, they were the soundtrack to my life. And I never knew it. Now I did.

McKayle was there to take a bow. His hair was a little grayer, but he still had those big glasses and that aura of gentleness. He has won many awards since those long-ago days when he taught awkward children on Saturdays to support his art. He has choreographed more than 50 ballets for companies around the world. He received five Tony nominations for his work on Broadway. In 1994, he won the American Dance Guild's Award for Outstanding Lifetime Achievement. He is a professor of dance in California.

I was so moved that I went back the next afternoon and saw the dance again at a matinee. Strong stuff, especially today, when some southern states are reviving the chain gang the way the Ailey company revived the dance.

You never know what will make an impression on a child. A good teacher can set a child's life on a course without that child ever knowing later why that course was taken. For me, that teacher was Donald McKayle.

(In 1991, The New York Times wrote a long story about Donald McKayle and his work. Although I didn't understand then how much his musical choices had influenced me, I wrote to tell him how important the classes had been, and that while I was no longer dancing, my mother still was. He wrote back in 1992: "It was marvelous to hear from you and to know that those classes on Saturday mornings at the New Dance Group meant so much to one little girl. I do remember them fondly...continued happiness to you and to your mother. She sounds great.")

September 6, 2001

THE STORY OF AXEL MUNTHE

How modern we believe our society to be! How advanced! How progressive in thought and deed! But as an antidote to such undeserved pride, I would like to recommend an encounter with a Swedish doctor who died in 1949 at the age of 92.

Axel Munthe was perhaps the first doctor to propose using pets to provide companionship for lonely people. He treated the poor for free and collected dolls for their children. He chastised the Pope in an effort to keep songbirds out of stew pots. He recognized the value of preserving the antiquities of Greece and Rome at a time when they were considered rubbish. He was an anti-war activist and a great humanitarian.

He was also a great writer. In 1929, at the suggestion of his friend Henry James, he published a best-selling book about his life. The book has been translated into 40 languages, including eight editions in Braille, and has never gone out of print. You can get "The Story of San Michele" today in paperback from Flamingo, an imprint of HarperCollins. It is not only witty and beautifully written, but so far ahead of its time that it humbles me.

I hadn't heard of Munthe until I visited the flower-filled and celebrity-drenched Italian island of Capri last year. There I came across lovely San Michele, the home he built on top of a mountain with his own two hands.

Now I keep his book by my bedside, dipping into it frequently. His warmth, intelligence, passion and, especially, his successes, are the perfect antidotes for the dismal culture we live in today.

In 1880, at the age of 23, Munthe was the youngest doctor of medicine to ever graduate from the Sorbonne. As a fashionable young doctor in Paris, way ahead of his time, he was gifted in using psychology to reinforce the limits of his era's pharmacology.

He was a passionate animal lover, yet he defended the use of animals for medical experiments in the face of virulent anti-vivisectionists who could have come straight from PETA.

"Pasteur's vaccination against rabies has reduced the mortality in this terrible disease to a minimum, and Behring's anti-diphtheric serum saves the lives of over a hundred thousand children every year," he wrote.

"Are not these two facts alone sufficient to make these well-meaning lovers of animals understand that (scientists) must be left to pursue their researches unhampered by restrictions and undisturbed by interference from outsiders."

His argument is even stronger today in the light of the political and religious hysteria surrounding (and hampering) stem cell research.

But Munthe went further. He suggested that animal lovers direct their protest against circuses and zoos instead, and that medical experiments might well be conducted on the living bodies of "born criminals and evil-doers," who could be given a choice of the gallows or submitting (under anesthesia) to substituting for "the wretched monkeys." Not even PETA went this far.

Sadly, from a feminist's perspective, I can find only fault with Munthe. He regarded most women as "neurotics." However, his practice was full of wealthy women who were not allowed the freedom to live and work outside the home. That gave them nothing to do except to try to account for their quite normal feelings of malaise with imaginary nervous illnesses.

"But it is not easy to be patient with hysterical women, and as to being kind to them, one had better think it over twice," Munthe wrote. "They remain what they are, a bewildering complex of mental and physical disorders, a plague to themselves and to their families, a curse to their doctors."

Today I believe that Munthe, who married twice, would revise his opinion of women — now that they are allowed to have jobs, lives, purposes and even opinion columns of their own.

My favorite story about Munthe involves the heroic measures he engaged in to save the songbirds that migrate to Capri each spring.

"It was a joy to my ear to hear them sing in the gardens of San Michele," he wrote. "They came in thousands: wood pigeons, thrushes, turtledoves, waders, quails, golden orioles, skylarks, nightingales, wagtails, chaffinches, swallows, warblers, redbreasts and many other tiny artists on their way to give spring concerts to the silent forests and fields in the North."

To Munthe's horror, the islanders thought of the birds as a lucrative cash crop; just hours after they arrived, they were already being netted and shipped to Marseilles "to be eaten with delight in the smart restaurants of Paris," Munthe wrote bitterly.

In fury, he went to war with Capri's primary bird butcher, who owned Mount Barbarossa, the mountain behind San Michele. It was a battle full of turmoil — it included pleas for government intervention, lawsuits, fines, and even a poisoned dog (Munthe's). In desperation, Munthe made a visit to the Holy Father, who, unfortunately had spent the very morning happily watching the netting of over 200 birds in the Vatican gardens.

Then the bird butcher fell ill. Munthe was called.

"Only on one condition would I come," he wrote, "that the man would swear on the crucifix that if he pulled through he would ... sell me the mountain at his exorbitant price..."

At first the man refused, but he capitulated after he received the Last Sacraments.

"I tapped a pint of pus from his left pleura, to the consternation of the village doctor and to the glory of the village saint, for, contrary to my expectations, the man recovered," Munthe wrote. "Miracolo! Miracolo!"

Thanks to Munthe, Mount Barbarossa is now and forever a bird sanctuary. "Thousands of tired birds of passage are resting on its slopes every spring and autumn, safe from man and beast," he wrote. "The dogs of San Michele are forbidden to bark while the birds are resting on the mountain. The cats are never let out of the kitchen except with a little alarm-bell tied around their necks."

"The Story of San Michele" is packed with vivid stories like this, including Munthe's horrifying description of the 1884 cholera epidemic in Naples. But its focus is the life and people of the town of Anacapri, his creation of San Michele, and his excavations of the Greek, Roman and Egyptian antiquities that fill it.

Munthe, blind, left Capri in 1943 for Stockholm, where he lived in the palace as the guest of the royal family. He died there in 1949.

After his book was published, tourists began visiting San Michele, and in 1948 he gave it, complete with his furnishings and personal effects, to the Swedish government. Part of the property now serves as the Swedish consulate, but his rooms and gardens are open to the public.

Reading "The Story of San Michele" makes me think of an old nursery rhyme: you put in your thumb and you pull out a plum — every single time.

January 31, 2002

CONSIDERING THE ALTERNATIVE

I've heard that when you reach middle age, you look into the mirror and see your mom or dad looking back at you. Well, what does it mean when you look in the mirror and see your grandmother? It means you're turning 60, turning the big 6-0, turning one of the last pages in the book of your life that you always thought would have been made into a movie by now.

Today that happened to me.

I was born in Brooklyn in 1942, so I was too young to understand about war, but just old enough to feel the full anguish and vulnerability of the Jewish community three years later when first the Holocaust stories, and then the film footage, and then the European refugees, arrived.

It's an odd year to be born, 1942, a cusp year. For example, I'm just a bit too old to be a Baby Boomer. And I spent my formative years without television, which came to our neighborhood when I was seven. Instead, I grew up on books, folk music and — because I was born to a theatrical mother — Broadway musicals; I could sing the entire score of "Carousel" by the time I was five. So television is something I can approach critically — it has not "always been there."

Being born in 1942 put me on the cusp of two radically different lifestyles when I became a teenager. Would my nature lead me to live a life modeled on the conformist 1950s, which were then winding down, or would I rebel against them? Which was it going to be, Joyce? Elvis or Pat Boone? Hip or square?

People like me became the original hippies, the ones who took the point in the liberation wars of the Sixties. And I've noticed that many of us — to our great financial disadvantage — have never let go of our idealism. It was our younger brothers and sisters, born after the war, the true Boomers, who morphed into the consumer-oriented yuppies — probably because television reached them earlier. Bill Clinton is not of my generation, thank you very much.

The models in my mind for being 60 are, naturally, my two grandmothers. Although I loved both of them very much, by 60 their lives were pretty much done. Not that they were dead — one lived to be 94 and the other to 89 — but they had followed traditional paths — caring for their aging parents, marrying, raising children. Then life

7

moved beyond them, but they lived on, watching television, talking to friends, burying husbands, babysitting for their grandchildren, killing time.

That may be the image of 60 that lingers in my head, but it's certainly not the truth about women's lives now. I feel like I'm just getting started. I feel like I'm entering my prime. A lot of the doubts and fears that tormented me when I was younger are gone. I know exactly who I am, what I do well, and what I can't do at all. I know that it doesn't matter how I look, it only matters that I'm here. I feel powerful. I'm raring to go.

But don't tell that to my body. Sixty also means that I'm wearing down — the famous "indignities of age" have arrived in force, and some of them make me furious. I take pills to keep my bones from shrinking and becoming brittle; in fact, I take pills for a lot of things. I have aches and pains, bags and sags, lines and bulges.

And then there's that mustache.

I still hike up and down mountains, but I also take naps. Twenty years ago, to face down turning 40, I started running. I was living in Panama then, and I ran two marathons in one year and set a mid-distance triathlon record for women my age. I stopped when I moved back to the States, defeated by the hills of Vermont. Three weeks ago, to face down turning 60, I started running again. I found that I couldn't read the dial on my sports watch without my glasses.

Turning 60 means that I'm coming closer to the end of my life. But when that thought gets me down, I just look at my mother.

I was visiting her in Florida a few weeks ago, where she's putting on a show. One day, she taught a line dance class in the morning, followed by a stretch class — doing all the exercises along with her students, naturally — and then she ran a two-hour dance rehearsal. Then she went home, started marinating a leg of lamb, and rested. At night she returned to the theater for a three-hour rehearsal in which she directed 40 people.

Mother admits to being 84. When I told her that I was planning to turn 60 by confronting it openly, partly by writing this column, she was horrified.

"Why would you ever tell people that you're turning 60?"

"Because it's a hard number to face. Didn't you have a hard time with it?"

"I had a hard time turning 30," she said. "But don't worry. You'll always be my baby."

A big part of turning 60 is letting go of dreams. I'm never going to win the Nobel Prize for Literature. I'm probably never going to get that call from the editors of The New Yorker. And those secret MacArthur Grant "nominators" will be passing me by forever.

Another part of 60 is accepting loss. There are friends I've loved who are no longer in my life, and I still miss them. I have friends who are really sick, and I'm scared for them. I've already buried my grandparents, my father and my brother. I've also buried much of my unbridled optimism about human nature.

Personally, however, I realize that I've been blessed. I, who was once quite literally homeless, now have a great loving bear of a husband, a quirky but welcoming home of my own, interesting and loving friends, and support for my writing in my community.

When I was a young woman, Edna St. Vincent Millay inspired me with these lines: "My candle burns at both ends/It will not last the night/But ah my foes/And ah, my friends/It gives a lovely light."

I expected those lines to be the story of my life, but here I am today, 60 years old, and ruefully — as the old joke goes — considering the alternative. Maybe it's true that only the good die young.

~ ~ ~

June 6, 2002

If You Can Read This Without Glasses, You Probably Don't Need To

The lure was an invitation to join an outdoor adventure trip and kayak, canoe, and raft on three lovely Massachusetts rivers, with a little mountain climbing thrown in on the side. I bit like a trout.

I was so delighted that I forgot an essential point: I can no longer read without my glasses.

As everyone who gets to a "certain age" knows, eyesight is one of the first things to go.

It isn't too much of a problem at home. You have three choices: buy a cord or chain and wear reading glasses permanently around your neck, or keep them pushed up on top of your head where, after a while, they will break, or scatter them around the house like wildflower seeds in spring.

That's what I do. Since my ever-diminishing eyesight remains in the over-the-counter, inexpensive drugstore range, I keep a pair of glasses handy wherever I tend to read: there's always one in the bathroom, for example, and another by my armchair in the living room. There's one at my desk, and one in the kitchen so I can read recipes and the small print on labels. I stash one in a case in my pocketbook, and another in the glove compartment of my car.

These are simple survival techniques, like printing out directions in 18-point type so you can read them while you're driving. Or keeping a pair of glasses with your gardening tools, so you can read the little sticks that come in the plant flats. That way you know that calendula, which can be grown in sun or partial shade, will reach a height of between 24 and 30 inches if you remember to water it. (Memory is a subject for another column.)

But who knew you needed reading glasses to go white-water rafting? Where do you put them in a wet suit?

We were at Zoar Outdoor in Charlemont, Mass., on the lovely Deerfield River. The guides inspired confidence, and I'd trust them with my life. But still, to get on the river, I had to sign a waiver that said, in part, "I acknowledge that my participation in outdoor adventure-based activities such as river rafting... entails known and unanticipated risks which could result in physical or emotional injury, paralysis, death, or damage to myself, to property, or to third parties."

Having left my glasses in my pocketbook in the van, I couldn't read the waiver. Someone handed me what they said was a large-print copy, but the print wasn't large enough for me. Having someone read the whole thing out loud would have taken too much time. So I signed it blind and had a wonderful time.

But it made me start to notice:

- Picnicking in a beautiful meadow, I couldn't see if the little packets were butter or margarine.

- Climbing the Old Indian Trail on Wachusett Mountain, I managed to get myself lost. Even though I had a trail map stuffed in my back pocket, I couldn't read it. Finally, a ranger noticed I was gone and came after me.

- The sign on the spa wall at the Wachusett Village Inn said in large letters, "Do not enter the hot tub if the temperature is over 104 degrees." But I couldn't read the thermometer. The water, however, was just what my aching body needed after the Old Indian Trail.

- Searching the hotel's store for bottled water, I couldn't read the small print. Because the shape of the bottle looked familiar, I ended up buying something sweetened, flavored, foul and undrinkable.

- And of course, I had to fish out my glasses to read menus and figure out the television's remote controls.

Even though I was having trouble with life's small print, it didn't stop me from doing what I wanted to do. Remember Little Feat's "Old Folks Boogie": "So you know, you're over the hill when your mind makes a promise that your body can't fill." But that's just the young smirking at their elders. And, as many of us know, the young have quite a few limitations of their own.

Aging seems to be a matter of determination, resourcefulness, compensation and self-knowledge. Asking someone to read the small print when you haven't got your glasses. Knowing that sooner or later, the ranger will come. Going to the hot tub while the rest of the group, after climbing the mountain, goes off on a two-hour bicycle ride up and down every hill in Fitchburg, followed by rock climbing. And trusting that you're smart enough to get out of the hot tub if the water is too hot.

Aging has nothing to do with age. There are 78-year-old women who can ski me off a mountain. It's mostly a question of knowing what kind of shape you're in, and also of working to keep yourself in the kind of shape you need to be in to accomplish whatever it is that you want to accomplish.

Aging also seems to be about recognizing that life is a never-ending course of self-knowledge, and about comfortably accepting the limitations this self-knowledge brings.

I will never stop adventuring. But maybe, if life stops being a cabaret, old chum, it will become a hot tub before it becomes a grave. And that will be fine with me.

January 2, 2003

My Perfect Divorce

Many people get a new family through marriage; I got one through divorce.

Let me tell you about Jerry Marcel, who is just about the dearest, gentlest and most generous man I know. I met him in 1961, when we were both students at Brooklyn College. He was a talented scene designer, I was a less-talented costume designer, and both of us were obsessed with theater.

We became close. I taught him how to drive. I met his mother, who disliked me. I met his step-father and his young step-sister, Marilyn. When Marilyn was 15, we all met her new boyfriend, Barry mutton-chop-sideburns Hoffman.

Jerry's father, Paul Marcel, had divorced Jerry's mother a long time ago. He died young, and Jerry only had a few memories, a picture of them together, and the name.

After graduation Jerry was offered a prestigious scholarship to Stanford University's MFA theater program. He wouldn't let me come with him unless I married him, and frankly, I was terrified of starting a career on my own in New York. Marriage was what women did in those days, so we were married in 1965.

We moved to Palo Alto, Calif., a stone's throw away from San Francisco and the Haight. I was the adventurous one and propelled us into free speech, free love, demonstrations against Vietnam, the civil rights movement, drugs, and dancing all night at the Filmore.

After Stanford, we spent a year in Europe and Israel, where we met Paul Marcel's sister. She told us that in Poland the family name had been Slud (pronounced "sludt"). Paul had taken "Marcel" from the side panel of a bakery truck as he passed through Belgium on his way to America.

We were on a Greek island, I think, when Jerry got a telegram from Brooklyn College offering him a job. We spent the next three years in New York, working in Off-Off Broadway theater.

By then our marriage had been through a lot, but it couldn't survive a brutal miscarriage in the dark ages when women were told to move on with their lives and ignore the love and joy that was curdling up inside of them. And it couldn't survive "The Feminine Mystique."

It was my idea to separate for a year while I "found myself." Jerry, distraught, waited for me in London. But once there, it didn't take him long to find Tessa, whom we had met on our travels together. Soon she was pregnant and that was that. I left the States and went on the road; I signed my divorce papers in La Paz, Bolivia.

But I didn't change my name. Marcel was a made-up name, and I figured it could belong to me as well as to anyone else.

Jerry and Tessa eventually moved to Ohio with their two young daughters, Rima and Gerlan, and he gave up theater for a Masters in Social Work in order to support his family.

In 1987, I returned to the States, settled in Brattleboro, Vermont, and started writing. It was only then that I found a picture of Jerry and me in Morocco in 1969. I saw my younger self looking up at him with such love in my eyes that I burst into tears. Until that moment, I don't think I had ever understood how much I had loved him, or how precious was this thing, our marriage, that we had thrown away.

One thing I have learned in my travels is that if you play with love, it will soon be playing with you. As Dylan says, "It falls on strangers, travels free." It refuses to die when you demand it to, and it resurfaces when you push it underground. Jerry and I started talking again.

Years passed. Tessa died very suddenly and way too young. Jerry's mother died soon afterward. When I flew to Ohio to console him, we started talking and we couldn't stop. We talked day and night. We drove his daughters crazy with our reminiscences. We were reclaiming decades of lost personal history.

By then I was living with my great love, Randy, who didn't mind that my ex-husband was turning into one of my closest friends. Jerry visited us often, and on one trip I introduced him to Barbara, my neighbor and gardening guru. I'm not the mystical type, but I swear that when they shook hands for the first time, a light went on over their heads. Soon they were married, he took a job in Burlington and they moved north.

Last week Barbara called to remind me that Jerry was turning 60. Marilyn and Barry, now a successful lawyer, were coming up from Florida. Gerlan was flying in from fashion school in London and Rima was coming from New York. Would I come, too?

It was a wonderful party. Jerry and I are so comfortable together now that we seem to float effortlessly through time and space. I see Marilyn and Barry whenever I visit my mother in Florida. Jerry's daughters have turned into charming, open and loving young women; I delight in their company. Sometimes I wonder if they are the children Jerry and I would have had if we had stayed together.

And there we were, surrounded by love and laughter, when Jerry said, "Some people get a family by marriage, Joyce; you got this one from a divorce."

And so, my love, did you.

We live in a culture of instant gratification and, at best, serial monogamy. Couples sign prenuptial agreements and divide their possessions before they even approach the altar. Husbands and wives are as disposable as dust cloths. Families break like cheap glassware. Personal histories get lost in the wreckage.

I am grateful that somehow — and I don't know how — Jerry and I have managed to forgive each other for the pain and damage, to cherish the stories of our married past, and to build, along with his loving wife and my loving husband, a present and a future together.

~ ~ ~

April 10, 2003

THE WINTER OF MY DISCONTENT

I don't mind admitting that this winter has me whipped.

Looking out the window, more snow is falling. The limbs of the trees surrounding our house, the ground, and even the rocks in our picturesque waterfall are all freshly blanketed with white. It's a Christmas card out there, a winter wonderland. But damn it, it's April.

Yes, it's April, springtime, and there's at least a foot of new ice and snow surrounding our house. That gorgeous waterfall? It long ago overran the banks of the brook and ate my driveway.

From Halloween to Easter, this year has been a six-month horror of a winter, and there is no end yet in sight.

We actually had a thaw a little while ago. The four feet of old snow surrounding our house on the hill quickly melted. Daffodil shoots pushed their way up through the wet dark earth. Downtown, people were running around in shirt-sleeves buying seeds and gardening tools.

Our town's many frozen dirt roads melted and became mud soup. Driving down our hill became an amusement park ride — without the amusement. My car careened from right rut to left rut, bouncing so hard that I was never certain from one minute to the next whether I still had an undercarriage, and my tires spun and spitted and splattered flying mud

An anonymous poet in our town was so mad that she or he posted this poem on the side of the sinkhole that used to be Park Laughton Road: "This road is impassable/Not even jackassable If you care to travel/haul your own gravel."

The day after the poem was posted, I watched the town's gravel truck sink up to its doors in that very same hole. Then it tipped over like a sinking ship.

For all the hard work our highway department has put in, our roads remain rutted and bumpy. But now they are frozen again. The deceptive thaw was followed by an April ice storm which turned the soft ruts sharp as razors. The ice was followed by more snow.

But if you think I'm having a hard time, you probably shouldn't talk to the bear.

Yes, the other day we woke to find bear tracks in the fresh show. Our garbage cans had been popped open and garbage was strewn everywhere. There was bear poop next to the cars, and Randy found three huge tooth puncture marks in a discarded can of Pam.

For this we have no one to blame but ourselves. Our house is tucked deep into in the woods, where deer regularly eat our garden and fisher cats eat our pets.

But we had not encountered a bear until last fall, when we unexpectedly found a black bear eating the carcass of a pre-roasted supermarket chicken in our driveway.

As if we were born yesterday, Randy and I were so excited that we stood in the open doorway taking pictures. The next day one of them appeared on the front page of the local paper.

Then I called the game warden and got an earful. Instead of shooting a segment of Joyce and Randy's Wild Kingdom, he said, we should have been banging on pots and waving our hands in the air and yelling and scaring away the bear. We should have defended our turf. Now the bear thinks we're his bitches. He thinks he owns us.

This year it might be a different bear, of course. But if you slept all winter, woke up hungry, went out looking for the first green shoots of spring and got hit by an ice storm, wouldn't you be pissed off? Wouldn't you hit up the easiest garbage can you know?

Worst of all, the bear's tracks lead up the stairs to our deck. There's only a sliding glass door between the deck and the living room, and there's nothing between the living room and the bedroom but a door that our cat can open. Now I'm sleeping with a pot, a metal spoon and my sneakers.

Yes, this is definitely the winter of my discontent, except that it is supposed to be spring.

This winter has not only been impassable but totally jackassable. I'm way past Seasonal Affectedness Disorder and a month deep into cabin fever. We need to get some sunlight, warmth and a few flowers up here soon, because I don't know how much longer I can hold on. And if you want to travel, bring your own gravel.

(After this piece appeared in the Reformer, a neighbor told me that the poem had been written in the 1950s under similar mud soup road conditions. I'll always be grateful to the poet who added the valuable new word "jackassable" to my vocabulary.)

∼ ∼ ∼

June 19, 2003

THE GREAT CHURCH OF THE WORLD

At this time of year, the birds at my house stage one opera early every morning and another one just before nightfall. Among the arias they sing is one of such clarity that every time I hear it, I envision a clean round stone dropping into a deep crystal pool, and in my mind I can see the rings widening in the water. Another three-note song ends in a minor key so soulful that it tugs at my heart.

Out of curiosity, then, I recently took the opportunity to do a little bird watching and maybe translate some of the libretto that wakes me up too early every morning in June. As soon as I learned a few things, though, I felt as though someone had handed me the key to another of God's mysterious kingdoms.

In the woods I mentioned my sense of magic to an experienced bird-watcher who understood exactly what I was talking about. "This is my church," he said with some passion, and then, thinking of how badly our environment is being damaged, he added, "and they're pissing in the pews."

A recent Nature Conservancy Magazine survey wanted to know, "How does your faith inform your conservation ethic?"

For me, the answer is that nature is as close to religion as I will ever get. I can't worship a male god in a beard and flowing robe, and I can't believe in any religion that spurs men on to kill other men or to repress women in its name. But I can believe in a Creator — a being or a force which is above mundane things like gender — The Greatest Artist of Them All.

The greatest human artist who ever lived, for example. could not have invented, say, the iris, the peony and the trillium. One of them maybe, or maybe two, but not all three, plus the complexities of the pink and purple columbines that are currently growing in my garden. No, it took a Creator God, an Artist God, to invent all the wildflowers and the perennials and the plants and the trees and the weeds. Marveling at their beauty and infinite variety, I am easily uplifted and feel I am in the presence of a Higher Power.

It is not only in the woods and gardens that I find this Creator.

I crewed on a yacht in the Abaco Islands once, when we ran into a school of whales. For about an hour we sailed beside them, watching them slip and dip and slide gracefully through the water. It was both heart-stoppingly beautiful and another of the earth's great mysteries. Now I keep a picture of a newborn gray whale breaching the waters of San Ignacio Lagoon — the "last untouched whale nursery in North America," according to the Natural Resources Defense Council — perched on my computer to remind me that there are larger creatures than human beings on this planet, and a little humility and reverence is in order.

I feel the same way about polar bears. I have a ficus tree next to my desk that I hang with polar bear pictures. These huge white creatures snuggling their babies or curled up in sleep or stretching out to get some sun fill me with awe.

People who do not revere the Creation, people who pollute and strip-mine our world for sport and profit — in my view they are committing sacrilege.

So whenever I have a little cash to spare, I give it to conservation groups to stop the clear-cutting of old growth forests, the drilling for oil in pristine Alaskan reserves, the strip-malling of America, and the pollution of our air, land, rivers, streams and oceans. It is why I love farms and forests and house plants and Vermont and our environmental planning law, Act 250. I want to protect what few lovely mysteries we have left.

I can only ask why our culture, instead of inspiring us to worship the natural wonders of our Creator's imagination, seems bent on destroying The Creation as fast as it can. For what? For money? For power? Is there a better way to describe it than "pissing in the pews?"

During my little foray into bird watching, by the way, I learned that the mournful minor-key song I love so much is that of a male chickadee marking out its territory, and the call that sounds like the sound of a stone dropping into a crystal pool comes from a wood thrush.

I've only scratched the surface of bird operas, but I know I'm not alone in believing they keep me in touch with the Creator as well as the best part of myself.

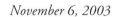

November 6, 2003

EULOGY FOR A LOVELY CAT

For five years, this was my small family: a happy husband, a happy wife, a happy little black and white and orange cat.

In the mornings, when Randy brought in my tea, little Dancer would jump up next to him and purr.

"We have a quorum," Randy would say.

But I'll never again see Dancer's little black, white and orange face at the back door, waiting to be let in. Or see her little black, white and orange rump facing the back door, waiting to be let out. Or, five minutes later, see her little black, white and orange face at the back door, waiting to be let in again.

If she was outside and I ignored her, she would jump onto the recycling boxes and bounce until they knocked against the door.

Randy was more susceptible to her knocking than I was. "My role is to make you and Dancer happy," he often said.

Randy was the one who rescued Dancer from what he calls "kitty jail," otherwise known as the Windham County Humane Society. She had a milky right eye, and other people were passing her by.

The Humane Society told us that she was left by an older woman who named her Precious. And she was precious, a well-petted, smart, loving and demanding cat that adored people's laps and managed to slide under their hands no matter what those hands were doing — talking on the phone, eating, typing, reading a newspaper.

Precious was too precious a name for us, so we called her Dancer, short for Lap Dancer, after a quote from Andrew Vachss.

"Cats are the lap-dancers of the animal world," he said. "'Soon as you stop shelling out, they move on, find another lap. They're furry little sociopaths. Pretty and slick — in love with themselves. When's the last time you saw a seeing-eye cat?"

But even though the name was apt, Vachss was wrong. Cats aren't sociopaths. They don't deserve their reputation for aloofness. They are intelligent. They are affectionate. They are creative. They are covered in a soft fur like velvet, and they enjoy having your hands run over their bodies. They are a sensualist's dream.

Dancer was a gifted and aware companion. Whenever she was outside and I left the house, she would run to meet me, scampering, leaping, flying up a tree and then turning her little head to make sure I was watching her with admiration, then jumping down to have her head stroked, then moving away on her own errands.

When I went on trips, Randy reported that she was listless. When Randy's car came up the hill, her little ears perked up. They didn't perk up for anyone else's car — just for his.

When I had trouble sleeping, her purring was my lullaby. When I watched television, she would curl up on my lap. I would stroke her head and her neck and hold her little foot in my hand. When she had had enough affection— and yes, cats can have enough — she would move to the foot of the couch and fall sleep. But she responded to the click of the remote control. As soon as I got up she took my place. I guess she thought I had been warming it just for her. I would say, "Goodnight, little girl," and go to bed.

I've never seen a cat with so many places. My unmade bed. The backrest of the couch when the sun poured in the window. The warm spot on the sofa after television. The top shelf of my closet. The old plastic lawn chair pillow that we kept for her on the deck. The hood of my car. The daybed in my office, next to the wood stove. The firewood box in front of the house — she would stand on it and press her front paws to the window, knowing somehow that I would see her little black, white and orange ears above my computer monitor and let her in.

I would watch her and think, "Nothing says a house has love in it more than a happy cat curled up, asleep."

When Randy and I sat together on the couch, with Dancer purring between us on the backrest, I would feel as if we were on a magic carpet and our little family was floating in space.

One of Dancer's jobs was to kill any stray mice that might get into the house. She was good at it. Outside, she never killed birds, but she was hell on smaller mammals. When she was young, she ate everything but the tails. Now that she was settling gracefully into kitty middle age — we think she was seven or eight — she only ate the heads. And she was selective. Sometimes a chipmunk could run right under her nose without attracting her interest.

Because we live in the woods, we trained Dancer to stay in at night. We understood that she was just another member of the food chain — as we all are — and that one day a fisher cat, or a coyote, or an owl, or a hawk, might get her, the way she got all those moles and voles.

Last Tuesday, Randy let her out in the morning. When she hadn't come back by noon, I knew.

I did all the right things. I walked down the road calling her name. I heard the full-running brook and the chirping chipmunks, but I didn't hear her answering meow. I called the neighbors. I called the humane society. I called the local veterinarians.

Her loss has left me swimming in an unfathomable lake of loneliness. I ache for her company. Watching television at night is painful. Many times I find myself standing at the back door, waiting to let her in, with tears running down my face. I look for her in all her favorite spots. I watch the chipmunks readying their winter nests in our woodpile and sigh, "Oh, Dancer."

I feel helpless because I couldn't keep her safe. In my dreams she's still alive, curled up on the backrest of the couch and purring.

Goodnight forever, precious.

~ ~ ~

June 3, 2004

THE UNBEARABLE LIGHTNESS OF DAFFODILS

D affodils can break your heart in so many lovely ways.

Two years after the poet William Wordsworth and his sister, Dorothy, wandered down by a lake and discovered a great mass of wild yellow flowers growing there, he famously wrote: "I wandered lonely as a cloud/That floats on high o'er vales and hills/When all at once I saw a crowd/A host of golden daffodils."

But he was with his sister, so how lonely could he be?

Dorothy wrote about the same yellow daffodils in her journal, and she wrote about them beautifully: "There were more and yet more... I never saw daffodils so beautiful. They grew among the mossy stones... some rested their heads upon these stones, as on a pillow, for weariness, and the rest tossed and reeled and danced, and seemed as if they verily laughed with the wind..."

I learned about Dorothy's journal from a little 1994 book called "Flora's Gems: The Little Book of Daffodils," by Pamela Todd, which Randy, bless his heart, brought home the other day from a thrift shop sale.

"Narcissus" is the Latin name for daffodils, Todd informs us. There are 12 classifications and hundreds of varieties, and all of them take their name from the Greek myth of Narcissus, the beautiful boy who became enamored of his own reflection in a pool of water and withered away from love of himself.

Percy Bysshe Shelley was referring to that ancient story when he wrote these sad and beautiful lines: "And narcissi/The fairest among them all/Who gaze on their eyes in the stream's recess/Till they die of their own dear loveliness."

It seems as though daffodils have been with us forever. "He that has two cakes of bread, let him sell one of them for some flowers of the Narcissus, for bread is food for the body, but Narcissus is food of the soul," wrote the Prophet Mohammed.

"In medieval times, high-born ladies occasionally cultivated daffodils in their gardens as they used the yellow dye the flowers yield to tint their hair and eyebrows," Todd writes. Those high-born ladies would be right at home with punk, wouldn't they? Minus a few piercings.

There's a wonderful story in the book about Fukien, China — a poor widow was so touched by the plight of a hungry beggar that she gave him her last half-bowl of rice. He ate it, thanked her, spit a few grains on the floor and disappeared. When she woke up the next morning, scores of graceful daffodils had appeared. She sold the blooms, became prosperous, and Fukien became famous for flowers. "So in China the flower symbolized prosperity and benevolence," Todd writes.

Randy thought I might like a book about daffodils because this has been the spring of the great daffodil wars — which, I'm not proud to say, I'm losing.

Daffodils breed prolifically in my garden, and if I don't separate them every few years, they grow mean. They gang up on each other and prevent their brothers and sisters from flowering. For the past three years I've been preoccupied with politics and watching the world going to hell in a hand-basket, so I've let my garden go — mostly to milkweed, I'm afraid.

As a result, this spring I was bereft of daffodils.

It was time to get to work. So I dug into a few clumps with a spade and a pitchfork, and soon I was drowning in daffodil bulbs. I was like the early American settler John Bartram, who in the 1730s wrote to tell his botanist friend in England that daffodils were plentiful in the Colonies and please, please, please do not send any more.

I was filling bucket after bucket with bulbs, so many bulbs and buckets that I couldn't lift them, much less find places for them. I spent an entire week on my knees, planting bulbs everywhere I could think of. I covered the hillside behind my house, and still I had more. I lined my garden path. Then I created another path and lined that, too. I became a welcome visitor at perennial swaps. I passed out handfuls to my friends — letting them commit bulbicide instead of me.

Just after daffodils flower, of course, everything else shoots up at once. Suddenly I had more work to do in the garden than time to do it. Digging up and planting daffodil bulbs took second place to raking, turning the ground, weeding, planting flats, mulching and fighting the deer who think my vegetable garden has a neon sign over it that blinks: "Salad Bar — All you can eat."

Now the daffodils are gone, leaving behind nothing but clumps of withering greens. Like spring, they fade so quickly that it heightens our sensitivity to the fleetingness of life itself.

"Fair daffodils, we weep to see you haste away so soon," wrote the poet Robert Herrick. "We have short time to stay as you/We have as short a spring.../We die, as your hours do/ And dry away like to the summer's rain/Or as the pearls of morning's dew/Ne'er to be found again."

∼　∼　∼

December 9, 2004

Rocking The Little Man In The Boat

Is it just me or is there an air of sexual repression wafting through this great country of ours?

For example, our president, such as he is, wants more money to teach — or is it preach? — abstinence to young people.

Promoting sexual abstinence ignores several large obstacles, including the danger of unprotected (ignorant) sex, raging teenage hormones and the highly sexualized American culture which stimulates those hormones for profit.

But the worst part of abstinence comes when impressionable young people go to their marriage beds inexperienced in the art of love and the workings of their own and their partners' bodies. Perhaps the young man has had a grope with a prostitute or seen a few porn videos, but that's not the best way to understand the complicated hydraulics of sexual activity.

23

Unless our young couple are extremely lucky in love, they will remain ignorant and dissatisfied throughout their lifetimes. If anything, they will have only idealized images of Hollywood sex to guide them. They won't know that rolling your eyes, rolling your head back on the pillow, opening your mouth wide and making strange sounds in the back of your throat is not usually the way sex happens. They won't know that laughter is a large part of healthy sex. And they won't know that unlike the movies, people don't always reach orgasm at the same time.

One of the most important things they won't know is the exact location of the clitoris. I speak as something of a published expert in this area, because the only time my byline has ever appeared in The New York Times Magazine, it was in a letter to the editor about clitorises. The Times had run a story about married southern Christian women who hold Tupperware-like parties in their homes to sample and buy sex toys. The women need the parties because — don't be too surprised here — they don't know much about sex. Or, to put it more bluntly, their husbands don't.

One shy woman whispered grateful thanks to the saleswoman for helping her find her clitoris, or, as she called it, "the little man in the boat." In my letter I saluted these women for learning about their bodies, but pointed out the disconnect between the gender of the euphemism and the female organ it represented.

Female sexuality has always put the male establishment — whether Christian, Jewish or Muslim — on edge. From our angry Biblical forefathers, who always seemed to be seeking a rationale for locking up their wayward daughters, to the even more drastic solution of female circumcision, the idea that women are equipped — by God, no less — to enjoy the greatest of sexual pleasures seems to drive authoritarian males (and the women who, for some reason, do their heavy lifting) mad.

That is why I was not surprised when, recently, a Food and Drug Administration advisory panel refused to recommend approval of a new medical patch, Intrinsa, which increases women's sexual pleasure. The panel claimed it needed more data before exposing women to heart attack and stroke for "a marginal increase in sexual satisfaction."

The FDA is right to be concerned about drug safety for women, given its dismal track record in the area: the first birth control pills featured scarily high doses of estrogen; then came the PremPro debacle — for decades the FDA assured women it was safe, and then we learned that it increased the risk of heart attack, stroke and breast cancer.

But with Intrinsa, how much do you want to bet that the idea of women having better orgasms was just a little too much for the good doctors of the FDA, who intend to remain gainfully employed throughout the long dark years of the Bush Administration?

Another example of repression is how the new biopic "Kinsey" has once again unleashed that hound of hell, Judith Reisman. She believes that Dr. Alfred Kinsey, whose groundbreaking work on sexuality was first published in 1948, was Satan incarnate, and the sexual revolution he sparked led to "fifty years of cultural terrorism," according to a recent article in The New Yorker.

Reisman, who just won a lifetime award for her work promoting abstinence-only sex education, is also against homosexuality, pornography and masturbation. She also believes that Nazi Germany and the Holocaust were the creations of German homosexuals, and that homosexuals today are planning a similar movement. The fact that Reisman currently enjoys strong credibility on Capitol Hill should give us all reason for concern.

Once again we are facing the great American sex dichotomy — the love-hate relationship which will not die: the $10 billion sex industry, the popularity of trash television, advertising, rap videos and the rest, vs. the hypocritical Bible-thumpers from the south — where they suffer the highest rates of teen pregnancy and divorce — and who want to repress sexual pleasure for everyone.

The sexual revolution was, for the most part, a positive thing for this country. As long as God created us as sexual beings, isn't it our duty to love one another, and to keep rocking that little man in his boat?

ALMOST A MILLION-DOLLAR BABY

In the end, it all came down to a racehorse's heart.

Odder still, it was the heart of Yankees owner George Steinbrenner's racehorse. And for a member of Red Sox Nation, that was a hard nut to swallow.

But that's my story and I'm sticking to it.

My interest in race horses began, a few years ago, as an aesthetic one. Up close, thoroughbreds are gorgeous animals, tall and gleaming and strong and beautifully configured with their tossing manes, well-muscled bodies and flying tails. At the Saratoga track, you get very close to these breathtaking animals. In fact, you can almost reach out and touch them. But you don't dare to do that, because you might spook them. Like the fashion models they in many ways resemble, thoroughbreds are quite high-strung.

At first I would just stand at the paddock rail, ooohhhing and ahhing and whispering "How beautiful" as each horse went by. Slowly, though, I started betting.

Betting on horses may be gambling, but it isn't anything like pulling the lever on a slot machine. For each race, you have to process information on past performances, track conditions, whether any post position that day is favoring winners, the records of the jockeys and the trainers, the Beyer numbers, what the turf writers are saying, your lucky numbers, your daughter's first name, and a host of other arcane facts and figures. In fact, you could call horses slot machines for intelligent people, if you wanted to call degenerate horse players intelligent, and I'm not the one to argue about that.

This was the year that Randy and I decided to get serious about racing. We took a room near Saratoga, and by Saturday, the day of the 135th running of the Travers, both of us were betting fools.

That day is the biggest one of the season, and the races for the Pick 4 — where you have to pick the winners of four consecutive races — were all graded stakes races with top-level horses. The guaranteed payoff of the Pick 4? One million dollars.

This was a good year for the Travers. Although Afleet Alex — the horse which won America's heart by first stumbling and then impressively winning the Preakness and the Belmont Stakes — was out for the season, there were top horses in the running. Steinbrenner's horse, Bellamy Road, was a big black beauty who had run an impressive 17½ lengths in front in the Wood Memorial. He was the favorite going into the Kentucky Derby, where he hurt his leg, decisively lost, and then retired for much of the season. His first race back would be the Travers, where he was again the favorite; the big question was whether he was ready to run again. Other Triple Crown horses like Flower Alley, Andromeda's Hero and Don't Get Mad were also in the race.

The morning of the Travers, by collating the picks of all the touts and factoring in speed and distance, Randy and I had worked out a bunch of possible Pick 4s — for the eighth, ninth, 10th and 11th races, the last being the Travers itself. We bet 12 combinations at a dollar each. By the first of the Pick 4 races, I had pretty much forgotten who we had bet on. But damned if four of our 12 tickets hadn't picked Leroidesanimaux, who won the eighth. In the ninth, the 101st running of the Hopeful, the touts' "unbeatable" favorite tanked, canceling all but one of our tickets. In the tenth, the 21st running of The King's Bishop, the touts' "unbeatable" horse, Lost in the Fog, turned out to be truly unbeatable.

Randy's sunburned face turned an even brighter red. Suddenly we were one race away from a million dollars. Our fate, of all things, was in the hands of George Steinbrenner and in the legs and heart of the beautiful Bellamy Road.

It's funny how you react when a life-changing million is on the line. My first reaction was, "Things like that don't happen to people like us." Randy's response was, "The Red Sox won the World Series last year." I was so nervous I had to go for a walk. When I came back, I found that Randy had shared his excitement with everyone at the rail.

"You're not going to faint if you win?" a woman asked me. "Be prepared for screaming," I said. "How does it feel?" another asked. "It feels strange to have my fate in the hands of something over which I have no control," I said.

And then they were off, with Bellamy Road in the lead from the start. I could hardly breathe, and that was only partly because Randy was holding me so tightly. When the horses came around the turn, Bellamy Road was giving it everything he had. And then, just as they passed in front of us, Flower Alley passed Bellamy Road by a nose. He went on to win the race by 2½ lengths and he took our million dollars with him.

You know, there is magic in the world and on some great days we are allowed to be a part of it. On Saturday our lives were entwined with the life of a great horse who was running his heart out. We were part of a crowd of more than 42,000 people cheering their lungs out for him — and some of them were cheering for us, too. And we were just a horses' nose away from becoming millionaires. You can't ask for more than that.

(I wrote this piece right after we came back from our vacation. It took another month before I realized that you <u>can</u> ask for more that. You can ask to win a million dollars at the racetrack. When I told Randy, he said, "What took you so long?")

TWO:
COLUMNS ABOUT MY FAMILY

SAVING SYLVIA

(I wrote this in 2001, at a critical time in the life of my beloved aunt, Sylvia Katcher.)

I'm someone who routinely surveys friends and Consumer Reports before buying something as uncomplicated as a toaster oven. So it was a shock last week when I was asked to make an immediate decision about whether my beloved Aunt Sylvia should live or die.

The situation was as difficult as it was absurd.

Sylvia, 85, is my late father's sister, and this is her year of medical hell. She went into the hospital for a colonoscopy — which always represents a risk, especially for someone her age — and her intestinal wall was breached. Rushed into surgery, she came out "trussed up like a turkey," as her daughter Ellen put it.

But Sylvia is a strong woman with a healthy cardiovascular system, and she recovered.

Back she went to her tiny apartment overlooking the Atlantic Ocean, where from the window you can watch swans riding on the waves like surfers. She resumed her quiet life of friends and television.

Unfortunately, she fell in the bathroom one night and ended up with a broken arm and hip. There was more surgery. Worse, the pin in her hip didn't take, and she had to have a hip replacement. More surgery, more pain, more recovery.

Sylvia is a widow, and Ellen, her only daughter, who is single and a teacher, bore the brunt of caring for her. She did it lovingly and well, but like many of us today, she is in the unfortunate situation of belonging to a small and scattered family.

In times like this, friends can be wonderfully supportive. But you really need your family — people who have known you all your life, who you can call at odd hours, and who you can ask for heavy favors.

Ellen and Sylvia live in New York. Sylvia's only cousin, Sybie, lives in Miami. Her sister-in-law, my mother, lives in Fort Lauderdale. I live in Vermont. On my father's side, that's all the family we have left. So we participated in Sylvia's recovery by phone.

Sylvia didn't want visitors while she was recuperating, so it wasn't until a few weeks ago that I visited her. I came bearing flowers, food and love, and was delighted to see her walking with a walker. Her eyes and her mind were as bright and as sharp as ever.

We had a wonderful visit, although she was tired at the end of it. We made plans for me to come down again and spend the night when she was stronger; we usually stay up late, talking and giggling like schoolgirls.

Unfortunately, soon after my visit, a blockage in Sylvia's intestine caused an infection. She was rushed to intensive care, where she fell into a coma-like stupor. One lung collapsed.

A doctor told Ellen that Sylvia needed immediate surgery, and that while she would have no chance of survival without it, she would have only a 30 percent chance of coming out of the anesthesia alive.

Sylvia and Ellen had never talked much about death and dying; they were focused on helping Sylvia walk again. Now Ellen was being asked to make immediate and unimaginable decisions for her unconscious mother. Should she sign a Do Not Resuscitate form? Pull the plugs? Inflict more surgery, pain and recovery? Hold her mother's hand and watch her die?

Ellen needed backup, so I raced down to New York, pulling behind me a suitcase holding a change of underwear and, just in case, my funeral clothing. Timidly, I entered the Intensive Care Unit and Ellen flung herself into my arms.

"Prepare yourself," she said as we approached Sylvia's bed.

My experience with ICUs has been limited to a few personal operations and a lot of television. What I hadn't realized from watching "ER" is that no matter how badly messed up the bodies on the gurneys are, they are actor's bodies, and they have put themselves on the gurneys.

My dear Aunt Sylvia, however, was so frail, so pale, so sunken and wrinkled, so fragile, so helpless and absent, that she could not have put herself anywhere.

At least three computers were registering her vital signs. Her arms were tied down. A large plastic tube was stuffed down her throat. Her mouth was taped open, making it look like she was screaming silently.

Another tube was stuck down her nose. Other lines dripped fluids into her poor body to fight the infection, stabilize her electrolytes and bring her back to consciousness.

Her hair was sparse and matted, her brow hot to my touch, her cheekbones way too sharp. It is terrible to see someone you love looking like that; I will not easily forget the sight.

"So, what should I do?" Ellen asked. "Should she have the surgery? Should we try to prolong her life? What kind of life will it be? You know, if she were a dog, we would know what to do."

It was hard to hear, but Ellen was right.

Who were we, I wondered, to be making this decision? We know nothing about medicine, nothing about Sylvia's wishes. We were in an inhuman, infuriating and intolerable situation.

When I was growing up, doctors decided these things. Then they came into the waiting room and told the anxious family what was going to happen next.

Now people live longer (after Sylvia's experiences, I don't know if that is a good thing), patients have rights (good), doctors fear malpractice suits (bad), and everyday people like me and Ellen are forced to accept far more responsibility than we can handle.

By the end of the day, it appeared that Sylvia might be coming back to consciousness. So we postponed making a decision.

Happily, the next morning Sylvia seemed to recognize us, and while she couldn't talk, she communicated by blinking. The antibiotics were clearing up the infection. The electrolytes were stabilizing her.

A kind surgeon told us that a less invasive procedure might clear the blockage. She said that Sylvia was strong, and her chances of recovery were good.

With Sylvia out of immediate danger, I returned to Vermont. The next day, she made her own decision about surgery. Ellen drew three boxes on a paper: "Yes," "No," "I don't know." Sylvia made an X in the box marked "Yes."

"But the look in her eyes was, 'How can you ask me to make such a decision? I'm so sick. How do I know?'" Ellen said on the phone.

"How does anyone know?" I said.

Sylvia will recover. She will be furious that she has to go through another period of pain and recuperation, but she will live, and for that, Ellen and I are grateful.

This is what I learned:

— No matter how difficult it is, have the end-of-life conversation with your loved ones — the older generation as well as your own — early and often. Get it down on paper. Know what you yourself want done. Tell people.

— In the hospital, don't allow yourself to be rushed. Talk to many doctors and nurses; collect as much information as you can; don't take one person's medical opinion as true fact.

— Hospice helps people who are dying, but Sylvia didn't have an underlying fatal disease. A great need exists for experienced, sensitive elderly critical-care guidance counselors.

— The loss of extended families and the scattering of nuclear ones can easily leave just one or two ill-informed people, themselves in crisis because a loved one is helpless, making life or death decisions, sometimes over the phone. Start building up all the family bonds you can, now, before it's too late. Ellen and I were never close before, but we are now.

Hopefully, this is the beginning of 10 more good years in Sylvia's life, and many more sleepovers.

(Sylvia recovered from the events I recount here. She is now 90 and living in a nursing home. Sadly, there have been no more sleepovers.)

~ ~ ~

May 10, 2001

HAPPY MOTHER'S DAY, MOM

(In 2001, when I was doing a lot of travel writing, I was invited to sample the pleasures of a five-day luxury European barge trip. The only costs would be airfare, connections to the south of France, and food and lodging in Paris after the trip. I convinced my mother to come along.)

Although the mother-daughter relationship is grounded in deep, deep love, it can also be a psychological minefield. Resolving its problems, I've found, can be a journey of discovery and delight.

Last month, for example, my mother, Rose Kagan, and I went to Paris. I had a long list of things I was going to do. For sure, I was going to visit all the flea markets. I was going to get a stylish French haircut. I was going to walk in picturesque neighborhoods and daydream that I lived there. I was going to see the Van Goghs at the Musee D'Orsay. I was going to eat pate every single day, and to hell with my cholesterol level.

I did one of the above.

I also had a list of things I definitely was not going to do. I was not going to play tourist. I was not going to visit historical sites. I was not going to gawk at the Eiffel Tower.

I did all of the above.

The reason? My mother.

Yet the trip was the best one I've ever had, and my mother feels the same way.

The idea for the trip came when I realized that since I had left my mother's womb, we had not spent very much time alone together. When I was young she was busy with my father, my brother, and our large extended family. Also, as a frustrated Broadway musical comedy star, she was fighting to make space in her rigidly structured 1950s suburban life for dancing, choreographing, and performing.

Back then, I never appreciated her struggle; I only felt abandoned by her ever-increasing involvement in amateur theatrics. Also, our family suffered from many of the more common dysfunctional family dynamics — we could be a heart-wrenching, best-selling memoir, if anyone had the heart to write it.

But people grow up. They change. If they're lucky, they learn to forgive. During the last 10 years, my mother and I have buried my father and my younger brother and started reaching out to each other. I happily gave her away at her second marriage, to Harold Filler, whom I love. They have started visiting me in Vermont, although Harold, who washes his white Lincoln Continental every day at home in Fort Lauderdale, has a hard time understanding why we like dirt roads here in Vermont.

I have started visiting them in their Florida condominium, timing my trips to coincide with the Broadway-style productions my mother writes, directs, choreographs and performs in. I've grown to love the dress rehearsals, the diva-like temper tantrums, the dancers — all over 70 and with great legs — the glitzy make-up and costumes. Most of all, I love watching my mother — a real star — on stage. I'm also impressed that with these shows, she touches the lives of over a thousand people every year.

All this was well and good, but as time went by, I longed to share a one-on-one experience with my mother. I suggested many things, but it was the idea of a leisurely cruise down the Canal du Midi in the south of France, followed by a visit to Paris, that finally drew her away from her busy life and into an adventure with me.

When we met at Charles DeGaulle Airport, however, I was afraid we had waited too long. The overnight Miami-Paris trip can be brutal for a woman in her 80s. She was nervous about not speaking the language, afraid she couldn't handle the money, scared to be in an environment where she had no control. She hadn't traveled without a tour guide for 30 years. She had vertigo. My dynamic, beautiful mother was a small, terrified, bewildered creature. I hadn't realized how frail she was. I had a moment of terror — was I going to kill her just because I wanted to spend some time with her?

Traveling south was difficult, but once we reached the barge, I was impressed with her good cheer and resourcefulness. When it was too cold to be on deck, she gave dance classes to the other passengers below. She studied her French. While I held my breath, she stole lilacs out of a walled garden in Homps. About the fine rich food, she joked that she would tell her friends we ate peanut butter and jelly sandwiches so they wouldn't be too jealous.

One day, on a visit to a winery, she tasted so many good wines that I found her alone and tipsy, humming and two-stepping in a corner. On the last night, she delighted the other passengers and the crew by writing charming limericks for them. (Sample: "There was a lady named Betty, and please don't think I am petty, but with a gin and tonic, she became supersonic, and they called her Betty Confetti.")

At one point, we talked about what I might write about this trip.

"I thought we would have two contrasting viewpoints," I said.

"But we don't," Mother said. "We both see things in almost exactly the same way."

We were amazed by this discovery.

In Paris, because Mom couldn't do much walking, we bought tickets for one of those circling buses with a tape loop describing the sights in four languages. We hopped on and off it at will. At the Musee d'Orsay, I loved the Van Goghs, while, with childlike wonder, she adored the Degas dancers. We ate in small restaurants to save money. I showed her how to read home-town newspapers on the Internet.

So I didn't do any of the things I had planned to do. Instead, I did something unexpected— I walked around Paris holding hands with my mother as we laughed at all the same things.

At the airport again, I watched Mom walking down the tunnel to her overnight flight. Her hands were trembling, but her head was tilted upward, her nose was pointed into the air, and her face was determined. She's quite a character, I thought, a formidable woman. How lucky I am to be so much like her. How much I love her.

Days after I got back to Vermont, I still missed her presence.

"I miss you too," she said. "After all, we were Siamese twins for thirteen very arduous and exciting days. I now feel the distance in miles between us."

So whatever happens to us in the future, Mom, remember this — and yes, I've been waiting the whole column to say it: We'll always have Paris. Happy Mother's Day.

~ ~ ~

March 21, 2002

YOUNG AGAIN, AND ALIVE

Well, I'm back in Vermont again, sitting at my desk, looking through the photographs I took in Florida. Here's one of Beth Greenberg on stage in her ruffled pink party dress, her mouth wide open, channeling Ethel Merman with all her heart and soul as she lip-synchs "Everything's Coming Up Roses" from "Gypsy." And here's Jeanne Max in a chef's hat and apron, lip-synching to, well, Jeanne Max. The song is "Be My Guest" from "Beauty and the Beast," but Jeanne has trouble remembering lyrics these days, so she pre-recorded her number.

And here's a picture of the beautiful set that Will Shulman painted for the "Fiddler" number, floating straight out of a Marc Chagall stained glass window. And here's one of Tony Scoppetta standing proudly in his workshop. He built all the sets and props, then fell off a tall ladder during the last dress rehearsal and had to take his bows using a walker.

They are some of the many people involved in "Broadway Banquet," a musical that was written, directed and choreographed by my mother, Rose Kagan, 84, for her Florida condominium, Lauderdale West.

Just in terms of numbers, what my mother does is impressive. This was her 26th show; there were 48 people in the cast, another 40 or so working behind the scenes, and they drew over 1,000 people to the three performances.

Two years ago I saw one of my mother's shows and was swept away by the excitement of it all. The costumes glittered. The performers had personalities. The chorus girls, average age 76. their great legs showcased in fishnet stockings, were all blonde and radiant.

So this year I decided to document a production. I went to Florida in November to sit in on auditions. In mid-January, I checked back in to see how rehearsals were going and dish the dirt (the politicking behind the scenes is fierce). Two weeks ago, I flew down again to watch the dress rehearsals, interview the cast, take lots of pictures, see the shows and go to the cast party. It was a revelation.

The Theater Club people were welcoming, generous with their time, and quite frank and open. No one minded my intrusive questions, the worst of which was, of course, "How old are you." (Some of the chorus girls, however, lied.)

I met remarkable people. Edith Levine, for example, is a small woman with white hair and an almond-eyed, expressive face. Her solo was "Some People" from "Gypsy," which she lip-synched in an elegant blue silk dress. Edith's husband, Lou, just as tiny, stood in the back of the audience every night, his proud eyes glued to his wife. She ran into his arms as soon as she got off-stage. At the cast party I asked how long they had been married. "Fifty-five years," Lou said.

Jeanne Max, 85, has a powerful voice and stage presence to burn. Two years ago she lip-synched Tina Turner's "Proud Mary," stomping her feet, shaking her wig, rocking and rolling and bringing down the house. She told me she always wanted to be a professional performer. When she was just out of high school, she had had the opportunity to tour with a band. But her parents hit the roof, so she found a regular job, married, and raised her children. But she never stopped singing and performing.

Several people in the club told me similar stories, stories about their thwarted longings for an artistic life. My talented mother always wanted a career in show business. And Will Shulman ran a children's furniture store in the Bronx when he would have been happier painting in Paris.

I didn't get Bob Wallach's age, but I would guess he's over 70 since he spent 40 years in the printing and binding business before retiring with his wife, Judy, to Florida. A rough-looking man with big eyes, a weathered face and large, strong hands, he specializes in drag.

Judy, who is one of the chorus girls, taught him feminine hand gestures, he said. He taught himself how to walk in heels. With grace, tenderness and wistful sadness, he lip-synched "Mascara" from "La Cage aux Folles," starting out with make-up, his own bald head, and a florid pink kimono. He ended in a blonde wig, a silvery beaded dress that brought gasps of wonder from the audience and a borrowed fuchsia marabou boa.

"I'm not gay, you understand," he told me. "But I like these songs. With songs like these, a man can express himself."

For me, what stands out most is the way that the performers carry on in the midst of illness and death.

During the course of producing this show, Beth Greenberg's husband died. So did Bo Salsberg's mother. Barbara Seltzer's mother had a stroke. Bob Wallach had knee surgery. Will Shulman was diagnosed with a heart condition. Lead dancer Sylvia Tannenbaum's back hurt so much that she couldn't bend down, and she needed an X-Ray and a cortisone shot to go on-stage. But she danced every night, and she was incandescent. Comedian Lenny Novie cares for a sick wife. When someone asked about her, he said, "She'll never walk or talk again. No matter how many times you ask me, it'll never change."

And then there was Red Gershon, 80, handsome, white-haired, a former mailman who lives to dance with my mother. He had such serious back problems that it was widely understood he couldn't be in the show. But only a few days after major back surgery, Red came to a rehearsal "just to watch."

Slowly, he and my mother gravitated towards each other. She put on the music of a number they had done before, "Ann on My Arm" from "La Cage." He took her in his arms, they gazed deeply into each other's eyes, and they floated around the rehearsal hall together as if they were alone in a ballroom. When the music ended the rest of the cast applauded and Red made a quick grab for his three-footed cane.

Making things even more difficult, Red's knee went out a few days before the show. He got "a shot" from his doctor and rested each day until it was time to put on his costume and makeup. Then he came out on stage with my graceful mother — always to applause — and they lit up the theater with their love of dancing.

Enchanted by all the heart and courage, I asked many of the performers how they could concentrate on performing in the midst of so much suffering, illness and death. All of them said pretty much the same thing: "When I'm out there, I forget about everything else. It makes me feel young again, and alive."

(This is a hard column to reread. Since I wrote it, Will Shulman has lost his sight, left his home and Lauderdale West, and moved to an extended care facility. My mother recently held a retrospective of his work which, I understand, touched him deeply. Sylvia Tannenbaum had to stop dancing in the shows, but I hear she continues to do ballroom dancing. Lenny Novie, well, his story is the saddest. He died in a car accident. I don't know who is caring for his wife now, but when my mother put together a retrospective show of his performance clips, the house was packed. The rest of the people I wrote about are still rehearsing and performing, joined by many newcomers. And as for my mother, read on.)

~ ~ ~

May 9, 2002

A Taste Of History

Our senses have a way of reconnecting us with our past.

For example, long ago I spent a summer on a Greek island, walking in the hills and picking fragrant mountain oregano, wild bay, rosemary and sage. As the herbs dried in the sun, I sewed little packets for them out of a rough-spun blue-and-white-checked cotton. I filled the bags, tied them with string, brought them home as gifts for my family.

Unfortunately, my mother thinks that spices grow in little glass bottles with McCormick labels on them. She never opened her packets. Ten years later I found them, tucked away in a dark corner of her pantry. I opened them and was immediately transported back to the island; I could see the dark Mediterranean and feel the sun on my face.

Sometimes I use cooking to bring back memories of a dearly departed ancestor. For example Lena Kagan, my father's mother, learned how to cook as young girl in Odessa, Russia. She carried her mother's recipes across the sea in her mind, but she never wrote them down. Once, as a school project, her niece watched her cook and took some notes. In that way, three recipes have been preserved.

Whenever I want to feel close to Grandma Kagan, who died at the age of 89, I take out a heavy pot, break an egg into it, and stir in raw kasha. As the scent of the roasting groats rises, I bend over the pot and inhale deeply. At once I feel connected to generations of Kagan women — to generations of Eastern European Jewish women — all bending over their stoves or fires, all smiling as they smell that wonderfully rich and earthy scent.

Grandma Kagan's recipes are precious to me, and they were the first thing I thought of when, a while back, my husband read about a Mother's Day recipe contest in The Boston Herald. The paper asked people to send in their mothers' best recipes, especially if they were brought from far away places like Italy, China, France, Russia or South America.

"Why don't you enter?" Randy said.

Instead of copying out Grandma Kagan's recipe for stuffed peppers or rice pudding or kasha varnishkes, I reached for the phone and called my mother in Florida. I asked if she had any interesting recipes. She didn't hesitate.

"Demph noodles, of course," she said.

"Huh?" I said.

"Demph noodles. My grandmother used to make them, and she taught me how. When I visited you a few years ago, and you had that party, don't you remember, I made demph noodles for your guests and they loved them."

"Oh, that cobbler thing with the sour cherries and the prunes?"

"That's the one."

"There weren't any noodles in that."

"I know. That's just what my grandmother called it."

"OK, how do you spell 'demph'?"

"I have no idea."

"What does it mean?"

"I don't know. It's all really strange, when you think about it. But my grandmother — your great-grandmother — came over from Germany late in the 19th Century, so it must mean something in German or Yiddish."

Frederika Kampler, my grandfather's mother, was by all accounts a wonderful cook who ran a popular boarding house in Yorktown, in New York City. When my grandfather became rich during the Roaring Twenties, he moved his family into a huge house in Far Rockaway, near the beach and abutting a mansion owned by Lillian Russell. My mother spent an enchanted childhood there. Frederika and her husband retired and lived in a small apartment on the top floor, where they had a small kitchen of their own. It's all very heartwarming so far, but this wouldn't be a family story if there wasn't a pinch of resentment and jealousy in it — at least, it wouldn't be a story from my family. So the truth is that Frederika disliked my grandmother, Flora Kampler, very much.

Even though Flora begged Frederika to teach her some of her wonderful dishes, she always refused. But Fredericka loved her granddaughter, swore her to secrecy, and taught her how to cook.

By the time my grandfather lost his money, sold his big house, and moved his family into an apartment by the subway tracks, Frederika and her husband were long gone. Demph noodles lived on only in my mother's memory.

Over the phone, Mom tried to give me the recipe, but when I asked, "How much sugar?" or "How many prunes?" she had no idea. It seems she made the dish each time by calling up and then duplicating her childhood memories of her grandmother's movements.

"But you have to use sour cherries," Mom said. "That's the most important thing."

My first attempt at making demph noodles was so sour that I couldn't eat it. It went into the compost pile. Then I doubled the sugar and sent the recipe to the Herald.

Last Tuesday, the paper's food editor, Jane Dornbusch, called and told me that demph noodles had won the contest.

"We received close to 100 recipes," she said. "We tested and tasted six. It wasn't even close. The demph noodles were very delicious — honest, straightforward and unique."

Although I never met Frederika Kampler, I think she, like her recipe, must have been "honest, straightforward and unique." And, considering the way she treated my grandmother, a little sour as well.

While the recipe's name will forever remain shrouded in mystery, ("We're guessing 'noodle' comes from 'knodel,' German for dumpling," Dornbusch wrote in a story that accompanied the recipe yesterday), I am delighted that food has helped me get to know another of my ancestors and unlocked another door to my past.

(After this piece appeared, I received several e-mails from people who knew about demph noodles. One wrote: "The 'demph noodles' are most likely 'dampf nudeln.' You are right that 'nudel' most likely comes from 'knoedel,' which is a fat, usually spherical dumpling, and the 'noodle' of course, from 'nudel.' The 'demph' must be 'dampf,' which is 'steam' in German. At least some recipes for Dampf Nudeln require that you use a sort of pressure cooker ('keep the lid closed and put a rock on it').")

$\sim \quad \sim \quad \sim$

May 1, 2003

TAKE YOUR MOTHER TO WORK DAY

Hey, Mom just got a job.

It's a big deal, and not just because she's over 85. It's a big deal because she belongs to a generation of women who were, for the most part, denied the opportunity to have professional artistic careers.

In my mother's case, she always wanted to be a Broadway dancer.

She has the talent. Even today, in the amateur musicals she's been writing, directing, choreographing and dancing in for her Fort Lauderdale condo, she can kick her leg over her head at least once in every number. And when she's dancing, she seems to glow from within; it's impossible to take your eyes off her. And I'm not just being a loving daughter here. Whispers run through the audience when Mom comes on stage. "There she is." "That's Rose Kagan." In her world, Mom's a star.

When Mom was growing up during the Great Depression, probably a few young Jewish women danced on Broadway, but most thought performing in public was one step away from prostitution. And not necessarily a step up, either, because hookers made more money than hoofers.

The sole mission of every good Jewish girl in my mother's day — and in mine, until Betty Friedan wrote "The Feminine Mystique" — was to love, honor and obey a man.

Pressure to conform was as strong as it was vicious. Even when my mother's generation was well over 65, women were dropped by their social circles as soon as their husbands died.

This never made any sense to me. Surely not every widow wanted to steal the husbands of her best friends, I argued. How could it matter if one guest at the table wasn't accompanied by another guest? What was wrong with being alone?

My mother would patiently explain, "That's just the way it is." She told me stories about widows chasing after the few remaining widowers, showing up at their doorsteps with chicken soup and casseroles, wanting to be married just to be socially acceptable again. Other widows defiantly formed female groups in order to have a social life. We see vestiges of this stigma today in women who are afraid to eat in a restaurant or go to a movie by themselves.

My mother never ostracized her widowed friends. But once my father died, I don't think she felt comfortable until she was married again.

If it takes a strong will to stand up to this kind of cultural pressure in 2003, I'm not surprised that back in the 1930s, my mother gave up her dream of dancing on Broadway, married my father and became a mother.

But even when people sacrifice precious parts of themselves in order to conform, the desires still bubble up. Creativity is as irrepressible as

Columns About My Familyegment>

sexuality or intelligence. So Mom never gave up performing; she just shifted to amateur theatricals.

The gap between amateurs and professionals in our culture is a vast one. Money is the only way our society has of placing a value on things. Money confers power and stature. The fact that the word "amateur" comes from the root word "love" has no meaning in 21st Century America.

At the start of this year, my mother announced that she was retiring. In March, her theater club put on the last show written, directed, choreographed and danced in by Rose Kagan. In the future she might dance in a number, or help out with the choreography, but she would never again be the creative force behind a show. It was the end of fighting with oversized egos, neuroses, jealousy, back-stabbing and exhaustion. But it was also the end of the work.

Until the phone started ringing. Suddenly other condos were calling my mother and begging her to put on shows for them. Bewildered, she started having meetings and going out on interviews. She set restrictions on her time that she could have never enforced in her own condo, and found that people were willing to respect them. Moreover, she found that there was widespread respect for her work out there.

Now she's choreographing a show for a nearby condo, and she'll have all the egos, neuroses and back-stabbing she can handle. But at the end of the day, she'll also have a sizable check.

Mom may never dance on Broadway, but she's become a professional choreographer. She has the career in dance she's always wanted — and it doesn't matter how long it might last. She gives hope to all the underpaid and under-appreciated artists who never give up their dreams. She's inspiring.

Mom may not realize it yet, but it's a very big deal.

43

AN UNCONVENTIONAL WEEK

My convention may have been different from yours.

As the Democratic convention began on CNN, I. Harold Filler, who was born in 1916, began to die.

The I is for Isaiah.

On the television screen, red, white and blue banners unfurl, Kerry and Edwards signs bloom and wave, and delegates put on silly hats.

But Harold, draped in a blanket, lies in a chair in his hospital room in south Florida. His head is back, his mouth is open, his eyes are closed.

Jimmy Carter speaks from his heart. I cannot speak. Harold's daughter, Beth, cannot speak. And Harold's wife, my mother, cannot speak. We are waiting for an ambulance service. It will take Harold to hospice.

"Today, our dominant international challenge is to restore the greatness of America— based on telling the truth, a commitment to peace, and respect for civil liberties at home and basic human rights around the world," Carter says. "Truth is the foundation of our global leadership, but our credibility has been shattered and we are left increasingly isolated and vulnerable in a hostile world."

I had flown in from Vermont that morning. Beth came from New York. Both of us were responding to calls from my mother: "Please, come quickly, Harold is dying. I can't do this alone."

Across the hall, a patient presses the nurse's call button and a buzzer begins to ring. It keeps time with Al Gore's speech. The buzzer goes on and on, and so does Gore. He gave up the presidency in 2000. He didn't fight for it. He has nothing to say to us today.

Harold is a great guy. He was big — 200 pounds at his late-life prime on the day he married my mother. He was tall and handsome then, with a full head of silvery white hair. He was frequently demanding — to the point of being a bit abusive — but he was also sweet and humble. He had a wicked sense of humor. He was thoughtful. He was always doing favors for people. He loved to serve.

He often told me that he was blessed because he had had the love of two wonderful women — his first wife, Lorraine, who died around the same time as my father, and now my mother. He sometimes had tears in his eyes when he told me this.

Now he weighs 130 pounds. He is all bone. Hard bone. Heavy bone.

Progressive terminal Parkinson's has him in its sharp alien teeth and it is eating him alive. He is dying.

I kiss him and wonder, not for the first time, if death is catching.

The buzzer is still beeping as Hillary Clinton starts to speak. Her face is shining with feigned innocence, her blond hair is crisply cut, and her manner is polished. She speaks of her great admiration for John Kerry, and how she wants nothing more than to be led by him. She is lying with enthusiasm. The delegates are delirious. She is their star, the first woman president of their dreams. And hers.

My mother listens to the speech. One of her bony hands worries the corner of her jacket; the other holds Harold's bony hand.

Hillary introduces her husband and the convention floor goes mad with joy. They wave their banners so hard they create drafts that make the buntings on the walls wave back. The EMTs come and strap Harold to a gurney.

Beth and I are to follow in her car. Bill Clinton begins speaking on the car radio as Harold is lifted into the ambulance.

I look at Harold, whom I love. For just one second, strapped to the gurney, he is upright. His eyes are dark and open, looking out at the world. This is his final journey, I think. It is a solemn moment. I turn off the radio.

The furniture in the hospice saves Harold's death. It is hand-me-down 1970s wood, country-tacky, ruffled curtains and the like. Beth moans, "I signed my father's life away." My mother falls to the floor crying, "I can't do it. I can't leave him here."

We get her into a chair and I drape a thin hospital blanket over her trembling shoulders like a cape. She makes an unlikely superhero.

Beth, so competent, learns that if Harold can come home to die, hospice will follow us. Mother wants him home. She know just how to set up the dining room as a hospital. She did it for my father.

Harold is awake now. He wants to knows where he is, and why. He wants to know who is paying for all this. He wants to know why my mother is crying. My mother can't find the words to tell him.

The next day we prepare the dining room. Carmen-from-Jamaica, a strong, wise, take-charge round-faced woman who was Harold's day aide, agrees to move in with us.

Sent from hospice, a hospital bed, a commode and a wheel chair appear, followed by an "egg crate" mattress, and then an air mattress. A hospital table called an "overbed" is delivered. Our vocabulary is increasing: Thicket, Nebulizer, chux, Atavan. Oxygen arrives, then medication. Then Harold.

We watch the convention at home. Barak Obama speaks, another man speaking from his heart. The crowd loves him. They wave his name in the air. Harold is sitting in a wheelchair, eating from the overbed table. My mother sits across from him, spooning food, tenderly into his mouth. "All you need is a bud vase and some candles," I say.

Carmen takes the spoon away. "Don't you take my job away from me, Miss Rose," she says. "Let me feed him. You eat your own dinner."

Mother picks at her chicken and John Edwards talks about hope. We have none.

We fall into a routine. Carmen does the heavy lifting. Competent Beth washes a lot of dishes very fast. I try to support my mother and feel useless.

Al Sharpton speaks, warning us that the next administration might have the opportunity to fill two seats on the U.S. Supreme Court. "It is frightening to think that the gains of civil and women's rights and those movements in the last century could be reversed if this administration is in the White House in these next four years," he says. "I suggest to you tonight that if George Bush had selected the court in '54, Clarence Thomas would have never got to law school. This is not about a party. This is about living up to the promise of America." I start liking Reverend Al.

John Kerry reports for duty to America. Harold's not drinking enough liquid and his kidneys begin to shut down. Beth and I cancel our flights home.

The Fleet Center, after the convention, is littered with balloons and posters.

And Harold is still at home, all bone, hard bone, slowly dying.

(Harold died soon after I wrote this piece. We flew his body to New York and buried him next to his first wife, Lorraine. When my mother dies, she will be buried in Florida next to my father. That's how they do things these days.)

October 7, 2004

LONELINESS OF THE LONG-DISTANCE DAUGHTER

It's funny how quaint it seems now, the idea of retiring to Florida (or having enough money to retire at all). But thirty years ago it was the dream of millions of hard-working Americans, many of whom actually pulled up their northern roots and moved south.

That particular American dream had dangerous underpinnings for the American family. It was one of the reasons that extended families disappeared, shrunk down to middle-aged couples separated from their own parents as well as their children, cousins and, eventually, grandchildren. It became a world of families joined only by airline tickets and the slender thread of land-line phones.

Thirty years ago, my parents retired to a part of Fort Lauderdale where there was nothing but scrub trees, narrow roads, cow pastures and new developments. Now there isn't a bit of open space left. The malls are huge. Roads packed with new cars run four lanes in each direction. New towns spring up all the time.

My mother, now 86, has had a wonderful life there. She is widely admired for the Broadway-style musical comedies she puts on in her condo. She has a full social life. She even remarried after my father died. She is vital and healthy. But since my stepfather died two months ago, she feels a kind of deep loneliness that friendship alone cannot alleviate. She has no close family left except me, and I live in Vermont.

Her generation is now paying a very high price for cutting the cords of family. In her world, visits from children are treated like visits from royalty — or saints. The sentence, "My daughter wants me to come north and stay with her for the holidays," has more status than a 4-carat square-cut diamond ring. "My children don't visit me anymore," is the saddest sentence in the world.

When someone sells their home and returns "up north," it means they can no longer live alone or advocate for themselves with the medical establishment. They need to be near a family member who will take on that responsibility, and thus they are on the certain path to deterioration and death. Seen in this light, returning north is something to be avoided.

This makes for a curious tension. My mother and I want — and need — to be near each other. But she wants me to move to Florida, while I want her to move to Vermont.

A number of people my age — generally but not exclusively women — move to Florida to live with their aging parents. These are people who have never married, or are divorced and at loose ends, or who were downsized or in some other financial difficulty. They are people to whom life in a Florida retirement community makes some kind of sense. My mother's condo even has a "50s-60s" club now.

For those of us who are leading complicated, demanding and rewarding lives up north, however, Florida is not a desirable option.

Mom has been depressed since my stepfather died, so last week I went down to keep her company. She has a beautiful house with plenty of space for me, and I've been visiting there so long that I'm now a part of the community. Last week, during auditions for the new show, for example, several people suggested I try out — they thought I would be good at lip synching Sophie Tucker's "Red Hot Mama."

I know it meant a lot to my mother to have me there. And naturally, living with her feels natural — so natural, in fact, that I forget all about my life in Vermont. I forget about my husband's kisses and the Red Sox and the clear, crisp light of autumn, and the ever-changing beauty of Spaulding Hill Road. It all fades away as if it has never existed.

While I was there, I helped Mom clear away some of the detritus of 30 years of pack-ratting. We tucked away photos of long-gone relatives. We donated sacks of paperback novels and hardcover books to the condo library. We cleared out multiple decks of cards, loads of antique electronic equipment, old magazines, bags of costume jewelry, yellowing pads of paper and broken watches. We worked hard. We made a great team.

Our parting was literally wrenching. I felt as if I was being torn away from a full, rich life. And I felt incredibly guilty about leaving my mother alone.

My first night back home, I barely knew where I was. I missed my mother. Green palms had morphed into flaming maples, but my head was in two places at the same time and my heart didn't know where to land.

At some cost to herself, my mother finally set me free. "Enjoy your wonderful husband," she said over the phone the next day. "Enjoy your beautiful house and your beautiful cat."

I'm beginning to understand why most marriage vows include the phrase, "And forsaking all others." It is not only about fidelity. It is also about transferring your emotions from your parents to your spouse, when the ties that bind you to your parents seem to be made of iron and rubber at the same time.

There is no solution to this problem; it is the price my mother and I are paying today for that long-ago lure of a happy, sun-drenched retirement. For now, we'll cobble together a life of daily phone calls. In emergencies, I'm just a plane ride away. And I'm guessing that she'll accept my invitation to visit Vermont for the holidays.

~ ~ ~

December 16, 2004

THE BATTLE OF THE BULGE

My uncle, Bernard Kampler, a kind young man much loved by his family, a high school swim star, newly married, died 60 years ago this week in the Battle of the Bulge. He died under unimaginably harsh and terrifying conditions. In my family, the repercussions of his death are still flowing outward, like circles from a stone dropped into a deathly still pond.

My first childhood memory is of my uncle. We were on the streets of Brooklyn, my mother and I, when her brother came walking toward us. He was tall and handsome in his uniform. I ran to him. He picked me up and held me above his head. We were both laughing. It was the last time any of us would see him.

The war in Europe was almost over when Germany made a last attack through the Ardennes forests of Belgium and Luxembourg. On the night of December 16, 1944, the Sixth Panzer Army came pouring through the American lines. This attack of about 200,000 German troops created a backward "bulge" in the line, hence the name.

"The weather was frightful — bitterly cold and snowing, with a high wind howling through the dark," wrote Gardner Botsford about the battle in his 2003 memoir, "A Life of Privilege, Mostly." "To make matters worse, the panzer troops were using a number of captured Sherman tanks still bearing their American markings. You could be shot dead by your own tanks. And there was more. To create even greater chaos, hundreds of German parachutists — *English-speaking parachutists, wearing American uniforms* — were being dropped in."

The slaughter was horrific. As men were killed, replacements were rushed to the front lines. These were often inexperienced, poorly-trained recruits who were unwelcome to the hardened riflemen at the front. They were also resented because they were alive, while the person they were replacing — a buddy — was dead.

My uncle was one of the inexperienced ones.

"He had a terrific job in the Coast Guard in Puerto Rico," my mother told me. "He swam every day and picked the bananas from the trees. But he felt guilty that he wasn't doing enough for the war effort, so he asked to be transferred to the Air Force. He went to Arkansas to train as a pilot. He did not make pilot, but he made navigator. While he was in training, the Germans were squeezing the Allied troops in the forests of Belgium. All the trainees were shipped out immediately, to train as privates in England. They trained there a short time and were shipped to the front. My brother and his whole platoon were killed in their first engagement."

My grandparents — Ben and Flora Kampler — were celebrating New Year's Eve with some of Flora's family when the telegram came. My mother, who was pregnant with her second child, had stayed home.

"We were all there for dinner," my great-uncle, Jack Goodman, told me. "They came to the door and rang the bell and gave Flora the telegram that Bernard was shot dead. One thing made me angry — why New Year's Eve? Everyone is sitting around peacefully eating and bang, your boy is dead. Why didn't they wait until the next day? When they brought the bodies back, there was a big ceremony in Central Park, and then Bernard was buried in Long Island. It was very sad, very heartbreaking. Flora and Ben were stunned. We all were."

The family couldn't bring themselves to tell my mother that her beloved brother was dead. For the good of her unborn child, the doctor advised the Kamplers to keep his death a secret. So they sat shiva without her, and when they visited her, they wore awful, strained expressions. My mother thought they were anxious because there had been no news.

My brother was born on January 10, 1945. Mother was ready to name him Ira Paul.

When she brought the baby home from the hospital, Ben and Flora told her. She screamed so loudly that the neighbors heard. She named the new baby Bernard.

Uncle Bernard's death affected us all. My grandmother never recovered from the loss of her son. She started keeping a diary addressed to him — it breaks your heart when you read it. She became bitter and clung to my mother. My grandfather's spirit was broken. My mother has mourned her brother's death ever since.

The new family Mom was creating — the one with me, my poor brother now saddled with my uncle's name, and my father — well, we never felt we were as important to her as the family the war had destroyed.

This feeling of unimportance affected our choices — what we did with our lives or didn't do, whom we married or did not marry, whether or not we had children. And our choices, in turn, are now affecting my brother's children's choices. The circles in the pond grow ever wider.

Since World War II, America has fought many wars. We have fought serious wars in Korea and Vietnam, and presidential ego-stroke wars in Panama and Granada. Now we are fighting a needless presidential ego-stroke war in Iraq.

Because every soldier's death in some way effects generations of a family, war must be considered the most serious and the most sacred of actions.

Because I can so easily imagine the confusion, terror and loneliness that my poor, gentle Uncle Bernard felt at the front during the Battle of the Bulge, unless my country is attacked, I will never support a war.

~ ~ ~

February 10, 2005

VALENTINE TO A LONG-LASTING MARRIAGE

The house in south Florida was low and white, with green trim and a tile roof. A huge rubber tree took up half of the front yard. I was walking past it last week when I happened to look over at the windows. I saw a small, frail woman alone in a large space, drifting over to close the curtains.

The woman's image remains with me because in another of those houses, my mother, recently widowed for the second time, is also turning into a small, frail woman drifting alone in a large space.

As Valentine's Day approaches, our culture of youth presses us hard to celebrate young love and young marriage — to celebrate with chocolate and champagne; to celebrate with diamonds.

Love is fun and marriage is even more fun, say the ads. But I am haunted by another of love's realities, expressed by G.K. Chesterton this way: "The way to love anything is to realize that it might be lost."

For my mother's generation, divorce was rare and marriages were "for better or for worse, 'til death do us part." Fifty-year and even 60-year marriages are not rare among my mother's friends. In fact, my late father's favorite joke was about a couple in their 90s who were applying for a divorce. "Why did you wait so long?" the judge asked. "We wanted to wait until the children were dead," the couple said. My father thought that was hilarious.

Some of those long-haul marriages were based on love and affection and others on frustration and contempt. In old age, the fault lines of marriage become brutally visible. Last week, down in Florida, I heard a story about a woman who was so angry about caring for her 90-year-old husband that she stopped feeding him. He grew weak, fell, and was taken to a nursing home. There he was fed and was starting to gain weight when he died, probably of a broken heart.

And I also heard about a woman who left her gravely-ill husband in the hospital alone because she had airline tickets to Europe. The doctors were kind enough to keep him there until she returned; they didn't want to send a dying man home to an empty house.

Whether a long-lasting marriage is good, great or terrible, the truth is that one partner is bound to die before the other. And the loneliness of the one left behind can be unbearable. Some die soon after their partners. One woman in my mother's community drowned herself in a lake the week after her husband died. One frail couple committed suicide together.

Even if, like my mother, you have children and grandchildren, friends, and volunteer work that you love, coming home to an empty house can be cruel. You find yourself drifting through empty rooms, turning on the television set just to hear voices, talking to photographs on the walls.

Still, life in the retirement community is not all about death and dying. Romance flourishes. The talk that week was all about the new affair between a lovely widow of 83 and her new, older lover. "He can't keep his hands off of her," one of their friends told me. "I'm not a prude, but they shouldn't act like that, not in public." Even juicier, before they became a couple, the man was double-dealing her with another woman. The two went on a cruise together; I was told she bought black lacy underwear for the trip.

Friendships also flourish, especially among the widows. One pair told me about their recent overnight at a Miami spa. "We were in our room, and a cruise ship was passing so close we could see the passengers" one said. "My roommate here lifted her shirt and flashed them!" "It was dark," said the other, giggling. "They couldn't see anything."

Our culture fears death so much that long life has become a fetish. Now that we are achieving it, however, it is common for people to outlive their eyesight, their hearing, their hip bones, their minds and, almost always, their partners. "Old age isn't for sissies," said the comedian Martha Raye, and neither is long-lasting love. Whenever I visit Florida, I wonder if I have the strength and the character for it.

"'Tis better to have loved and lost than never to have loved at all," said Alfred Lord Tennyson, and who could argue with him. But as we celebrate the friskiness of young love, we should also recognize the strength it takes to be part of an older, long-lasting love. And we should realize that at the end of love, we can find ourselves drifting through a large space, sad and too much alone.

~ ~ ~

March 24, 2005

Two Red Shoes

Glitter. Thick stage makeup. Eighty-year-old dancers with great legs. Women (and some men, of course) in fancy gowns. Big egos and small talents. Lip-synching to popular songs. Usually, when the Lauderdale West Theater Group of Plantation, Fla., puts on a show, that's what it's all about.

This time, my enduring memory will be of red, high-heeled dancing shoes, worn, scuffed and cracked, sticking up from a gurney being wheeled into the emergency room.

Two weeks ago, I flew down for another of my mother's famous, Broadway-style condo shows. She retired at 87 last year, so this was the first show in decades that she didn't write, direct and choreograph as well as dance in. But she kept her hand in, writing the prototype script and choreographing the dance numbers. And because she's the star of Lauderdale West, she had a star turn — a solo in the second act, lip-synching and dancing to Liza Minelli singing "New York, New York."

Giving up the reins wasn't easy for Mom, but she's also had a rough year. The sad death in August of Harold Filler, her second husband, took its toll. They say that grief seeks out the lungs, and in December she was in the hospital with pneumonia. But by February she was back at work, training her dancers, teaching exercise classes and rehearsing for the show.

I flew down in time for the last dress rehearsal, which was the usual melange of bar mitzvah dresses, Jewish/Italian bling (long before there was ghetto bling, there was Jewish and Italian bling), and upstaging. "Look at me!" "No, look at me!" the performers silently cried.

Although I didn't know it when I arrived, Mom wasn't feeling well. She barely made it through her number, and she fainted on the floor of the kitchen when we got home. I hydrated her and fed her toast and she seemed to recover. She was determined to go on.

On opening night, she began dressing at home. She put on her flesh-colored tights, her red dancing shoes and her stage makeup. Then she began to tremble. "I'm not going to make it," she said, clutching at my hand. "Take me to the emergency room."

For the first time in 29 years, my mother was going to miss a performance. In the space of an hour, we had gone from musical comedy to epic tragedy. We sat in the emergency ward all night, Mom wearing her red dancing shoes and stage makeup and looking like an 87-year-old hooker. But the hospital sent her home.

Saturday night, with my heart in my mouth, I again helped her prepare. This time, we made it the theater. It was a full house — maybe 500 people. The parking lot was full. Fifteen walkers were lined up against the wall. Five motorized wheelchairs were parked in a corner.

The spotlight hit the glitter ball, the theater came alive with sparkles, the music started and I burst into tears. I've been coming to these shows so long that I not only know the cast and the crew, but half of the audience, as well. Watching them all age has been a special circle of hell. The performers didn't always lip-synch, for example. They used to have voices, they used to sing. But as they got older, they found they couldn't remember lyrics any more. Still, nothing can keep them from going on stage. It makes them feel young again, and alive.

The show had a Las Vegas theme. It opened with the whole cast lip-synching to "Happy Days are Here Again." Then Bob did his Liberace impersonation in a swirling black cape with gold sequins. Fran stopped the show singing "God Bless America" — don't ask what the song has to do with Las Vegas; I can only tell you that the new director's wife is a supporter of President Bush. Sylvia did a fantastic rendition of Marilyn Monroe singing "Diamonds are a Girl's Best Friend."

Then it was time for Liza. The audience started chanting Mom's name and applauding as soon as she stepped on stage. She was herself again, young and sparkly and full of personality. Her eyes were shining. Her delicate wrists, dancing inside the beat, illuminated the music. She went slow during the first part, but after the bridge I could see her thinking, "The hell with it." And she started doing Liza kicks — maybe not as high as before, but Liza kicks just the same. The audience stood up and cheered. I was screaming, "Bravo!" as the tears rolled down my cheeks. A woman I didn't know ran down, slapped me on the back and said, "You can't keep a trouper down." It was a magic moment, one that repeated itself at the Sunday matinee.

We returned to the emergency room on Monday morning. Mom was old, cold, pale and trembling. I told the nurse that her patient was a star who had been on-stage the day before, but looking at Mom, she said she couldn't understand how. I thought about it as we sat in the ER all day, waiting for a diagnosis and a hospital bed. Just before they diagnosed Mom with pneumonia again and sent her upstairs to her room, I looked for the nurse.

"It was will power," I said. "It was iron will power, and the need to be loved by her audience one more time."

It seems to me that old age is like a thief, stalking its victims, coming up behind them when they least expect it, whacking them with something hard. Whack, you're old. Whack, your back is bent. Whack, you walk slow now. Whack, you have to lean on a cane or a walker. Whack, you're in a wheelchair now.

Whack, you're on a gurney in the emergency room, with your red dancing shoes sticking up as they wheel you away.

Whack.

~ ~ ~

July 28, 2005

WHEN ART WAS POLITICS

When I was a young girl, my mother enrolled me in modern dance lessons at a professional school in New York. It was called the New Dance Group Studios. Every Saturday morning I took the subway from Brooklyn to Manhattan, rode up a tiny, creaky, scary elevator in a narrow old building on West 47th Street, changed into a black leotard, and, with other children, learned movement to the beat of a drum.

My mother, Rose Kagan, who is a far more talented dancer than I, took classes there on Wednesdays. And sometimes, in the evenings, she would take me to the 92nd Street Y to watch our teachers perform.

This is only a distant memory now, but it seems that if you manage to live for a certain number of years, some of the pieces of your life enter the history books without your even realizing it. To the astonishment of my mother and myself, that's what happened last week.

Mom, who is now 88 and living in Florida, was visiting me in Vermont. For a treat, we went over to Saratoga, N.Y., to see the New York City Ballet in its summer season. While we were there, we stopped in at the National Museum of Dance & Hall of Fame. To our surprise, we found an exhibit curated by two sisters, Carolyn Adams and Julie Adams Strandberg, along with the American Dance Legacy Institute. It was called "Dancing Rebels: The New Dance Group."

We were astonished to see pictures of our former teachers on the walls of a museum. Videos of their performances were showing on monitors. Their costumes were on mannequins. Their words and their history were on the walls. Our history, our lives were on the walls.

The New Dance Group, it turns out, was formed in 1932 at a rally protesting the killing of a young labor organizer named Harry Simms by the New Jersey police. Right then, a group of idealistic modern dancers and choreographers joined together to make "great ideas real" and use them "to create works of truth and beauty."

They had two rules. The first was that they must perform dances about subjects that mattered to them personally — no dying swans and handsome princes allowed. The second was that the dances must be crafted in such a way that they would be understood by "the masses."

Yes, there was a certain amount of intellectual arrogance and pretentious romanticism along with the artists' good-hearted desire for social justice. When choreographer William Bales said, "I have tried to capture the unsophisticated quality of the peasantry because I believe it is the most direct way I can communicate the simple emotion of simple people," it was clear he never met a peasant in his life. If he had traveled in the developing world, as I have, he would have found in the jungle people quite as sophisticated — and life quite as complex — as it can ever get in Manhattan.

But that is a small point when we now live in a world where art is separated into categories, "fine" and "popular," and never the twain shall meet. Here was a group of dedicated artists from a variety of ethnic backgrounds — Eastern European Jews, African-Americans, Caribbean islanders — who created dances from their cultural roots with "a sense of feeling deeply about things and having them spill out into the body, into the movement," as Joseph Gifford said.

These artists were not interested in "pretty." They were not interested in uniformity. Their hallmark was to "place great value on their differences and the specificity and rigor of each dance style. They were not a melting pot. They were richly diverse."

The New Dance Group dancers achieved a limited fame. I'm not sure how many people know the names of Sophie Maslow, Anna Sokolow, Jean Leon Destine, Muriel Manings, Jane Dudley, Jean Erdman, Hadassah, Pearl Primus or Donald McKayle. But these names are very real to me. My mother and I sweated in their classes, watched them teach and rehearse, and applauded them at performances that are still fresh in my mind 45 years later. It was thrilling to see these artists and their work elevated to the importance of a museum show.

My mother walked through the exhibits with her eyes shining and her hands clasped to her breast. "I learned everything from these people," she said in a whisper. "How to fall forwards and backwards, how to do splits, how to kick. I accomplished so much for someone who started so late." For 35 years as a dancer, choreographer and teacher in Florida, my mother has been using what she learned at the New Dance Group.

Dance is an elite art now, with little or no political content. In fact, it's hard to find political art of any kind in America, outside of comedians, some theater, and the occasional singer-songwriter. But for the passionate dancers of the New Dance Group, art was about politics and politics was about social justice, and that's quite a legacy for an obscure dance studio in New York.

~ ~ ~

THE MINK COAT

It must have been 50 years ago. My father was doing well in his Brooklyn Army & Navy store, and my thin and elegant mother, Rose Kagan, bought a girdle.

Into the girdle she tucked $2,000 in cash. Then she took the subway into the city, where she met an old friend of the family, a furrier named Kelly Kalish. She came home with a glossy, stylish full-length mink coat.

It was the time then, in the 1950s, when middle-class husbands who survived the Depression and World War II and now found themselves with a little success and disposable income bought mink coats for their wives. If they weren't doing *that* well, they bought mink jackets or mink stoles.

My mother proudly wore the coat for 15 years. Then she and my father decided to retire and move to Florida.

The coat stayed in the north and ended up in a plastic cleaner's bag in my closet. It was so long ago that I don't remember how it came into my possession. It never fit, and was too ostentatious, so I never wore it. I think I planned to make a blanket out of it at some point, but you know what happens to projects like that... down quilts came into my life and the coat hung in the closet, along with my old skunk coat from the Seventies and a series of colorful native Panamanian and Bolivian dresses I collected when I lived in those countries and never wore in the United States.

And that would have been the end of the story, except for the fact that my mother, now 88, agreed to come north for Thanksgiving.

She's been very lonely since her second husband died, and I didn't want her to be alone for Thanksgiving. But I have spent a lot of time in Florida this year, helping her through a series of health crises, and I couldn't face another trip south. So over time, I convinced her to face the frozen north for the first time in over 30 years — she had been visiting, of course, but only in summer.

My not-so-secret motivation in inviting her was to start getting her used to the cold, with an eye to a future when she would sell her home and move north. I was thinking she could live a) with me, b) in an apartment on Main Street in Brattleboro or c) in a retirement home and have an interesting life closer to people who know and love her.

Mom was brave to come. I met her at the airport with a down coat, a fuzzy hat and suede lined gloves, but even bundled up, she winced in the cold air. Randy and I heated our house to what we considered Amazonian jungle levels, with sweat dripping from our bodies, but still she was cold.

When it was time to go to Randy's family for Thanksgiving dinner, I had an idea. Why not wear the mink? She had forgotten all about it, and was surprised I still had it. I pulled it out of the closet and it was still elegant and glossy even after all those years. She put it on, and it glowed on her. It was heavy and a little dusty, but it looked wonderful on her. She was a bit abashed at its luxuriousness, but she wore it for the rest of the week.

It brought back a lot of memories. She stroked it and remembered the girdle and my father and how he had surprised her when he said he wanted to retire and move to Florida, and how worried she was that he wouldn't know what to do with himself after spending 12 hours a day, six days a week, for 35 years in his Army & Navy store. And how he had surprised her by finding friends, joining clubs, and having a wonderful and active retirement. And how he always said that Mom fell "into a pot of gold," because the retirement community had an active theater group, and Mom became their playwright, choreographer, director and star.

She stroked the coat and remembered how my father died in the house in Florida, and then, a few months later, how her mother died in a nearby nursing home. And then, a few months after that, how my younger brother, my only brother, died in Woodstock, N.Y.

She stroked it and remembered coming back from my brother's funeral and spending time with Harold Filler, and eventually marrying him. I gave away the bride, in the same room in which my father had died, and Mom and I were both crying when we started walking down the aisle because Pop wasn't there.

She stroked the coat and remembered the good life she had had with Harold for 10 years, and then, how he died in the same spot in the same room where my father died.

She stroked the coat and said, wistfully, "So many memories."

It did nothing but snow while Mom was here, and the mink coat served her well. Her worst fear, of driving in a snowstorm, well, we did that twice.

The day she left, we gently put the coat back in its plastic bag and rehung it in my closet.

The conversation has been opened. Mom is willing to consider renting an apartment on Main Street and spending the warmer months up here in Vermont. She is not ready to sell her house in Florida and leave her many friends, but she is starting to think about it. She knows that she has family here — me. Randy's family, my friends — who love her and will take care of her. My brother's daughter will give birth in January, and Mom will have a great-grandchild in Kingston, N.Y.

And when she is ready, she can stay here all year. Because she has a mink coat.

THREE:
THE NEW HOPE TRILOGY

April 22, 1992

CONCERT: RAPTURE FOLLOWED ECSTASY

(When the posters appeared — overnight, all over town — I couldn't believe Brattleboro's luck. The 11 O'Clock Mass Choir of the New Hope Baptist Church of Newark, N.J. was coming to town! One hundred black faces in one of the whitest towns in the country! Gospel music! Gospel passion! Can you tell how excited I was? I knew the power of gospel. I knew it was the front side to the raunchy old-time Rhythm & Blues that I loved. I knew it was the progenitor of rock 'n' roll. I knew this choir would sing wonderfully and I would be in heaven. As this piece shows, heaven wasn't the half of it.)

Like a fool, I took a reporter's notebook to the gospel concert at the First Baptist Church on Saturday.

I only needed to take my heart.

When the 100 members of the 11 O'Clock Mass Choir of the New Hope Baptist Church of Newark, N.J., draped in long navy robes, marched into the jammed church and gave out that first, full-throated power chord, I totally lost it.

These beautiful people — this beautiful community of people — chose to bring their music and their deep, deep faith in God to Brattleboro. They chose to share so much joy, so much emotion, so much love with the audience that words mean nothing beside it.

For me, ecstasy was followed by rapture, and there I stayed for the two-plus hours that the band played and the choir sang.

Sometimes I was standing and dancing, sometimes sitting and swaying. Sometimes the power of the voices raised goose bumps on my arms and shoulders, and sometimes it raised the hair on the back of my neck.

I thought my mouth was open in astonishment the entire time, but after the concert, one of the singers told me I had a beautiful smile, and that she had enjoyed watching me use it during the concert.

She was watching me. I was watching her. Two cultures met and stared at each other. We made eye contact.

Saturday night, the meeting of two cultures was probably as much of a shock for the gospel singers as it was for Brattleboro.

The New Hope Gospel Choir, of course, is composed of African-Americans. Dignified, God-loving, long-married, talented, hard-working black people.

People like us, only better dressed.

We in Brattleboro, of course, are mostly white.

The choir's 24-hour visit probably doubled the black population of Vermont.

We had to get used to each other. They were "down home" with their warmth, smiles and elegant suits. We were "down home" with our welcome, our wonder, our blue jeans and our flannel shirts.

Finally, our hearts joined as one.

It was intense.

Some of the people in the audience had driven 200 miles to be there. The choir had driven hundreds of miles, in three buses, to be there. Family and church members accompanied them and sat in the audience.

Before the music started, Selectman Charlie Miller read a proclamation that declared Saturday and Sunday "The Weekend of New Hope" in Brattleboro, Vt.

"The joyous coming together of people from very different backgrounds symbolizes the possibility for oneness for all people," he read.

The elegant director of the choir, Anne Moss, took the proclamation and held it to her heart.

Bruce Talbot, the producer, is a white guy who loves gospel music. He has a long-standing relationship with the New Hope Church, and he was the one who brought the choir here. He only moved to our area a month ago.

"The purpose of my life is to enable people to have joy-filled, fulfilled lives," Talbot told me. "I make it up as I go along. I'm not looking at church or religious work. There's a love that occurs in the music, that to me goes beyond all differences and transcends everything."

"Bruce, you have fulfilled your purpose," Anne Moss replied.

It wasn't the music that brought us all together, although the music was superb.

It wasn't the astonishing quality of the voices, male and female, soprano, alto, tenor and bass — although every soloist could have (and might well have, for all I know) a professional singing career.

It wasn't the excellent rhythm section, consisting of electric bass, organ, drum and percussion — although they supported the singers beautifully.

It wasn't the fascinating sizes, shapes, faces, clothes, hairdos and ages of the singers — although their diverse characteristics were a hundred novels, the audience, with pleasure, tried to read.

It wasn't even the humanness of the choir — although I liked the fact that by the end of the evening, almost every singer in the front row — and that included the elegant Anne Moss — had kicked off their shoes and were singing in their stockinged feet.

It was the joy.

Music, when it hits right, brings joy up from a deep place. But the joy in our hearts that night came from a deeper place. Call it the spirit. For the singers, the spirit was God.

I admit, I was slow to get it.

I thought we were at a concert. I was responding to the beauty of the music.

Then the first soloist, Victor Williams, started talking. He walked back and forth, testifying to an early life of drugs and alcohol. Then he sang.

I thought it was a powerful performance.

But when he finished, he broke down and sobbed in Anne Moss's arms.

Then I got it.

The emotion was real. His life story was real.

These extraordinary people had brought us a church service, not a show. They were openly displaying their love of God.

"God is a good God; he's a great God," they sang.

Because I put my notebook down, I can't remember a lot of detail about the evening. I can't tell you the names of the all the songs, for example, or the singers. The exquisite Felicia Moss, Ann's daughter, singing "Let There Be Peace" stands out, but so does her proud mother's victory dance at the end of the song.

But there were other women with extraordinary voices. I remember the woman in front translating into sign language. The deaf man she was signing to was swaying to the music. I remember afterward, when refreshments were served, I naively wanted deep conversation about the black experience, and about how rhythm and blues and gospel are intertwined. I wound up instead talking about diets with a woman who had lost 64 pounds by fasting and was guiltily wrapping up almond cookies in a plastic bag to take back to her hotel room.

I guess that's the message. We're not all that different.

I'll let Anne Moss describe the weekend: "It was an experience that will never be forgotten. All our hearts came together, and we were one in the spirit. If Jesus had come walking in the door, I wouldn't have been surprised. It was the best experience the choir has ever had. It didn't have anything to do with black and white. The exuberance that the audience had was so great, we responded accordingly, and sang our hearts out."

Amen, hallelujah and please come again, 11 O'clock Mass Choir.

(The concert was not the end of the story. Down in Newark, my column was read, passed around, and proudly pasted into the church scrapbook.

Talbot brought the choir up two more times — each time to bigger venues. Then he moved north, to Barre, Vt., and began specializing in cross-cultural exchanges.

We kept in touch, and he issued frequent invitations for me to visit Newark with him. I finally did, in February of 2001.)

February 8, 2001

A STORY OF NEW HOPE

It all started back in April of 1992, when the African-American 11 O'Clock Mass Choir of the New Hope Baptist Church of Newark, N.J. appeared in Brattleboro.

The concert's producer, Bruce Talbot, was just about the whitest white man I've ever met. How, I wondered, did he hook up with a black church in Newark, N.J.?

It seems that a few years before, he had had an epiphany with an Aretha Franklin gospel record. Then, with trepidation, he and his friend Paul Erlbaum began seeking similar gospel music epiphanies in the black churches of Harlem. They were surprised to find how welcome they were.

Eventually, they found their way to the New Hope Baptist Church in Newark, where the world-famous gospel singer Cissy Houston (yes, mother of Whitney Houston and aunt of Dionne Warwick,) runs the sacred music ministry.

Talbot and Erlbaum were immediately adopted by the New Hope congregation, especially by church stalwarts Mom and Pop Sullivan.

Mom — or Rose — Sullivan, 84, is a woman of intelligence and power. She became clerk of the church in 1947, but Talbot says that when you ask anyone what her job description really is, they just say "boss."

It was Mom Sullivan whom Talbot called when he wanted to bring the choir up to Brattleboro. She thought it was a wonderful idea, and soon the 11:00 A.M. Mass Choir, along with many of New Hope's congregation, came, sang their hearts out, spread joy and levitated the town.

According to Talbot, when the congregation returned to New Jersey, their pastor, the Rev. Dr. Charles E. Thomas, told them this story: When he was a boy in the south, he said, he walked five miles to school and five miles back every day, while white students passed in buses and mouthed hateful things at him. But after returning from Vermont, "I now judge people by who they are, not what they are."

"The church erupted," Talbot said.

Talbot eventually moved to Barre, but he continued to bring African-American choirs to Vermont. And he and Erlbaum started taking Vermont groups down to Newark and Harlem for cultural exchanges.

I hadn't seen Talbot in years when he called a few weeks ago. Pop Sullivan was gone now, he said, the Rev. Thomas had retired, and now Mom Sullivan was retiring, too. New Hope was honoring her amazing 54 years of service in a special ceremony; would I like to come? Of course I would.

That Sunday morning, we were a warmly welcomed group of seven white people, including Talbot and Erlbaum, among about 1,000 African-Americans. Many hugged us and thanked us for coming.

Mom, elegant in a pink bubble of a hat, a tailored pink brocade jacket over a pleated pink skirt, white tights and pink shoes, called us her "Vermont family."

When the congregation was seated, we — Mom's family, black and white, Newark and Vermont — marched down the aisle behind her. Applause rang out. Mom was seated up front, facing the congregation, in a throne of a chair decorated with ribbons and balloons.

Then the Male Chorus, elegant in black suits and yellow satin ties, strutted down the aisle, clapping, dancing and singing while the band — an electric bass, keyboard, drums, and guitar — played.

"A treat for the sisters," wryly remarked the new pastor, a strong young man named Joe A. Carter.

The service was filled with music, prayer, song, dance, clapping, shouts, and tithing. Backed by the electric bass, Carter started his sermon slowly and built to a James Brown-ian climax — shouting, ululating, singing, gesticulating, falling back, rising again, as his deacons rushed up with white towels to mop the sweat from his closely-shaven head.

Some people were carried away by the spirit; they were gently scooped up and comforted by nurses in white uniforms and caps (Mom Sullivan had a hand in founding the nursing ministry). About 12 people came up to the rail to be saved.

Then it was time to celebrate Mom Sullivan's extraordinary life. We learned that besides being church clerk and singing in the chorus, she had been instrumental in establishing the Newark NAACP, the church's Senior Citizens group, the young people's choir, and had done, it seems, a significant amount of marriage counseling.

Talbot told me this story about Mom Sullivan: A new member of the church, who didn't know many people, needed a hysterectomy. She went to the hospital to be prepped for surgery at the ungodly hour of 6:30 in the morning. When she walked in, she found Mom and Pop Sullivan sitting there, waiting to help her through the ordeal.

For over an hour people showered Mom Sullivan with praise, plaques, bouquets of roses, gifts, cards and "love offerings" in the form of serious money. Carter himself started the giving with a $250 check. Pew by pew, everyone lined up and dropped bills or envelopes into her open arms.

Moved, Mom thanked the congregation for giving her these tributes now instead of waiting for her funeral.

Then Cissy Houston sang, from the depths of her deep, deep heart, two of Mom's favorite hymns. Her voice was rich and powerful and full of emotion, and it sent chills down my spine. Then we repaired to the basement for fried chicken, more tributes, and cake.

Someone told me recently that "a community is defined by the people it excludes."

Maybe that's true for most of our divided, individualistic, niched-to-death world. But it wasn't true at New Hope. Just think of all the people who were included in that service: old, young, healthy, ill, wealthy, poor, gay, straight, married, single, divorced, black, white, Baptist, Jew. We were lifted high by the music, the passion, the rejoicing, and the preaching. Our differences temporarily forgotten, we melted into a single unit — a community — sharing one rich experience. For that short time, we were a single body with a thousand different heads.

Later, Talbot said that his becoming part of this community was a surprise.

"There was such a big, built-in cultural rift," he said. "Yet over the years, Paul and I and others from Vermont have been completely and unexpectedly embraced. All we had to do is reach out a little bit, and snap, there were these instant loving relationships — not just cordial or nice, but loving. With nothing on our part. We're all inherently anxious, if not downright fearful, of other people. If someone just makes a little step, boom, snap, these things just open up."

ANNE DRINKARD-MOSS: SINGING FOR THE LORD

(Bruce Talbot called one day to tell me that Anne Moss had died. So I wrote this piece as both an obituary and a tribute to the people I had met at New Hope. After it was printed in the Reformer, I offered it around to all the African-American gospel magazines I could find. Many of them ran it as a tribute to a remarkable woman who had lived a remarkable life.)

A murmur ran through the bus when it pulled into Brattleboro, Vt. "Everybody's white here. What're we going to do?" Then someone said, "We're going to sing to the Lord," and that's exactly what they did.

This is the story of a remarkable cross-cultural exchange that took place in the 1990s between Vermont, one of the whitest states in the Union, and the incredibly powerful, all-black, 100-member 11 A.M. Mass Choir from the New Hope Baptist Church in Newark, N.J. The woman behind that exchange, the beautiful, musically gifted and devoutly spiritual Anne L. Drinkard-Moss, died on New Year's Day at the age of 75.

Moss was one of eight children in a remarkable family. One of her sisters was Emily, or Cissy, later Houston, who sang lead with the Sweet Inspirations; they backed everyone from Elvis Presley to Aretha Franklin and had a hit of their own in 1968. Houston's daughter, Whitney, took the family's gospel roots into the commercial sphere, with enormous success.

When Anne was only 11, she, Cissy, and two brothers, Nick and Larry, sang gospel professionally as the Drinkard Four. Sister Marie was their instructor, and sister Lee, later Warrick and the mother of Dee Dee and Dionne (later Warwick), was their manager. The group expanded to become the Drinkard Singers; they were the first gospel group to sing with Mahalia Jackson at the National Baptist Convention, the first to sing at the Newport Jazz Festival, and the first to be recorded by RCA.

Moss then formed the Drinkard Ensemble, which toured the country with Warwick and served as the inspiration for Alex Bradford's famous play, "Your Arm's Too Short to Box With God."

While she was still in high school, Moss met Felix Moss; they married in 1944 and had three children, Kenneth, Gregory and Felicia, a powerful singer in her own right. Felix Moss died in 1997.

Rather than continuing to sing commercially, Moss created a ministry out of her music. At New Hope she lovingly and demandingly directed a children's choir as well as the 11 a.m. Choir, which sang with such power, passion, joy and spirit that they lifted the hearts of everyone who heard them.

The choir came to Brattleboro in 1992 through the efforts of Bruce Talbot and Paul Erlbaum, two passionate gospel fans who have become honorary members of New Hope.

"A friend suggested I invite the choir to Brattleboro, where I had just moved," Talbot said in a three-way phone conversation with Erlbaum and myself just after Moss's funeral. "I wondered, 'Why would they ever want to do that?' But Anne was enthusiastic about the idea. She'd never been to Vermont. But she expected to be singing for a black audience."

"She was nervous when she recognized this was a white town," Erlbaum said. "But she was there to sing the praises of the Lord. Whatever she did, she was doing it for God."

I was waiting at the church that first day, when the buses arrived, and I'll never forget my first sight of Moss. She was a strikingly beautiful women, even in her 60s, and she was wearing an exceptionally lovely full-length, glossy fur coat that floated out behind her as she inspected the church.

When it came time for the concert, Moss, now changed into robes, marched down the aisle with the robed choir behind her, all of them singing at full throttle. "The look on her face was so childlike and radiant and happy," Talbot said.

Like Moss, the music that day was ecstatic, rapturous and deeply emotional. We testified and sobbed, danced, clapped and shouted. We joined arms and swayed. We were overwhelmed and transported.

"All our hearts came together, and we were one in the spirit," Moss told me afterward. "If Jesus had come walking in the door, I wouldn't have been surprised. It didn't have anything to do with black and white. The exuberance that the audience had was so great, we responded accordingly and sang our hearts out."

The town's selectboard proclaimed the weekend, "The Weekend of New Hope," and the choir, along with about 50 of their Newark "boosters," were welcomed with opened arms.

"A few years ago I was talking to Russia Thompson, since deceased," Erlbaum said. "She said that when she was shopping for souvenirs in downtown Brattleboro, people gave her special greetings in every shop. She walked into one store and a tape of the choir was playing. In another store she found a pair of shoes she really liked, and the owner, who had been at the concert, made sure there would be no charge."

Two more Brattleboro-area concerts followed; when Talbot moved north, he and Erlbaum produced two concerts in Barre. And they continued to attend Sunday services in Newark whenever they could.

"I remember one time, two members of the choir had had very dangerous strokes," Talbot said. "They were no longer able to sing. Anne worked with them, and during the choir's anniversary program, she brought them down to solo. Although they couldn't articulate the words, they could carry the melody beautifully. Very quietly, Anne articulated the lyrics for them. At one point she plunked her head down on the piano, she was so overwhelmed with emotion."

The choir was an open one; there were no auditions. "I once asked Anne, 'How do you get such an incredible sound out of them?'" Talbot said. "And she said, 'I just lead them to the source of their experience.'"

Characteristically, Moss had prepared for her death; she had even designed a pink robe and pink hat for her laying-out. "She looked beautiful," Erlbaum said.

Both the church and the choir were packed for the funeral; people who had left long ago came back to sing for Moss.

"There were at least 1,000 people in the church and 200 people in the choir," Talbot said. "Cissy sang. Whitney Houston and Felicia sang; they were sensational. At the end, when the choir sang the 23rd Psalm, former members came up out of the pews to sing, and the song went on and on and on."

For the last leg of her journey home, Moss's coffin was transferred to a white wagon drawn by two white horses; she remained elegant to the end.

"One pastor said, 'She made it,'" Talbot said. "He meant she made it to heaven. She made it to the other side."

FOUR:
THE TOWNS I LIVE IN:
BRATTLEBORO AND DUMMERSTON

(My first job as a journalist was as the metropolitan reporter for the Brattleboro Reformer. Covering Brattleboro and its surrounding towns — usually lumped together as "Brattleboro" — has meant a never-ending stream of interesting personalities and stories.

To quote the late musician Dave Carter: "This is my home/ This is my only home/This is the only sacred ground that I have ever known/And should I stray in the dark night alone/Rock me goddess in the gentle arms of Eden."

I will never tire of writing about this place.)

September 16, 1992

JUDITH KNEW IT WAS COMING

(In 1992, Brattleboro Reformer reporter Judith Hart Fournier and radio personality Bob Sawyer were a well-known media couple. I met Judy when she was doing public relations for a local music producer. If I remember correctly, after the producer left town, I was the one who told Judy that a stringer's job at the newspaper was opening up. She applied and was hired.

Then Judy met Robyn Burke and everything changed. Suddenly, Fournier and Burke were a couple, and Sawyer seemed to be out of his mind with rage. As you will see, he stalked the couple long before he attacked and killed Fournier at a gas station on Putney Road in Brattleboro on September 15, 1992. She was 33 years old.

When I heard about the attack, I didn't think, I just picked up a reporter's notebook and ran to the hospital.

At the entrance to the emergency room, Police Chief Bruce Campbell stopped me. "Are you here as a friend or a reporter," he asked, and it was the first time I realized there might be a difference — and a conflict —between the two. "Both," I blurted out, and he was sensitive enough to let me come in.

71

Judy was lying on a gurney, alone, in a quiet room across from the ER. She was still alive, but she was dying. Robyn and I went outside, sat on the steps, and she told me what had happened.

Later, still in shock, I went back to the newsroom. Without speaking, I sat down at a computer and wrote this. It appeared on the front page the next day.)

Judith Hart Fournier knew she was going to die.

"The past few days she kept saying she wanted to be buried in Putney," said her lover, Robyn Burke, who was with Judith when she was fatally stabbed Tuesday afternoon. "She picked out her spot in the cemetery. She said, 'I need to call the cemetery man and see how you reserve a spot.'"

Robyn was talking on the steps of the emergency entrance to Brattleboro Memorial Hospital. Inside, Judith, pale and silent, her eyes closed, breathing through a respirator, lay on a table in a room in the emergency ward, her knife wounds covered with a sheet.

It was 7 p.m. Robyn was waiting for Judith to die.

In the past few weeks, Judith wrote a living will and left instructions for her funeral.

"It's bizarre," Robyn said. "She's talking about how she wants to be buried in Putney, and then this guy comes and kills her."

Bob Sawyer, who has been arrested in the slaying, had been stalking Judith, Robyn said.

Judith and Sawyer had lived together "as roommates," Robyn said. Then Judith met Robyn.

"The first week he was OK about it," Robyn said.

Then Sawyer, according to police, assaulted Judith and Robyn on the Main street of Putney. Since that day, there has been a court order saying that, "the defendant (Robert Sawyer) shall not associate with Judith Hart Fournier or Robyn Graham Burke, nor personally contact, harass or cause to be harassed, the same."

"He would get his toes just up to the line of the Vermont court order," Robyn said. "We reported everything, all the calls, to Captain Henry Farnum of the Windham County Sheriff's Department. Even if nothing came of it, they had it documented. But they couldn't do anything until he did something. I had to wait for him to kill her before we could do anything."

Tuesday, on the afternoon of the day Judith died, she was writing a story at the Reformer office. While there, she received four "hang-up" calls, Robyn said.

"When I picked Judith up from work, she said, 'Call the sheriff's Department'" Robyn said. "She'd had four hang-up calls, spaced every two minutes. A lot of weird stuff like that has been happening in the past week and a half."

Judith and Robyn walked out of the Reformer and got into the car. When they reached the end of the driveway, they saw Sawyer parked in his car in the Spiral Shop driveway next door, Robyn said.

"We waited for him to go, and he wouldn't," Robyn said. "We drove down to Putney Road to see if he would follow. He followed. I pretended I was turning into Fireside (True Value hardware store) to see if he would follow. I swerved away at the last minute. He swerved. Then we knew. It was obvious that he was following us."

Robyn said they pulled into the Mobil Station on Putney Road because they knew they could drive up to the cash booth.

"I yelled to the woman, 'Please call the police. This guy is after me,'" Robyn said.

In a matter of seconds, Sawyer was in the car, Robyn said.

"He was stabbing Judith," Robyn said. "Judith was screaming. He was pushing and pushing against her. Blood was everywhere."

Robyn said she got out of the car and ran around behind Sawyer.

"I grabbed him around the neck," she said. "He held on to my thumb. He bit me on the thumb while he was stabbing her. I got him out of the car. I was screaming to Judith to shut the door and lock it. The window was down just an inch or two. He got his hands in there and broke the glass right out. He was saying, 'I'm going to kill her. I'm going to kill her.'"

While all this was happening, Robyn said she was screaming for help.

"A guy showed up with an ax handle in his hand — no ax, just the handle," Robyn said. "I asked him to start hitting Bob. He told me he couldn't because he'd just had open-heart surgery. He showed me the scars!"

Then Judith got out of the car, Robyn said. She staggered across the lot.

"I was trying to deal with Bob and watch Judith at the same time," Robyn said. "Judith fell down a few times. She got up once or twice. Then she collapsed. Right then, the cops came."

The police moved Sawyer away, Robyn said.

"Oh my God," Robyn said. "There was a huge butcher knife all the way in Judith's back. You could only see the handle, but from the size of it, it must have been 10 or 12 inches long. There was blood all over her head and all over her chest. She was all sliced up."

As Robyn talked, hovering in the background were her parents, who were visiting on their way back from a Canadian vacation, and two of Robyn's neighbors. They were there to support Robyn.

"Judith's on life support until she dies," Robyn said. "They're not even going to move her into intensive care. It's not worth it. They did everything they could do. Even if they called LifeFlight, it wouldn't help. He did so much damage. They sewed her up. She's on a respirator. She's basically dead. It's just a matter of time until it's over."

Judith died while Robyn was talking, at 7:10 p.m.

"I really thought this was it for life," Robyn said. "We really loved each other. I thought we were going to be together. What am I going to do now?"

(Brattleboro being Brattleboro, a candlelight vigil for Judy drew 400 people the Saturday evening after she was killed. And later, an exorcism ceremony was held at the gas station to drive away evil vibrations. Sawyer told a packed court that God told him to kill. He remains in jail.

Three months after Judy's death, a polished black stone heart, inscribed with drawings of Judy by her two children, plus messages of love from them and Robyn, plus lines from a poem that Judy had chosen to be read at her funeral — the night before she died! — was put over her grave in the Putney cemetery. And that was the end of that. Even today, whenever Randy or I pass by the cemetery, we wave hello to Judy.)

July 2001

LOVE LETTER TO A FLEA MARKET

Smoke starts rising from the cookhouse in the center of the Newfane Flea Market very early on Sunday mornings in summer, and people line up to buy donuts, coffee, fried-egg-and-sausage sandwiches and home fries.

Flea market people, I've noticed, fall into four general categories: vendors who come to sell; dealers who come to buy cheaply and resell somewhere else; collectors like myself; and civilians, for whom a morning at the flea market is an entertainment instead of a passion.

I collect antique fabrics, 1930s ceramics, and overheard conversations. I collected my best one a few years ago, as I was walking behind two men.

"Look at that," one man said, pointing. "Don't you want to buy a pith helmet?"

"You know what that's for, don't you?" said the other man without missing a beat. "So monkeys don't pith on you."

I come early so I can watch the vendors setting out their goods.

The first aisle tends to be populated by weathered men who gently lay out old rifles, shotguns, stuffed animals, and, in a touching tribute to eternal boyhood, baseball cards and marbles. I used to think their gruffness meant they were unfriendly, but then one morning a friend of mine brought her Labrador retriever, and I discovered that most of them are softies who carry dog treats in their pockets.

The second aisle is the domain of women laying out patchwork quilts, decorated plates and costume jewelry. Then there are the rest: the woman who only sells kitchenware, and the family that sells its own maple syrup, and the elegant elderly Massachusetts couple who sell perennials, and the man with the (I think) counterfeit Coach purses.

I often meet my friend Anne when I'm picking my way down the aisles. She is a second generation antique dealer and knows a great deal about Mission furniture, Arts & Crafts and flea market competition.

"It's always painful to pull up and see lots of cars here," Anne says. "I think, 'Oh my God, the good stuff will be gone. Why did I bother to eat breakfast?' I used to leap out of my car with great anxiety. Now I have learned that first, there's always good stuff out there, and second,

I've developed radar. It's almost as if all the junk fades out, and I can focus on the good stuff."

When Wayne and Pam arrive in their white van, dealers from all over the field converge on them like sharks smelling blood. They joke with each other, but the tension in the air is palpable.

Wayne buys "ends" — all the things that are left unsold after an auction. The standing joke is that he has never unpacked his own van. When he opens the doors, a feeding frenzy begins. Dealers elbow each other aside, grab cartons, take them away, hunch over them, unpack them, and make small piles of treasure.

"It brings out the worst in people," Anne says. "That carefully-structured social self completely disappears. It becomes opportunistic."

The thrill of the hunt obsesses these dealers, and for each one it is a different thrill: 1940s mixing bowls, vinyl records, old milk bottles, letters and photographs, a collection of received Christmas cards, picture frames, a rare book, an old piece of fabric.

Some collect only men's tools – rusted chisels, saws, hammers, screwdrivers, folded measuring sticks, pincers. Some collect only women's tools – kitchen implements, sewing needles, thread, scissors. After all the cartons have been unpacked, the dealers confer with Wayne; he never bargains but always sells cheap. Then the rest of us pick through what is left.

My friend Ned comes over. He is usually a buyer, but recently he set up his own stand.

"I sold two pairs of snowshoes," he said, amazed. "I bought them years ago at the flea market for $30 each, wore them out completely, and then sold them last week for $35 each. And that was selling them cheap!"

Speaking of shoes, an antique textile dealer I know came over to show me a wonderful find — two tiny leather ladies' slippers. He said they dated from before the Civil War.

"How do you know?"

"They are made on the same last," he said. "The idea of a right foot and a left foot came later."

Flea markets almost became an endangered species a few years ago, as collectors and dealers flocked to eBay.

"How can I compete?" one dealer said. "Those people on eBay sit at home and sell all over the world, 24 hours a day. Here I have to get up at 3 a.m., drive, rent a booth, and stay and watch my stuff all day."

But now I'm hearing dealers complaining about constant e-mailing and trips to the post office, so maybe things have become more balanced.

"It would be a shame if flea markets died out," another dealer told me. "This is one of the most democratic places on earth. There are people here with PhD.s, and people with grade school educations. They're all here because they love stuff. They love to buy it and they love to sell it."

For me, a flea market is a living collage. It's a place to see a variety of unexpected things, to study human nature, to meet my friends and neighbors, to catch up on gossip.

I connect with my ancestors when I touch an old kitchen clock, a piece of cabbage rose curtain, or an 18th Century ship painting, things they bought, used and left behind a long time ago.

I connect with the whole country's past, with traditions that exist in our lives.

The flea market helps me celebrate life and, at the same time, wryly acknowledge death. After all, it's hard to look at the contents of dead people's houses without wondering what your own stuff is going to look like spread on rickety tables in the sunshine, selling for ten cents on the dollar a few years down the road.

But most of all, the flea market is a precious Sunday morning ritual. It's one I love so much that when winter comes, some Sunday mornings I drive out to Newfane, sit in my car on the rise above the deserted lot, and replay the market in my mind. I can see the smoke rising from the cookhouse, and all the familiar faces.

And here's a secret: sometimes I'm not the only one there.

June 13, 2002

WELCOME BACK, BRATTLEBORO

(A friend — I called him "Deep Buttercup" — tipped me off that a group was organizing, as a tourist event, a parade of cows down Main Street in Brattleboro. I thought that it was the dumbest idea I'd ever heard, and wrote a column about it.

The parade, sponsored by the Holstein Association, would cost $56,000 to produce. It amounted to approximately $200 per cow. I carried the idea further, writing that the town fathers were missing a beat. "If the event really goes over, they should give laxatives to the cows and sell the resulting patties to tourists, possibly in Chinese takeout boxes decorated by Vermont artist Woody Jackson." I also suggested that if people wanted to see a herd of spots parade down Main Street, they might consider Dalmatians.

One of the parade's organizers, publicist Lynn Barrett, called me when the piece appeared. Instead of being angry, she thanked me for being the first person to take the parade seriously.

Of course, it turned out that I was completely wrong. The parade was a great success, and no one had a better time during the weekend than I did, as you will see from the following column. The Strolling of the Heifers, now in its fifth year, has become a four-day event filled with agricultural seminars, balls, art auctions and a huge dairy fair on the Brattleboro Common. It is a major Vermont tourist attraction now, and always a lot of fun.)

A formal black-and-white ball was the climax of last Saturday's Strolling of the Heifers parade and farm festival, so the town's power elite put on tuxedos, while Alfred, the town's premiere African-American drag queen, chose a white satin ball gown with a closed square back, tight bodice, umbrella skirt, and Jackie Kennedy pearls.

Oh, Brattleboro! Where have you been so long?

When the idea of a cow parade was first announced last year, many residents, myself among them, were dismayed. I thought the idea of marching a bunch of cows up Main Street as a ploy to attract tourists was ridiculous. For a place that prides itself on rural sophistication and calls itself "The best small arts town in America," the idea seemed manufactured, lame and humorless — nothing more than a staged media event.

Once, in the 1950s, this area was dominated by dairy farms; this event supposedly harks back to that time. But the Brattleboro area is better known today for its ecclectic mix of aging hippies, pierced neo-hippies, native Vermonters, rock-ribbed Republicans, farmers, working class people, artists, and, lately, computer folks with lots of new money.

There is an inherent free-spiritedness here that the Chamber of Commerce doesn't advertise but which makes the area a joy to live in. It's a mixture of the steady along with the wild and slightly woolly. We have one of the most successful organic food co-ops in the country, but we also have a nuclear power plant.

Once, Brattleboro's Fourth of July parade epitomized this wonderful combination of the goofy and the serious. Anyone could march, making it the ultimate expression of real American values. There were American flags galore, Shriners, the American Legion Band, and also anti-nuke protesters and samba dancers — a sensuous group that wriggled down Main Street to the beat of wild drums.

But then Brattleboro came under the control of uncreative types, the Chamber tried to sanitize the parade and remove its political content, the samba dancers disappeared, and the whole thing became just another dull, small-town Fourth.

The cow parade was a good chance to bring back some of the town's creative weirdness. Almost in spite of the organizers, who were looking to create a serious, money-making, career-building, Chamber-style tourist event, the genie jumped out of her bottle and started to boogie.

It may have been because Saturday was bright and sunny, or because it's been a rough year for Americans and we're all feeling the need to break loose a little. But people left behind their serious, conservative, or critical demeanors and seemed happy to make joyous fools of themselves for a day.

Thousands of applauding, laughing and mooing people lined the streets for the parade, most of them with cameras. Children were holding cow balloons in the shape of udders.

Some of the worst puns in the known world were released from protective custody. For example, an elegant woman wearing a tailored jacket and skirt decorated with cows told me her outfit came from Paris and it was "cow-toure." T-shirts proclaimed, "I'm having an udderly good time," "Moochas gracias," "Let's party till the cows come home," "Deja mooo," and, of course, "I'm in the mooood for love."

Many people — in and out of the parade — wore cow costumes, with the black-and-white Holstein pattern predominating. A horn player from the American Legion Band marched in one while playing "Yankee Doodle." Several men wore udders as codpieces.

The sole protester from People for the Ethical Treatment of Animals — a man who had driven up from North Carolina for the event — wore a Holstein costume, carried a sign that said, "Love Cows, Don't Eat Them," and blended right in. Hood ice cream sent its cow mascot, and Tony the Tiger was there, probably because Frosted Flakes go so well with milk.

The real cows were black and white Holsteins, brown Jerseys and russet milking short horns. They were groomed and shining and bedecked with wreaths of flowers. One little heifer wore an American flag cap. I was charmed by both the cows and the kids who so clearly love and care for them. And although the cows themselves were unavailable for comment, they didn't seem overly freaked.

A story had been circulating that the cows were going to get enemas before the march, so I asked Putney School junior Margaret Chapin, who was walking Lupine, about it. She was offended. "I'd definitely never do that to a cow!" she said. "Besides, they've already pooped all over the truck."

The parade turned out to be a circus.

The Costume Ladies, who wear overstuffed fat-lady outfits which regularly offend the politically correct, put black-and-white print bikinis on their bulges and danced down Main Street. The anti-nuke people and the anti-hormones-in-food people marched, and so did members of the Fire Department of New York City.

Alfred sashayed down the street wearing a short black skirt with a sequined top, plugging his vintage fashion shows. A swinging Jazzberry Jam played "I'm in the Mood for Love" from a hay wagon. Clowns, jugglers and unicyclists entertained us, as did a slightly out-of-control Dairy Fairy, and one politician, Jeb Spaulding, who is running for state treasurer, marched on stilts. This will inevitably irritate his opponent, a progressive who makes much of the fact that he is openly gay. Walking on stilts trumps being gay any time.

The parade ended up at the Commons, where we all enjoyed a festival of delicious free dairy products — mostly in the form of hand-crafted sheep, cow and goat cheeses. Not a glass of soy milk was to be found.

C&S Wholesale Grocers, the state's largest business, got into the spirit by giving out refrigerator magnets decorated with black and white spots. The maple syrup people spun maple cotton candy that melted in your mouth. A reggae band played — play that funky music, white boys! — and Sen. James Jeffords and Congressman Bernie Sanders participated in a milking contest. Woody Jackson, the man who began the artistic deification of cows in Vermont with his Ben & Jerry's packaging, set up a tent and sold his work. People caught up with friends they hadn't seen in years.

It's a good thing to celebrate farmers; these days they have a hard time getting by. They're a lot like artists — hard-headed and individualistic enough to believe they can make a living by doing what they love, failing most of the time, and still plugging on. Maybe that's why this parade let loose such a spontaneous combustion of cows and creativity. All in all, it was quite a party.

~ ~ ~

February 13, 2003

VALENTINE TO A SMALL TOWN

At the drive-thru teller's window at the River Valley Credit Union the other day, a fresh daisy came along with my receipt.

"Why?" I asked.

The response was muffled by the microphone, and the only two words I understood were "Joyce" and "spring." And suddenly, that cold, gray day, which happened to be my birthday, was a great deal brighter.

More and more, as the world feels like it's spinning out of control, it's important to appreciate the many small good things. For me, that includes the joy I get from living in the Brattleboro area.

I moved to Brattleboro in 1987 with not much more than a duffel bag and a nameless cat which had become my familiar in Panama. We lived in an apartment downtown; I was paying $400 a month in rent and earning $600 a month. Times were hard.

For me, not for the cat. Within a few months, the tellers around the corner at the Brattleboro Savings and Loan (BSL) had named her Bissel and were feeding her every day. Hospice was next door then, and the cat took to going through an open window to sit on people's laps while they grieved. She often went down the road to the Brattleboro Music Center, where she climbed the fire escape for even more food and attention. Occasionally, she crossed Main Street and hung out at the library.

In time I followed her excellent example and made a life for myself here. I found my calling as a writer here. I met my beloved husband here. I learned about small-town living here.

Early on, for example, I was covering Vernon for the Reformer. Late one night I was speeding back from a selectmen's meeting when a policeman pulled me over. When he saw my name on the driver's license, he waved me through. "Keep on telling us what those bastards are up to at the town hall," he said.

Being a local reporter wasn't always easy. Once I wrote a piece about the terrible pop music on the local radio stations. A number of letter-writers agreed with me, and I was feeling pretty pleased with myself until I went to a Brattleboro selectman's meeting and discovered that at the press table, I had to sit between the owner of one station and the chief reporter of the other.

That's when I discovered what journalists call the "Afghanistan Principle," named long before Sept. 11, 2001. It means that the further away from things you are, the more openly you can write about them. It's been easy to rail against the policies of President George W. Bush. It's a lot harder to write something negative about someone you might be meeting the next day in the supermarket.

Almost every day I have a little adventure here, something to cheer me up, something like getting that flower. For example, a few weeks ago I was annoyed — at myself — because I left a rented video at home on the day it was due. I brought it in the next day, but I was still grumpy. "Here's the video of 'The Good Girl,'" I said. "It's overdue and I have to pay extra, but I'm really disgusted because the movie sucked."

I started to apologize for being rude, but the young man behind the counter only said, "I'm not going to charge you for the extra day. I didn't like the movie either."

I love the quirks of living in a small town. I smile every time I drive by the Chinese restaurant Panda North and see the towering sign that says "TEA," because that's my favorite Brattleboro story.

Why does it say tea? Glad you asked. There used to be a steak restaurant there, and the sign said "STEAK $5.99." Then the restaurant went out of business, and Panda moved in.

Around the same time, the town changed its signage regulations and made it illegal to build a tall sign visible from the Interstate. This one, however, was grandfathered, and the owner of the property refused to take it down.

The new restaurant owners were unhappy. People were coming in for a $5.99 steak and they didn't serve a $5.99 steak. What to do? Well, one night the owner went up on a ladder and took away some of the letters. When the town woke up the next morning, the sign was offering tea, which was definitely served at a Chinese restaurant. Everyone was happy — except maybe the planning commission.

I like living in a place where I know the stories, a place where I can get a flower every now and then. I like living in a real community, with a real downtown that Wal-Mart couldn't kill. This place could be precious and full of itself, but somehow it isn't. Hippies, woodchucks, working people, yuppies, New Agers, hipsters, artists, internationalists, neo-hippies, skate punks and the occasional mental patient co-exist here. I like it that the main downtown parking lot is called Harmony.

I like the variety of ethnic foods here, the multiple independent bookstores, and the fact that on a freezing night, hundreds of people are willing to go downtown to see the newest art. I like it that the local paper's op-ed page would give Bill O'Reilly and Ann Coulter a heart attack.

Two rivers run through this place, along with a great deal of heart and small-town spirit. Happy Valentine's Day and thank you for this really good life, Brattleboro, Dummerston, Putney, Newfane, Vernon and the entire Brattleboro area.

May 22, 2003

LT. SPAULDING'S HILL

Auction March 2, 1871. That's what the poster said, the one announcing the sale of a 65-acre farm belonging to "the late widow Spaulding."

The farm offered "running water to house and barn, plenty of wood on the place and a very good apple orchard." Also, one pair of oxen weighing 3,800 pounds together, two cows, a three-year-old steer "nearly fat," a spring calf, a horse, a "cosset sheep" and a cart.

The farm and its contents were put up for auction by Hoyt Thomas Spaulding, the widow's son, but something interesting must have happened on that day in March, because by the end of it, Hoyt still owned the farm. Sixty-three years later, his great-grandson, Tom Johnson, was born there.

And Johnson, 70, hasn't moved very far away. He now lives just down the road from Dummerston Center, in the house where the first Dummerston Town Meeting was held in 1771. And I live on part of his ancestor's property, on Spaulding Hill.

Dummerston was chartered under the name of Fullum back in 1753, which is why the town is celebrating its 250th anniversary this weekend. But its history goes back much further.

It seems that back in 1713, when the government was trying to figure out the boundary between the Massachusetts Bay Colony and Connecticut, it found that 107,793 acres lay outside the legitimate limit. So Massachusetts gave that land to Connecticut, in exchange for equivalent land in the south.

Since the land Connecticut received was not contiguous, the state put these "equivalent lands" up for public auction on April 24 and 25, 1716. On that day, 43,843 acres were sold to William Dummer, Anthony Stoddard, William Brattle and John White. Later, in 1741, when New Hampshire and Massachusetts were figuring out their borders, the land became part of New Hampshire. Give me a few minutes and I'll get to what happened next.

One of the nicest things about Dummerston is that people have a strong sense of history here. That's why, when the covered bridge over the West River needed to be replaced, the selectboard voted to rehabilitate the old wooden bridge instead of building something modern and suitable for trucks. Many of the houses in the town center have been here since the 1700s, and some of the oldest families are still here, too.

One of them is Johnson's. He's a great storyteller, a retired banker who calls himself a "farmer historian." In his huge barn, made out of timbers from the very first Dummerston meeting house, you can see the whole history of New England farming. Back in the 1700s, he said, there were more sheep here than cattle.

"Cattle and horses came later," he said. "There was no grass as we know it today for pasture. It was all woods. Then a man from Keene, N.H. went to England and found a grass seed that would grow in the shade. He brought it back and sold it to the Vermont farmers."

It was a hard life back then, but not a bad one.

"Everyone had more or less the same thing," Johnson said. "Maybe your dad had a few more cows than my dad, but that's about it."

Johnson has collected some of the old record books from Dummerston and Vernon. These are fragile and faded and written in a graceful hand on lined paper in browned ink. They are interesting to read, giving us a perspective on life back then. In Dummerston in 1814, for example, Enoch Cook, who built the house where Johnson now lives, paid only $1.43 in property taxes, while the Town of Vernon "spent and raised" $145.32 for the entire town budget. Of that, they spent $90 for "keeping paupers," $2 on paupers' coffins, and the rest on powder and lead. They spent another $134 on the school.

My hill is named after an interesting character, Lt. Leonard Spaulding, Johnson's "great-great-God-only-knows-how great" grandfather. He was an adventurous, spirited and strong-minded soldier whose ancestral family came from Spaulding, England. The name Spaulding comes from a tribe named Spaldas, and means "fortification" in Latin.

Lt. Spaulding fought in the French and Indian Wars (1689-1773) and settled in Dummerston in 1772. When King George III turned over the New Hampshire lands to New York, the Sheriff of New York told Lt. Spaulding to get off his own land.

He refused and the sheriff burned down his house; the Spaulding family barely escaped to New Hampshire. So Lt. Spaulding again picked up his gun and fought against New York with Ethan and Ira Allen and the Green Mountain Boys for a state of their own, Vermont.

"People don't know this, but Ethan and Ira were land speculators," Johnson said. "They owned thousands of acres. New York State, for a fee, offered to honor the New Hampshire grants, but Ethan couldn't afford the fee, and that's why they revolted. Vermonters didn't want to pay twice for their land. But they could have paid without having a war or getting burned out."

According to the town's history, "Dummerston 1753-1986," Lt. Spaulding was jailed in 1774 for "throwing out remarks" unfavorable to King George III. (The remarks concerned the king's intelligence.)

"The first effective organized defiance to the king's authority in all the colonies was in Dummerston when they called a meeting on the 'green' October 29, 1774, to release Lieutenant Spaulding from jail," the history book reports. For a time after that, Lt. Spaulding fought again, this time against England in the Revolutionary War. In October of 1776 he was wounded at the Battle of White Plains.

When he returned to Dummerston, the warrior settled on Spaulding Hill. He was the father of 11 children, five sons "all over six feet tall — one of them 6'7"." His wife, Margaret, was no slouch either. She lived to be 94, and "every two years she would go alone on horseback to Providence to visit her mother."

Late one Fall afternoon, Johnson took me up the hill to see the foundation of Lt. Spaulding's house. An apple tree grows outside the front stoop, and there were apples on the ground. I picked one up and ate it, felt a connection to Lt. Spaulding, and was thrilled.

Lt. Spaulding is just one of a number of interesting characters connected with Dummerston. George Aiken, Rutherford Hayes, Rudyard Kipling and Ellsworth Bunker are some of the others.

This Saturday, Dummerston will celebrate its long and remarkable history with food, parades, animals, antique cars and tractors, quilting, dancing and more. It's a rain-or-shine all-day party, and the public is most welcome.

Happy 250th anniversary, Dummerston!

ANDY WARHOL MEETS SMALL-TOWN AMERICAN VALUES

One has to wonder.

America, in the middle of a presidential election cycle, is wrapping itself in the flag, proclaiming its kindness and compassion and trumpeting its small-town morals and family values. So why is Andy Warhol, who represents the antithesis of those values, getting such a big play in a small New England town?

"Andy" fever is sweeping the good burghers of Brattleboro — the kind of unstylish people whom Warhol and his crowd held in total contempt. The reason is an art show, "Intimate & Unseen: Andy Warhol," which opens on Sept. 18 at the Brattleboro Museum and Art Center.

Why Brattleboro? Why now?

For complicated reasons involving a late-in-life Warhol love affair, the object-of-desire's twin brother, plus some middlemen — including one from Brattleboro — the town's tiny but elegant museum is hosting a large show of never-seen-before Warhol paintings and photographs, along with many snapshots from the artist's life.

The show should provide an extended visual rush. Warhol's work, often scorned as a triumph of self-promotion when he and his cohorts were making it, now looms quite a bit larger than life.

What were then vibrant, jewel-colored copies of photographs and pop culture rip-offs — the stealing of other people's hard-crafted iconic images — have long since become the icons themselves. Marilyn, Mao, Campbell's soup cans and the fashion and cultural leaders of the 1970s and 1980s now live vividly on the walls of museums and private homes. Their celebrity reinforces the value of the art, just as the art reinforces the value of the celebrity, as a clever Warhol long ago figured out. As long as these pictures sell for millions of dollars, these people, like the ones in paintings by Vermeer and Rembrandt, will ride into eternity on Andy's shoulders.

So it is reasonable that the town should celebrate. Before opening day, the museum is hosting an expensive preview event for its patrons. It features three parties — the last one a "Club 54 Disco" — all for a contribution of $54. For the general public, there will be a film series and a lecture series. I've heard they're selling white "Andy" wigs at $6 apiece.

All of this raises one amusing problem, which is Warhol himself.

In today's world, where "values" are crucial, the values that Warhol represented were these: decadence; cynicism; greed; the abuse of power; cruelty; exclusion; the worship of money and beauty; a profound love of drugs, especially methamphetamine and, later, cocaine; and wildly transgressive sexuality. These are not exactly the things you would put on the stage at a Republican convention, or expect to see celebrated in Brattleboro, Vermont.

I never met Warhol, but as fate would have it, a long time ago I knew many of the people in his entourage. The early "superstars" I knew were the ones who were immortalized in Lou Reed's "Walk on the Wild Side," and who starred in "The Chelsea Girls." They were glamourously tacky transvestites like Jackie Curtis and Holly Woodlawn, razor-tongued speed freaks like Pope Ondine, and truly fearless women like Mary Woronow.

These people, exhibitionists every one, were also actors. At the time, the early 1970s, I happened to be designing stage costumes for what is now called Off-Broadway, but back then was Off-Off-Way-Off Broadway. While I wasn't part of the scene, I had a front row seat.

I would be fitting dresses on the transvestites and, at their direction, padding with socks the crotches of their boyfriends' jeans. And when we were done, they would rush off to their other, wilder lives. "Let's go have sex with the bums on the Bowery," was one such cry, although whether they actually did it or said it just to see the shocked look on my face, I don't know. Probably both.

They seemed to spend a lot of their time circling Warhol like orbiting moons, longing for his approval, trying to see themselves reflected in his light while giving him all of theirs. They rehearsed saying the word "fabulous" until it they could extend the syllables in just the right way— it was a kind of code word for them. I enjoyed their passion, cruelty, creativity and intelligence. I benefited from their kindness. I admired both their glamour and the heartbreaking courage it took for them to go out on the street every day in the costumes of their own personas. I sensed their longing for some of the cultural acceptance that I, a married heterosexual woman, took for granted.

I especially admired their defiance of convention, which is badly needed today. But I also witnessed betrayals and drug overdoses. Well before AIDS, serious diseases like cancer and leukemia took some of them — or maybe these were early manifestations of AIDS before the disease had a name.

There were too many broken hearts, too many broken jaws and too much sadness and desperation in that world.

I left New York in 1974. Soon after that, Warhol started wining, dining and snorting with a much more elite entertainment and fashion crowd — people who didn't need 15 minutes of fame the way the downtown self-described "freaks" did, people who had their own wealth and fame. The drug of choice switched from speed to cocaine, and the scene went from Max's Kansas City to Studio 54, which would never have let me inside.

It wouldn't have let inside any of the Brattleboro people who are now celebrating Warhol, either. So they're having their own party, but without the sex and cocaine spoons. And they're talking about putting Warhol wigs on schoolchildren as a way of promoting this very unlikely role model!

These days, Republicans and Democrats alike have taken stands against decadence, self-degradation, cocaine, methamphetamines and transgressive sexuality.

They do, however, still support cruelty, torture, exclusion, and the worship of money and beauty. Maybe Warhol was on to something after all.

Has Warhol's success rehabilitated his reputation? Has his dark side been eradicated, until all we're left with is a happy-face cartoon? Have his values slipped into the mainstream? Is it all about time and distance, when the only thing left is the art and not the destructiveness of the artist's life?

Brattleboro is indulging in a bit of celebrity worship, and why shouldn't it have its 15 minutes of fame, even if it is two or three decades too late?

But as I said, one has to wonder.

(The next four columns were written in response to a symposium at Marlboro College's Brattleboro campus on the idea of building a "creative economy" for Brattleboro.

The concept has been gathering interest in Vermont for some time. Studies have been done, week-end long seminars have been held all over the state, and a lot of people have weighed in on the topic.

Over the years, the Brattleboro area has attracted many artists. Recently, since the town's industrial base disappeared, people have been studying and organizing around the idea of tying Brattleboro's economic development to the arts.

I've been covering the concept of a state-wide creative economy for several years for Vermont Business Magazine, so I was very interested to hear what people in my own back yard had to say — and what they refused to say — especially about the big gray elephant in the middle of the room: gentrification.)

~ ~ ~

September 15, 2005

THE GENTRIFICATION OF BRATTLEBORO

When I first moved here, I thought Vermont was similar to the Third World countries I had been living in for years in South and Central America. It was cheap, difficult to survive in, and very, very beautiful. That was fine with me, because I wanted a quiet place to write and wasn't sure I'd ever make any money at it.

By the time I got here, there were already many artists — writers, poets, painters, photographers, sculptors, musicians, dancers, cooks — living here, all drawn by the same things that drew me. Tucked away in the woods, they worked at their art and lived by their wits. It wasn't easy and there was never a lot of money, but they survived. And along the way, they created the cultural stew we enjoy in Brattleboro today.

Greg Brown, in his prescient 1994 song, "Boomtown," describes the scene perfectly: "Here come the artists with their intense faces, with their need for money and quiet spaces. They leave New York, they leave L.A. Here they are — who knows how long they'll stay."

Yes, who knows? Maybe we should all start packing? Because damn if the city fathers haven't decided to make Brattleboro the next artistic boomtown.

Yes, they've looked around, and what do they see? Manufacturing has disappeared down a rat hole to China. Warehousing has slip-slidded away to New Hampshire. What's left? All those artists living in the woods. Hell, let's make some money off of them.

Trying to turn artists into something akin to a gushing oil well in the backyard is called "the creative economy," and it's a hot topic in Vermont these days. It can mean anything from using art to draw tourists who will spend money and then leave, to nurturing entrepreneurs who might someday create new businesses and provide jobs — like the successful Cotton Mill Hill business incubator.

A creative economy sounds like a great idea, and that's why there was a well-attended two-day symposium on the topic at the Marlboro College Graduate Center earlier this week.

The keynote speaker was Bill Ivey, who created the Country Music Association and helmed the National Endowment for the Arts before becoming director of the Curb Center for Art, Enterprise and Public Policy at Vanderbilt University. He pointed out that "knowledge workers," or creative types, are a growing part of the national economy — only the service sector is growing faster. And these people are mobile. They can live and work anywhere, but they are attracted to "funky" cities and towns, places with "street-level cultures, large gay populations, bohemians, places with participation in the arts. It's not about sports stadiums or big performance centers."

According to Ivey, it's desirable to attract these people to your area. But once you have funky — and the Brattleboro area excels in funky — these creative money-making types come. They, in turn, attract second-home and McMansion-building wealthy people who like to rub shoulders with art and culture. And as more and more of these people arrive, the property values and the property taxes climb. The original artists — those who were funky by nature instead of nurture, as well as working people, the young and the retirees, are forced out.

As Greg Brown says, "The rich build sensitive houses and pass their staff around. For the rest of us, it's trailers on the outskirts of town. We carry them their coffee, wash their shiny cars, hear all about how lucky we are to be living in a boomtown."

One word for this process is gentrification. It happened in Soho in Manhattan. It happened in Woodstock, NY. It's happening in Waitsfield, Vt. Now it could be happening in Brattleboro, too.

When pressed, Ivey admitted he had no solution for this problem. The original artists are always, eventually, pushed out, he said. Indeed, he said he has come to think of artists as Johnny Appleseeds — sowing their seeds and moving on. Change his gender and put a powdered wig on him and to me he looks a lot like Marie Antoinette saying, "Let them eat cake."

Personally, I don't want to move on. I want to live here, work here, die here and be buried here. Haven't I paid my dues? Haven't I earned that right?

It's hard to make a living anywhere, but in Vermont it's especially difficult. The winters are from hell. We learn to drive on ice and heat with wood while trying not to burn our houses down. Salaries are low. Rents are high. And don't even get me started on the property taxes.

Whether we're artists, newspaper reporters or factory workers, everyone in this country is facing a coming era of scarce resources. As we saw in New Orleans, the wealthy survive and the poor - who, in New Orleans, created that city's deeply revered culture — they just float away.

Greg Brown has it right: "The guy from California moves in and relaxes. The natives have to move — they cannot pay the taxes. Santa Fe has had it. Sedona has, too. Maybe you'll be lucky — maybe your town will be the new boomtown."

Lucky us.

~ ~ ~

September 22, 2005

ARTISTS AND AFFORDABLE HOUSING

Affordable housing is a jargon term that puts most people to sleep. It also raises interesting questions. Affordable to who? Isn't all housing affordable to somebody?

But whether or not the term is sexy, the concept of affordable housing is at the root of Brattleboro's ongoing gentrification problem. As the area continues to reinvent itself as an "arts community" to reap the financial benefits of the "creative economy," many creative people are, frankly, running scared about how they're going to continue to live and work here.

In gentrification. a group of poor but creative types move into an inexpensive area and, being creative, create an agreeable lifestyle. Stores follow , and soon other creative types with higher incomes — advertising execs, gallery owners, restauranteurs — want to get in on the fun. Property owners start raising rents. Property values increase. Soon the artists can no longer afford to live in their own scene. The gentry — the wealthy — take over. Hence, gentrification.

Downtown Brattleboro is already in the process of gentrifying, and the fears are real. Remember, Brattleboro may have a thriving arts community, but it is not an "arts community" per se. Like most other towns, it is owned and run by a community of burghers — retailers, property owners and the like. Philosophically, the burghers' main goal, to maximize profits, frequently conflicts with the goal of artists, which is to push the boundaries of the status quo.

It is also important to remember that in Vermont, every town is an island. While it is a polite fiction that Guilford, Newfane, Dummerston, Vernon, Townshend and Putney are not just bedroom communities — suburbs! — of Brattleboro, when it comes to making — or changing — the rules, someone from Dummerston, creative or not, will have no say in the political life of Brattleboro, and vice versa.

Artists are often regarded as an elite. Why should they be targeted for special treatment, people argue, when there are so many in need of affordable housing? This is true, even though most artists are just poor people with college degrees. But if you want a creative economy, you have to help the artists so they can keep on creating it.

In a capitalist society, the best way to survive is to own the means of production. Artists need spaces in which to live and work. At best, artists should own those spaces. At the very least, rents on apartments, homes and studios should be reasonable. This is where the conflict between art and commerce stops being philosophical. But there are solutions.

For example, 10 years ago, as a poor writer, I couldn't afford much in the way of housing. But I found a small house on a hill, deep in the woods, and partnered with Connie Snow and the Brattleboro Area Community Land Trust to buy it. I sacrificed my equity down the road — and permanent access to central heating — for the joy of living in a space of my own that I could never afford any other way. And the land trust added another home to its stock of permanently affordable housing.

The land trust remains open to this "found housing" model, although it is more difficult now for artists to follow it because of the current real estate bubble: few available houses, inflated prices. But artists still might want to explore the option; mortgages are surprisingly available, and owning your own home keeps you out of the hands of developers. Of course, then property taxes become your biggest threat, but that's a threat we all live with, whether we rent or buy.

If buying seems overwhelming, then artists should know that the land trust is currently creating studios/offices and living spaces in the fire-damaged Wilder Block. The land trust is not targeting artists — its apartments are for everybody. But Snow told me that they want to encourage artists to get on the waiting list and be eligible when the apartments — eight apartments and six studio/office spaces — become available (construction should start in December or January). In the next few weeks the land trust will be spreading the word to arts organizations. You heard it here first.

Another model was created by Robert McBride of RAMP (Rockingham Arts & Museum Project) in Bellows Falls. McBride is an artist as well as a very savvy arts administrator, and he partnered with as many state funding sources as he could to create the Exner Block — 10 affordable apartments with studios for artists in downtown Bellows Falls. Some retailers complain that the artists are too poor to be good customers, but they are there, they are working, they are eating and drinking coffee, galleries are opening (and closing), and there's even a small gallery tour every month.

Artists' co-ops are another interesting idea. Artists get together, buy a property and convert it to living/working space. This approach worked in downtown Burlington, where artists partnered with the Burlington Community Land Trust to create 11 units in the Rose Street Co-op. The artists are paying off the land trust over time. In North Bennington, there's also an artists' cooperative, developed by the Vermont Arts Exchange in partnership with Housing Vermont.

Affordable housing may not be sexy, but it is a problem that can be solved. As McBride says, "Put creative people together and they do creative stuff. Put whiners together and they do whiney stuff."

(After this piece appeared, I received a phone call from a downtown retailer who resented being called a "burgher." As a gallery owner, she saw herself as straddling the line between shopkeeper and artist and didn't see any reason to label people as one or the other. She made a good point.

As Brattleboro Town Manager Jerry Remillard told me when I did a profile of him for the February 2006 issue of Vermont Business Magazine, "The presumption made here for 100 years-plus is that (Brattleboro) was a small mill town turned into a little industrial and commercial center. That's what we've always been. We're not an arts community. We're a business community. We used to be a very strong industrial community and we're not that any more. There's an economic disadvantage for the town. That's something that's not going to change.... We've always struggled down here, and we're always going to struggle. There's no magic answer. There's no industry that's going to come in, there's no business that's going to come in, no arts or tourist thing that's going to be the magic answer. It's going to be all of the above.")

~ ~ ~

September 29, 2005

How A Creative Economy Can Create Community

There was a time when I thought creativity was for writers, painters, musicians and other artists. And then there was business.

But in the many years that I've been a contributing editor at Vermont Business Magazine, I've changed my tune. Now I think that business might be one of the most creative occupations of all.

Think about it. As with art, there's the same anticipation each day of not knowing what will happen but knowing that you will have to respond creatively. There's the invention of strategy, the creation of product, the thrill of problem-solving, the design of ways to reach out to the market, the excitement of success, the despair of failure. And as icing on the cake, you can make a living at it.

Best of all, you can create jobs so that other people can make a living.

In Vermont, some of the very people scorned as "flatlanders" or "Birkenstock-wearing, Saab-driving liberals" have created the most jobs. Ben Cohen and Jerry Greenfield, of course, spring to mind. But they're just the tip of the creative iceberg here. Susan Dollenmaier, for example, was a Sixties hippie and a flea-market hound. She turned her passion for old textiles into a $10-million-plus luxury textiles business. Say what you want about spending $800 for a top sheet, she is now the largest employer in tiny Tunbridge.

David Blittersdorf liked to tinker with engines and windmills while his wife, Jan, worked as a nurse. David's tinkering turned into the fast-growing NRG Systems, which makes wind assessment technology. It also makes about $16 million a year, employs 45 people in Hinesburg, and — oh yes — Jan is the CEO.

Thomas Fricke and Sylvia Blanchet were do-gooder Third World development types — the kind who usually work for non-profit agencies. Then they realized that you need money to make real social change. Now they own and run ForesTrade in Brattleboro, importing spices from exotic locales like Indonesia and India. Sales last year? About $10 million. And they employ about 200 people around the world.

Annie Christopher was an artist working in tempera and gold leaf back in the days when SoHo in New York was still a place where artists could afford to live. To support herself, she waitressed in an artists' bar. That's where she met Peter Backman, a printer's representative and a publisher of Tibetan books. Now they own and run Annie's Enterprises, Inc. (yes, the Star Trek reference is deliberate) in North Calais. You know them better as Annie's Naturals. The company has about $15 million in yearly sales, 39 delicious products, and leads the natural food industry's salad dressing category.

Fred and Judi Danforth were struggling artisans working in pewter when they used their creativity to design a new business model. Now, although Fred still keeps an eye on the financials, other people handle the business and sales of Danforth Pewterers in Middlebury — with around $2 million in sales and about 40 employees at the height of the gift-giving season — freeing Fred and Judi to work at their craft.

Then there's Hinda Miller, who became a multi-millionaire at 40 because in 1977, when she was a costume designer, she and two female friends created the ubiquitous sports bra. The Washington Post said the Jogbra and Title IX were the two things most responsible for the explosion in women's athletics — and women's health. After Miller left the company she became a Democratic state senator from Chittenden County. She's now running for mayor of Burlington.

Miller's baby is the "creative economy," but she's not talking about artists and musicians. She's talking about entrepreneurs.

"The people who are going to come up with those creative ideas enjoy being in a state where there's stimulation from the arts and creative people," Miller told me. "But the creative economy itself is about moving towards business that creates cutting-edge ideas and intellectual property, rather than trying to live off the manufacturing of commodity products."

The creative economy is "any business that improves upon what is," she said. "We are looking for people who look at the world, find a niche that they can leverage globally, and want to live in Vermont. We can't stop people from leaving the cities and coming to our state. I'd like to tap into their creativity and context and let them bring something to Vermont. After all, I was an outsider who came to Vermont."

Rather than just talking the talk, she and her cohort, Senator Matt Dunne, D-Windsor, made real legislative progress. They created a new committee in the Senate for economic development. They created grants for broadband service in rural areas — Dunne told me that Gov. James Douglas's staff testified against the grants in committee, but when the bill passed anyway, Douglas went around the state giving out the money and taking the credit. They got a seed capital fund started. They got a brownfields bill passed to make it easier for people to revitalize old mill buildings. They developed a tax credit program targeted to renewable energy. They started a program to attract overseas business to Vermont.

Creative business is how a creative economy starts to make sense. It starts at the ground level. When a community has good jobs, people can buy homes. They can own cars instead of living in them. They can spend money at local stores. They can raise families. They can pay property taxes. They can become involved in their communities.

And here's the beauty part, where everything comes around full circle: they can provide a solid community structure in which other creative people, the artists and writers and musicians et al, the ones who created the creative atmosphere which attracted the entrepreneurs who created the jobs, can live and thrive.

(As I was writing this series, a loosely-knit group of arts entrepreneurs created the Brattleboro 05301 Festival — a collection of over 60 concerts,

gallery shows, readings, the Brattleboro Literary Festival, Gallery Walk — a long-running downtown Brattleboro party held on the first Friday evening of every month, which features new art shows at over 40 galleries and stores — and a bunch of other events, all gathered into a month-long festival.)

~ ~ ~

October 6, 2005

Brattleboro Under Glass

That creative economy symposium a few weeks ago opened up a floodgate of discussion about the future of our area, and I've been proud to contribute a few columns of ideas — although I must say, given some of those phone calls and letters, you people might want to retire that "Hate has no home here" bumper sticker.

A great many people here are punch-drunk on the power of Richard Florida's book, "The Rise of the Creative Class." As Florida says, "My core message is that human creativity is the ultimate source of economic growth. Every single person is creative in some way. And to fully tap and harness that creativity we must be tolerant, diverse, inclusive."

How can we argue with that?

But life is more complicated. So I'd like to sum up my own thoughts before I retire the Afghanistan Principle and return to bashing the Bush administration.

First, creativity in the form of innovation has always been the key to economic success. Just ask Henry Ford. But this discussion is about something else. It is an attempt to brand Brattleboro as an "art town" for economic purposes.

What is an "art town" anyway? Arcosanti out in the Arizona desert and a few earthworks projects come to mind. But in reality, while an area may be home to artists, it also needs to be a home to tractor-trailer drivers and house painters. The beauty of Windham County lies in its gritty mix — artists, yes, but also farmers, retailers, real estate owners, political activists, contractors, retired folks, educators, road crews and the wonderful cooks of the Dummerston Grange.

If a town focuses only on the arts, it is inevitable that it will quickly attract people who want to capitalize on the arts. The question is, as always, who benefits. The people who win most are the arts administrators, the developers and real estate speculators, and the upscale retailers. Among the losers, oddly enough, are often the artists. When a place becomes chic or "hip," the middle class and the poor become endangered. Provincetown is having a hell of a time holding onto its original wild and woolly character, while in the Northampton area, the price of real estate has reached astronomical levels.

Brattleboro is not so much an "art town" as it has been, historically, a thriving market town. It's economic underpinnings were the many warehouses and factories that have now closed down. While there has been an admirable — and creative — attempt to turn the town's many empty warehouses and factories into duty-free zones or new-business incubators, the fruits of these endeavors, to mix a metaphor, are a long way down the pike.

Politically, the town of Brattleboro isn't "creative" but conservative. From what I gather, the arts community had a seat at the table when it came to designing the new parking garage. In the end, their suggestions were ignored in favor of that eyesore we love to hate. When young people started congregating in the Harmony Lot, did the town congratulate them on establishing a unique community? No. It proposed installing surveillance cameras — the very antithesis of a creative response. Not to mention the machismo-drenched circling-of-the-wagons done by the Brattleboro police and the old guard after an agitated Robert Woodward was shot by the police in a church in 2001.

If the "creative economy" means that theaters, artists and galleries, festivals and the like are driving the economy, then the inmates, if you'll pardon the expression, are suddenly running the asylum. Thomas M. Keane Jr., writing a few weeks ago in The Boston Globe Magazine, described an analysis of 240 American cities done last year by Harvard economist Edward Glaeser, who concluded that the number of artistic people in an area has no correlation to economic success. "Support for the arts doesn't produce economic growth," Keane said. "Rather, strong economic growth creates enough wealth so that the arts can flourish." He also pointed out that art isn't "supposed to be good for a balance sheet; it should be good for the soul."

The current Brattleboro 05301 festival has pulled together an impressive amount of creative activity, and the Strolling of the Heifers put Brattleboro on the national map. But festivals like these are designed to attract tourists. Many people fear a "Brattleboro under glass", or even worse, a "Vermont under glass."

If Vermont becomes a theme park, then the jobs available will be turning down bed linens and putting chocolates on the pillows of our guests. And if the price of gas climbs much higher, what will we do when the tourists stop coming?

Florida might be right about one thing: entepreneurship could be the state's saving grace. To encourage it, the state must do creative economic development. Working for state-wide high-speed Internet and cell phone access, more seed money for innovative businesses, an affordable health care system and much more is not as sexy as creating "art towns." What we need most is a creative governor, something we do not currently have. That might be a good place to start.

So I hope everyone enjoys the Brattleboro 05301 festival and has a great time at Gallery Walk on Friday night. And if you see me on the street and want to throw rocks, I'm partial to emeralds and aquamarines from Renaissance Fine Jewelry. And how about that George W. Bush?

FIVE:

SEPTEMBER 11TH

(My mother was visiting from Florida, so I wrote that particular week's column ahead of time. We were happily browsing in a Putney resale clothing shop when someone burst in yelling, "Turn on the radio, turn on the radio!" We rushed home, listening to the horror in the voices of the National Public Radio commentators without fully comprehending what was happening. When we got home, we turned on the television set and watched the second tower fall. At first the events of that day were too difficult to grasp, and writing about it did not seem like a real possiblity. But at the urging of Randy and my mother, I went to the computer the next morning and wrote this, the first of four pieces I eventually did about the tragedy. They are all included here.)

September 13, 2001

AMERICA'S LOSS OF INNOCENCE

As I write this early on Wednesday morning, all I can think is that now it's about us.

I don't mean that in the movie sense, although Tuesday played more like a movie than anything real. And not in the "now it's personal" sense that will make Sylvester Stallone Bush and Jean Claude Van Cheney fly into action, beat up the villains, and make the world safe for capitalism. We're at war now, and we don't even know, really, who the villains are.

But now that — as the newscasters repeated endlessly on Tuesday — "the skyline of Manhattan has been changed forever," and thousands are dead in New York and Washington, and thousands more are grieving, we Americans are finally, personally, involved in the suffering of the world.

We, the ones who lie on our couches and stuff our faces with junk food as we watch 23 minutes of world and national news every evening. We, the people whose most serious thoughts are about joining Weight Watchers some day soon, or who Julia Roberts is dating.

We, the people who have been so safe and secure and bored that for entertainment, we put good-looking strangers on desert islands or cruise ships or drop them in the middle of nowhere and let them have adventures that we vicariously watch and judge.

I think Tuesday was enough reality television for anyone.

Tuesday brought it all home. We've watched Palestinians dying on television for years. We've watched bombs explode in Israel. We've seen people whose arms and legs have been hacked off in Africa. We've seen child prostitutes in Asia, raped women in Bosnia, avalanche victims in Peru, hurricane victims in the Caribbean. Safe, happy and comfortable, we've watched it all from our living rooms.

But now it's about us. Now the struggles which have devastated millions of people across the world have reach our well-protected, self-absorbed, greedy shores, and they have devastated us.

Whoever was behind this wake-up-call of an attack on America knew our country well. The "weapons of mass destruction" were not bombs or missiles; they were airplanes from our very own "friendly skies." The symbols of American power that were destroyed — the World Trade Center and the Pentagon — were chosen well. There is even speculation that the fourth plane, which went down in a field outside of Pittsburgh, was headed for Camp David, the White House or the halls of Congress. I almost expected a hijacked Lear Jet to slam into the Statue of Liberty as a finale.

Our posturing leaders talk about vengeance, but how can that be? Even if we are certain that Osama bin Laden or his organization, al-Qaida, were responsible for these vicious terrorist attacks, what can we do?

We can bomb Afghanistan, of course, but we'll just be hurting thousands of innocent Afghanis who are already oppressed and miserable under the control of the lunatic Taliban. Will we actually get bin Laden, if, indeed, he is the person responsible? It's doubtful. We can't penetrate his forces or his defenses. We've had a $5 million bounty on his head for years. He'll be like Saddam Hussein, who laughs in our faces, stuffs his bank account with money from illegal oil sales and writes a romance novel while his people suffer and die.

On Tuesday, pompous officials called this a "sophisticated, large-scale, well-financed, coordinated attack." They implied that only an armed and organized enemy with massive resources could attack the mighty United States like that.

But when you think about it, all it really took were four suicidal pilots — and these days, doesn't the world seem too full of people who are so angry they are willing to die for a cause? — a few airline timetables, some plane tickets, four synchronized watches and a total disregard for innocent human life. According to people on the planes who managed to make cell phone calls before they died, the hijackers were armed with "knives and box-cutters."

At least this puts the ridiculous "Star Wars" technology in the garbage can forever. We have to get used to the idea that we are vulnerable. Even though bin Laden warned three weeks ago that something serious was going to happen in the United Sates, we seem to have had no warning about this tragedy from our intelligence community. Missiles in outer space wouldn't have helped us here.

The horror of Tuesday will remain in our memories forever. I may never get out of my mind the innocent silhouette in the bright blue sky of that second plane just before it flew into the World Trade Center. I will never forget the images of those poor people who jumped, or dropped, or were blown from the top of the building. "We thought it was debris, but it was people jumping," said a survivor as I wept.

The attack touched us all, even those of us who live in the relative safety and quiet of Vermont. Like millions of others, on Tuesday I worried about my friends and loved ones. I was grateful when a friend who works on Wall Street called to let me know that she was safe, even though she was in tears, wondering if her friends and co-workers were still alive.

My cousin Ellen e-mailed from Queens Tuesday night, "Things are unreal here. My friend's daughter had to walk home 30 miles on a broken toe. My 10-minute drive home was two hours. TV stations — all but one — are down. They were transmitting from the WTC. I used to see the towers from my terrace. No more. Scary."

The Washington-based president of a foundation to which I am applying for a fellowship also e-mailed, "Sorry about the delay. I'm watching the Pentagon burn from the view of my office on this awful day."

"America has been attacked; it has been changed," said Tom Brokaw. A country filled with ordinary people who lead daily, hard-working lives has lost its innocence. Certainly we must pray for the victims and their families, but most of all, we must work everywhere against injustice and for peace.

(My mother was scheduled to fly home the next day, but her flight was canceled. The first day that planes started flying again, I took her to the airport. Security was intense — armed soldiers were everywhere. Both of us were terrified. We held hands and quivered until her flight was called. Just before she went bravely through the gates, she slipped off her wedding ring and pressed it into my hand. It was the small circle of diamonds that my father had put on her hand they day they were married. If anything happened to her, she said, she wanted me to have it. It is too small for me to wear, so I have kept it in my jewelry box ever since. Just recently, she asked if she could have it back.)

~ ~ ~

October 11, 2001

In A Dangerous Time

It's been exactly a month since the Sept. 11 attacks, and I still return to the World Trade Center every night in my dreams.

In one dream, I'm rooting through the rubble and hold up the severed head of either a baby or a doll. I can't tell which one it is, but the neck is ragged and stained with blood. In another, I'm in one of the buildings, but instead of escaping, I'm waiting for the elevator to take me up. There are other dreams, too, but you don't want to know about them.

I'm a relatively adventurous person, so I'm surprised at how fearful I've become lately. I happened to spend last week visiting my mother at her retirement condominium in Florida. While I was packing, I identified with the passengers on the hijacked flights. Had they been in their bedrooms on the morning of that fateful day, fretting like me over which clothes to pack? Had they folded a sweater? Tucked toothpaste into the corner of a suitcase?

On the mini-van from the parking lot to Bradley Airport, I thought, "I'm like a lamb being led to slaughter." When I saw a plane take off, I thought, "flying bomb." I racially profiled everyone in the check-in line. A middle-aged couple speaking a language I couldn't identify made me nervous. So did a raw-boned young man. Over the loudspeaker came the startling warning, "It's a federal offense to make jokes about hijackers, bombs or concealed weapons."

In Florida, I wasn't surprised to learn that 14 people in the condominium complex had died in the two weeks following the attack. One was my mother's best friend.

It made a crazy kind of sense to me. In their 70s and 80s, the children of immigrants, they had managed to assimilate only in time to go through a fierce Depression and then plunge into the chaos and loss of a world war. Next they enjoyed a little peace and prosperity in the shadow of a potential nuclear holocaust, and then were thoroughly upended by the Sixties — a different kind of chaos caused by their own children. I could understand some of them looking at the crater that used to be the World Trade Center and saying, "Been there. Done that. I'm checking out."

In south Florida, the television stations were having a field day with the anthrax story. I tried to count the times in one hour that I heard the word and lost track at 32. Of course, the newscasters prefaced their comments with statements like, "This does not necessarily relate to terrorism," but it was that unusual and sinister word — anthrax, anthrax, anthrax — that came through the commercial din. That story continues.

I am not alone in my fear. The country has gone mad with it. People are buying gas masks and stocking up on antibiotics. They're buying guns in record numbers. Many are wearing "God Bless America" t-shirts, but I wonder how many are expressing nationalistic fervor and how many are simply afraid that they will be attacked by their fellow Americans if they don't display the flag.

Mr. Osama bin Laden must be happy about how fearful we suddenly are. In his little videotaped address to the nation Sunday night, he crowed: "America has been filled with horror..."

For decades, we have been a nation of fearful people who demand security in everything we say or do. Look at the warning labels we put on everything, and the way babies in cars are buckled and padded to within an inch of their lives. Our mothers drank highballs and martinis, but woe to the pregnant woman who drinks in public today. We demand safe cars, toys, clothing, music and entertainment, and we sue when accidents happen — as they always do.

But why am I personally afraid, when I know that the chances are small that Mr. bin Laden will be leading an army of Islamic

Fundamentalists up the dirt road to my mountaintop home any time soon?

First — and this might sound melodramatic — I'm afraid for Western civilization. As much as I criticize the United States for its many flaws, I cherish our civilization and its great achievements in art, literature, medicine, technology. I can't help thinking about the many other storied civilizations that fell apart — Greece, Rome, Alexandria. I can't help but wonder if ours won't be next. If we plunge ourselves into a third world war, we run that risk.

I worry about the similarities between the Afghanistan bombings and the Vietnam War, when American arrogance went to a foreign country to fight against entrenched, battle-hardened, patriotic zealots who had already beaten back one large and powerful nation.

I worry about the similarities between Mr. bin Laden, who appeared robotic and oddly emotionless on television, and who lives in caves and worships a deranged ideology, and Mr. Mao Tse Tsung, and I remember the damage that particular dictator heaped on his ancient — but also corrupt —civilization.

I worry that even though I long for peace and write columns calling for a sharing of American prosperity throughout the world, in the end my personal safety depends on my country continuing to support foul dictatorships that deprive their own people of any vestiges of their liberty or prosperity.

I worry, but perhaps not as much as Mr. William Safire, who said, in The New York Times on Oct. 8, that the terrorists' goals were to drive Israel out of the Middle East and remove the sanctions against Saddam Hussein. "These are not mere street-acclaimed goals adopted to gain fundamentalist adherents," he wrote. "These are steps to gain weapons of mass destruction by which to intimidate and dominate the world. Crazy? Hitler was crazy, too, but he almost won."

When the attacks were finally over on Sept. 11, my husband whispered to me, "We're lovers in a dangerous time." That's the title of a Bruce Cockburn song; the last lines are: "But nothing worth having comes without some kind of fight. You've got to kick at the darkness 'til it bleeds daylight."

With so much darkness all around me, where do I start to kick?

October 25, 2001

A Visit To Ground Zero

They say that television doesn't do it justice, that you can't feel the full horror of the tragedy until you see it for yourself, that only a visit to lower Manhattan makes it "real." So I went.

Ground Zero, that huge depression in the ground that once was the World Trade Center, has become our nation's newest tourist attraction. It is the latest in a long line of carnivals of deaths, souls, flowers, cheap souvenirs and costly heroics. My husband calls it the new Via Dolorosa.

We took the subway downtown, where rat poison warnings were our first warning that we were close. At Chambers Street, six weeks after the attack, the smell of burnt still clings to the air — burnt plastic, burnt paper, burnt wood, burnt metal — everything but the scent I feared most, the scent of burnt people.

A gray and powdery ash of pulverized concrete still clings to store and apartment windows, to the subway steps and railings, and, especially, to the garbage trucks, concrete mixers, and huge, twisted steel girders that tractors are carrying, one by one in a somber funeral procession, out of Ground Zero.

Looking south at the corner of Greenwich and Chambers streets, you can see in the distance smoke rising from a vast emptiness. The street is blocked, though, and the barricade has been turned into a memorial decorated with flags, flowers, poems, signs and notes from all over — Florida, Ohio, Minnesota, Argentina. Many say "God Bless America." But life also goes on: a sign for a check cashing service says, "We're back!"

By blocking the road, a plaza has been created in front of Washington Market Park. On Saturday morning it was full of friendly police officers and soldiers in camouflage who kept the crowd moving, plus a bustling Saturday farmers' market selling exotic breads, fragrant eucalyptus branches, vegetables, plants and flowers. Gourmet food at a memorial site —very New York.

There were also lines of port-o-potties and lots of tourists, some crying, some holding flowers, and all taking pictures.

We were too far away from Ground Zero on Chambers, so we started walking east and then south down Broadway. Approximately every 10 feet we passed someone selling American flag pins and ribbons and pictures of the World Trade Center. There were also many people selling NYC fire and police department hats and t-shirts, and others selling their own versions of God.

By the time we walked past City Hall, draped in purple and black bunting and American flags, I realized that we had become part of a slow-moving line. A fire engine rushed by, and I was relieved that it was racing to a new, probably less devastating fire than the one it had raced to on Sept. 11.

Drops of water brushed our faces. Looking up, I saw that many of the tall buildings were being cleaned. The famous Woolworth Building was getting a renovation ("State-of-the-art in 1913, state-of-the-future in 2000," said the sign.)

The fire engines stopped on Vesey Street. "How 'bout a cheer for the fire department of New York City," yelled a woman as we passed, and I had the sense that she was only doing what she had seen people do on TV. "Ready? Yeaaaa!" Very few people joined her.

A flute player was playing an emotional version of "The Star Spangled Banner" as we walked past a Chase 24-Hour ATM covered with hand- and type-written poems and notes. Someone had copied out lines by Dylan Thomas: "Do not go gentle into that good night ... rage, rage against the dying of the light." A person from Texas wrote, "Hate kills he who hates." Pictures of Jesus were plastered all over.

A fiddler played a jig as the line, guided by police barriers, shuffled slowly along, always a block away from Ground Zero.

At John Street we started getting glimpses directly into the site. Two huge cranes, lit by rays of sunlight, crossed each other in a V, while smaller cranes shot streams of water.

At Dey Street I saw a building that looked like a modern sculpture — from its top flowed a motionless curving waterfall of iron girders.

We passed a sign on Houlihan's Bar that said, "You are looking at hallowed ground... Please give it the dignity it deserves."

The crowd must have numbered over a thousand by then. I was hearing a whole world's worth of languages and accents, and was surrounded by people wearing everything from saris to lederhosen. Ghouls, I thought, hating them for being there. But then of course, I was there too.

At Maiden Lane I could see a building that had been shredded; it looked like a huge pile of used, unraveling sweaters knitted from rebar and girders.

Given the distances of time and space, if there's going to be an emotional punch in the stomach, a sense of the tragedy becoming real, it will come at Liberty Street. That's where you first see the famous verticals, the walls which are the only things left of the World Trade Center, and in front of them "the pile," the mass grave of over 3,000 people.

These walls now have a terrible and ancient beauty. They might as well be Angkor Wat or the Roman Coliseum, they look so weathered and so old. Silently they stand, a reminder of a lost culture and a lost time.

Across from them, a building stands intact except for one corner, which looks like a huge panther has raked its claws down it, looking for meat. It screams silently in witness to the intense hatred that has caused all this pain and sorrow.

In the nearby Trinity Church graveyard, somehow untouched by the attacks, I read some of the tombstones: "Here lies the body of Elisabeth, wife of John ... March 4, 1764." Elisabeth's was a much simpler time, I thought, but she's just as dead.

As I moved slowly with the crowd from one street to the next, I noticed that my eye had become a video camera; I was making a moving picture in my mind. It wasn't a silent film, either. Under the subdued noises of the crowd there was a constant rumbling of truck motors and generators and engines.

Past Trinity, the crowds dispersed and the line ended just as informally as it had begun. We walked uptown to Chinatown, which was crowded, and had lunch. We went shopping for used books and saw a Broadway play. New York was its usual lively, crowded and colorful self, and I was bewildered because away from Ground Zero, except for the large number of buildings decorated with American flags, it was as if nothing had ever happened.

But when I got back to Vermont, I gathered up the papers and magazines from the week of Sept. 11, studied the pictures again and reread the first-hand accounts. Then, because I had been there, it all became horribly, viscerally real.

September 11, 2003

A NATIONAL DAY OF MOURNING

A month ago, while making a appointment with my dentist, the secretary said, "How's Sept. 11 for you?"

And I was startled.

"You're working on Sept. 11?" I said. "Somehow that doesn't seem right."

And it doesn't, does it? Today, Sept. 11, should be a national day of mourning in America, not a day of typing, shopping, dental hygiene and automotive repair. We should be grieving for the dead — the American dead, the Afghani dead, the Iraqi dead, the others dead. We should be engaged in a day of reflection and discussion. We should be mourning the loss of our innocence. We should review the path we as a country have taken since that tragic day.

Sept. 11 calls for nothing less.

Many people scoff at the idea that "things are different now," that the date has special meaning. After all, planes still fly, the stock market still operates, George W. Bush is still president, television still dominates our lives with silly sitcoms and sillier reality shows, and Julia Roberts still makes movies.

And in fact, in the world of reality, which strangely is also the world of denial, nothing really has changed.

After Sept. 11, we talked about the death of irony. Irony never died.

We said the news would become more serious; no more shark attacks and Chandra Levy. Now we have Laci and Kobe.

We said we would re-examine our dependence on Arab oil. Instead, we have flooded the country with SUVs.

But everything did change on Sept. 11. On that day, the lid of a Pandora's box was ripped open and every evil known to man came flying out.

Instead of beginning a national discussion on how best to bring to justice the criminals who attacked us, we embarked on a national policy of wanton revenge. And as many of us predicted, the violence has not brought peace, but only more violence.

We have killed thousands in Afghanistan. In Iraq, the latest civilian death toll is about 37,000. Hundreds of Americans have been killed, and thousands more have been wounded. We hear of new casualties every day.

We threw away 60 years of good will and cooperation with our allies around the world. We squandered every bit of sympathy and respect the world has had for us. We attacked our own precious freedoms at home. We hired other countries to do our torture for us; surely, if torture is really necessary, we should do our own dirty work and face the consequences. We have turned our armed forces into some kind of antiquated Western posse assigned to bring in Iraqi officials "dead or alive." We hold men like dogs in cages in Guantanamo.

Yet Osama bin Laden remains free. Saddam Hussein remains free. And those two do not really matter. What matters is that the Taliban is regaining control of Afghanistan in the wake of the chaos we created there, and now, for the first time, al-Qaida has taken root in Iraq. Violence breeds hatred, and there does not seem to be a shortage of suicide bombers in the Middle East.

To do the things we've done in the past two years in Afghanistan, Iraq and the United States in the names of those who died in the World Trade Center, the Pentagon and in Pennsylvania is an obscenity.

We need a day in which we can acknowledge that our decent, lawful and generous country has been taken away from us — and not by men who wear turbans, but by the very men we trusted to lead us.

That is what has changed: a group of American men have cynically grasped the horrors of that day to embark on an earlier plan to create a global American-cum-British empire based on our excessive addiction to oil.

British Prime Minister Tony Blair has acknowledged this. He was quoted in The Times on July 17, 2002 saying, "To be truthful about it, there was no way we could have got the public consent to have suddenly launched a campaign on Afghanistan but for what happened on Sept. 11."

"The overriding motivation for this smoke screen is that the US and the UK are beginning to run out of secure hydrocarbon energy supplies," said Michael Meacher, the UK's environment minister from 1997 to 2003, in The Guardian recently. "By 2010 the Muslim world will control as much as 60 percent of the world's oil production, and, even more importantly, 95 percent of remaining global oil export capacity.

As demand is increasing, so supply is decreasing, continually since the 1960s... The 'global war on terrorism' has the hallmarks of a political myth propagated to pave the way for a wholly different agenda — the US role of world hegemony built around securing by force command over the oil supplies required to drive the whole project."

Unquestionably, we in the industrialized world are dependent on oil; surely there must be better ways to secure our supplies and/or reduce our dependency besides shedding the blood of innocent people and dominating countries halfway across the globe.

Many of us will always be scarred by Sept. 11. I myself am haunted by the nightmare images of the people — the people just like you, the people just like me — who jumped from the top of the World Trade Center. In the latest issue of Esquire, Tom Junod writes that between 50 and 200 people jumped to their death that day.

"They jumped to escape the smoke and the fire; they jumped when the ceilings fell and the floors collapsed; they jumped just to breathe once more before they died," Junod said. "For more than an hour and a half, they streamed from the building, one after another... as if each individual required the sight of another individual jumping before mustering the courage to jump himself or herself."

Sept. 11 should be a national day of mourning so we can muster the courage to reflect whether we, if we were unfortunate enough to be trapped in the Windows on the World or the offices of Cantor Fitzgerald, would have jumped. To talk about how to stop America's blundering aggression in the world. To talk about repairing the damage we have done. To think creatively about how to restore justice, mercy and rationality to the world and still remain relatively safe and economically sound.

Sept. 11 should be a national day of mourning so we can all breathe once more before we die.

SIX:

Our Political Life

February 4, 1996

How Do They Explain The Duke?

(This piece was written in frustration in response to the discussion sparked by "The Bell Curve: Intelligence and Class Structure in American Life" by Richard J. Herrnstein and Charles Murray — just another of many attempts to stuff the African-American genie back into the bottle and cork it up for all time.)

Whenever I read some strange racist theory that black people are somehow more deficient than white and Asian people in intelligence, I wonder, how do those people explain Duke Ellington?

Not that racists think very clearly. Or, for that matter, how do they explain the brilliant Louis Armstrong, Miles Davis, who changed the course of music two, maybe three times, the early Nat "King" Cole (I can't explain the Nelson Riddle period), Charlie Parker, all the early bluesmen and women like Charley Patton, Richard Johnson, Sippie Wallace, Bessie Smith, Lightnin' Hopkins, and Muddy Waters. Or the creators of rock, James Brown, Little Richard, Chuck Berry, Jimi Hendrix and the rest.

I could fill this column with names of great black musicians, but some racist bigot might say it only proves that black people have rhythm. So let's throw in some writers, like Langston Hughes, James Baldwin, Richard Wright, Alice Walker, Zora Neale Hurston and Toni Morrison. Add some movie stars like Denzel Washington (sigh) and Wesley Snipes, just for the hell of it.

Think of the enormous dignity of the December 1994 Kennedy Center Gala, when Sidney Poitier and B.B. King were honored.

But all these lists are silly, because of all the names I'm leaving out — the names of the great painters, political figures, opera singers, scientists, inventors, sports figures, business men and women, freedom fighters. Their names are legion.

Back in the early 1970s, men used a similar argument about women. According to this theory, women weren't as intelligent as men because there weren't as many great female artists, architects, writers, etc.

Of course there weren't. Women of talent and greatness — who weren't lucky enough to be born with protective royal titles — were sometimes burned at the stake, more frequently buried in marriages or tucked away in convents. It was difficult for them to have enough control over their energy to fully realize their talents. Now that so many barriers have been removed, we see women's talent flourishing everywhere.

Intelligence and talent are carried in the genes, and fall equally on the male and female members of all the human races. How that intelligence and talent is nurtured determines how or how not they are used. All the rest of the discussion is smoke.

Because racism is so prevalent in our society, there must be few African-Americans, male or female, who have not felt the venom of this dreadful thing. That so many have gone on to contribute so greatly to American culture can only be called inspiring.

Here is a story from "Sweet Man; The Real Duke Ellington" by Don George. One sunny morning around 1950, Ellington and the author visited Lena Horne and her (white) husband, Lennie Hayton, for breakfast at their home in southern California. With them was Ellington's friend Billy Strayhorn, the arranger, collaborator and composer of the classic "Take The 'A' Train." While they were eating, a neighbor called to warn that some other neighbors had been seen sneaking onto Horne's property and burying something on the lawn. When the group checked, they found a freshly buried coffee can full of marijuana. Naturally, they flushed the dope and waited for the police, who soon came with a search warrant. The police didn't search the house. They went right for the spot in the lawn.

"Perhaps it was not only because Lena was black but because they had seen these other black fellows arrive..." George said.

This incident is such an insult to the whole of American culture that I am astounded by it, yet it is only one small incident. Ellington — perhaps the greatest American composer of them all, a man adored all over the world, a man entertained by royalty — in good times toured the United States by rail instead of by bus, so his African-American musicians could live, eat, and sleep in dignity and luxury instead of being shunted off to segregated southern hotels. He later developed the habit of eating in hotel rooms because, it is theorized, he didn't want to risk being refused service in restaurants.

Not long ago, I saw a professional revival of the Broadway musical "Raisin," closely based on Lorraine Hansberry's powerful and award-winning 1959 Broadway play "A Raisin in the Sun." The title comes from a Hughes poem: "What happens to a dream deferred? Does it dry up, like a raisin in the sun? Or fester like a sore — and then run... Maybe it just sags like a heavy load. Or does it explode?"

Nearly four decades later, the poem and the play still ring with truths.

It's about a poor, church-going black family living in a Chicago slum, and what happens to them when they receive a large insurance check. The matriarch puts a down-payment on a house in an all-white neighborhood and the offended neighbors try to buy her out. Her son, the chauffeur of a rich white man, takes the rest of the money and invests it in a liquor store. He wants desperately to be his own boss, away from the servile jobs open to him as a black man. Unfortunately, he loses the money. In the end, the play is about loving people for their weaknesses as well as their strengths — a lesson we all need to learn, especially those of us who write books about black people's intellectual inferiority. I think we need to question the intelligence of some white people.

~ ~ ~

January 1, 1998

THE TIMES THEY ARE A'CHANGIN'?

Is it a sign of schizophrenia or cynicism that our government gave the Kennedy Center Honors treatment to Bob Dylan?

There he was, on television on Dec. 26, his mother sitting behind him, Lauren Bacall to one side, Charlton Heston to the other, his face carved out of stone, being honored for what has really been his biggest problem for the last 30 years: being a legend.

Our government doesn't usually honor creativity. It tries to censor the Internet, put V-chips in our televisions and warning ratings on the programs. It tries to eliminate rap lyrics, stop risk-taking performance art, and cut financial subsidies to thousands of small orchestras and ballet companies around the country by dismantling the National Endowment for the Arts. On an ordinary day, our government seems to consider performing artists one step higher than welfare cheats.

So it was weird to see Dylan, who spent his early years correctly excoriating the government for its hypocrisies, lies and self-satisfied arrogance, sitting a few seats away from a president, Bill Clinton, who seems to epitomize everything Dylan once railed against.

Dylan's contributions to music are so great that in the end, he will be put in the company of jazz greats like Louis Armstrong, Charlie Parker, Miles Davis and others who changed the course of music and the culture. And unlike Elvis Presley and Frank Sinatra, he didn't ride to fame on the force of his performance personality; he doesn't seem to have one.

After experiencing a creative streak unparalleled in this century, igniting in a generation a revolutionary demand for social change, and creating electric folk, a genre so rich it is being profitably explored 30 years later, Dylan found himself so famous and revered that he spent the next 30 years practically in hiding.

Then he went on a long performing streak, exploring and refining his songs. As everyone who saw him at Tanglewood or Smith College this year knows, the songs never sound the same way twice. And as explosive gospel singer Shirley Caesar showed at the Honors, there's still much to be explored.

Now Dylan has released a gorgeous new and mature work, "Time Out of Mind," which, with the help of Daniel Lanois (U2's "Joshua Tree," Emilylou Harris' "Wrecking Ball"), takes folk-rock as far into the realm of jazz as it can go, considering the essential squareness of its beat.

In the light of this creativity, Dylan's mid-period mistakes like "Dylan at Budokan," the mumble-and-stumble shows, and the selling of "The Times They Are A' Changin'" to an accounting firm, are forgiven.

Still, why does Newt Gingrich, who led the charge to savage the funding of the NEA, now rave about the inspiration of Dylan's lyrics? And why does Clinton, who loves every piece of censorship legislation that comes down the pike, now honor him?

Is the older Dylan now safe and sanitized for public consumption? Have the politicians been able to appropriate the important symbols of his work to suit their own needs? Has his bite been muzzled by giving the same award to rabid NRA-supporter Charlton Heston? Can we expect to see Dr. Dre and Ani DiFranco being honored at the Kennedy Center 30 years from now?

Artists should be nurtured and honored throughout their lives. The Kennedy Center Honors is just a feel-good thing, the government patting itself on the back and rewarding artists who, by some miracle, have managed to survive and flourish, while it tries to strangle the newest generation in the crib.

~ ~ ~

February 13, 1998

GRANDMOTHERS ARE "TITANIC"

Over drinks the other night, a friend explained the "Grandmother Hypothesis." It is based on the idea that the human race has progressed so far in its evolution — progressed over animals, I believe, not over its own instincts — because, unlike animals who die after their reproductive life is over, humans continue to live. That gives the race, as a whole, a large number of women with free time and energy who can help nurture their grandchildren, protect their families, gather food and generally devote themselves to the welfare of the species.

The hypothesis, developed by a team from the University of Utah led by Professor Kristen Hawkes, an anthropologist, appeared in an article in the journal Proceedings of the National Academy of Science.

It tied in nicely with something I have been thinking about since I saw the film "Titanic."

I loved the movie. Not because of its special effects, and certainly not because I thought Leonardo DiCaprio was an attractive lover — he looked way too young for the ripe Kate Winslet.

I loved it because its story was told by a 101-year old woman, Rose DeWitt Bukater, with amusement, wisdom, bite, intelligence and fierceness. I loved her from the moment I first saw her, sitting in a lush greenhouse throwing a pot, then walking into a kitchen where every wall and surface was filled with something interesting, beautiful and meaningful.

I could have happily spent an hour in that room, listening to Rose tell stories to her granddaughter. The sinking of the Titanic, which cost hundreds of millions of dollars to get on film, was less interesting to me than being in that room with Rose.

As played by Gloria Stuart, herself an 87-year-old woman who is now, happily, a nominee for an Academy Award for Best Supporting Actress, Rose told the story of the sinking of the Titanic from what she called "the bottomless well of secrets" that is a woman's heart.

The real story of the Titanic is a bottomless well of destructive machismo, egotism, arrogance and classism, but Rose's perspective was clear-eyed and humane. I was grateful to "Titanic" writer-director James Cameron for writing the script from Rose's perspective. I took from her demeanor and her life a sense of lasting calm and purposefulness.

As it turned out, the very next evening, on public television, I found myself in a similar state watching "Porgy and Bess: An American Voice." The program, created by James A. Standifer, a music professor at the University of Michigan, examined with intelligence the artistic and racial issues raised by the Gershwin opera. But the epiphany, for me, came at the end, when the stars of the first 1935 production sat in an album-lined room listening to their young selves singing.

The camera, with Zen felicity, lingered for a long time on the faces of Anne Brown, now 86, and Todd Duncan, 95, as they listened with looks of wonder to the great beauty of their voices so many years ago. At intervals, we saw them young and on film, playing the parts of Porgy and Bess — Brown so beautiful that she took my breath away, Duncan, so strong and yet so crippled that I was afraid for him when he tried to walk.

At the end, Duncan asked about the music they had made together, "Did we deserve it?" And Brown, her face glowing, patted his hand and told him that indeed, they had made the music; it was their achievement, certainly they deserved it.

Right now there is a hunger in me for older women's stories, for stories not of women's abuse but of their achievements, for stories from that bottomless well of secrets that is the female heart.

I find myself in the odd position of being old numerically but in the middle of my life emotionally and professionally. I'm at a loss to make the number that represents the years I've lived compute with the person who has lived them.

It has long been a truism that our society discards women after menopause. Actually, women are discarded all the way through their lives: when they become, for some reason, crippled; when they put on 20 extra pounds; when they stop dedicating their lives to being attractive to men; when they are pregnant; when they are mothers; when they are old.

It is possible that the Baby Boomers will change this, because there are as many vital and productive women out there who are turning 50 as there are men. These women have become accustomed to — and enjoy — jobs, power and money. They have voices and, perhaps, will refuse to be discarded.

It is possible that "Titanic" was — pardon me — the tip of the iceberg, and in the coming years we will be fortunate to know the stories of many accomplished women, so that Toni Morrison, Maya Angelou and even Gloria Stuart will not be so alone with their great achievements and white hair.

It makes sense that older women are a treasure, a resource, a source of wisdom, a repository of history. Maybe the "Grandmother Hypothesis" is true, and they are an important reason for the evolutionary success of the human species.

After a cognac or two, however, my friend and I could not help but wonder, "While the grandmothers were evolving the species, what is it, exactly, that the grandfathers were doing?"

~ ~ ~

June 14, 2001

Thou Shalt Not Kill

(Every now and then, those of us who are opposed to the death penalty have new reasons to speak out. The film "Dead Man Walking," for example, reintroduces the topic into the culture. Or the release of another innocent man from prison or worse, death row. Or the execution of another man

or woman. Since there are only a limited number of ways to say "Thou Shalt Not Kill," I tend to repeat myself. This version was written after the execution of Timothy McVeigh, the Oklahoma City bomber.)

So, are you "healed" now, America? Have you found "closure"? Can you get back to your "normal life" now that Timothy McVeigh no longer walks (or sits in a jail cell) among us? Doesn't it feel good to lash out, to punish? Isn't revenge great?

It's a shame the feeling doesn't last, isn't it?

Blame, punishment and revenge, as sweet and satisfying as they might be, are drugs. You always need more.

It was never about Timothy McVeigh. No matter how the justice system dealt with that sad, hateful and demented young man, it wouldn't bring back one single soul from the tragedy and insanity of the Oklahoma City bombing, or provide more than a single moment or two of self-righteous vindication.

I am sick of all the pontificating, the call-in shows, the screaming tabloid headlines, the conspiracy theories, the death penalty arguments, the pictures of that ugly chair monument, the regret that McVeigh didn't show "remorse" at the end, and — in a perfect example of how our country has lost all sense of proportion — of Peter Jennings on national television worrying that some of McVeigh's ashes might find their way back to Oklahoma City.

So I'm going to keep it simple: Thou shalt not kill.

The death penalty isn't wrong because innocent people might be executed, although they are. It isn't wrong because some murderers can be rehabilitated, even though that's true. It isn't wrong because some murderers are mentally ill, even though that's certainly the case. It isn't wrong because one or two of them can paint like Picasso.

It's just wrong. By killing, we lower ourselves to the level of the killer. By embracing the death penalty, we degrade and coarsen our society. An eye for an eye is the law of barbarism.

This isn't the first time I've said all this, but to my surprise, the first time I said it on the Internet, I was flooded with e-mails condemning me for being soft-headed and liberal (is that now a punishable offense in the United States?), not to mention irrelevant.

The general opinion of my Web correspondents was that while the Ten Commandments say, "Thou shalt not kill," what they really mean is, "Thou shalt not murder." Around the time of King James, I was told many times, something got lost in the translation.

Most of my correspondents quoted the Bible as a passionate supporter of killing in every possible form and degree. Not being a Bible student, I was surprised to hear that the Lord had revised Exodus 20:13, so I checked a concordance for the words "kill" and "killeth." Among the entries:

- "And he that killeth any man shall surely be put to death." Leviticus 24:17.
- "That whosoever killeth any person unawares might flee thither, and not die by the hand of the avenger of blood, until he stood before the congregation." Joshua 20:9.
- "A time to kill, and a time to heal." Ecclesiastes 3:3.
- "He that killeth with the sword must be killed with the sword." Revelation 13:10.

Still, the Bible was written in another time and for other cultures. Now we build huge restaurant chains centered around the eating of shellfish. We don't slaughter rams and offer them to the gods when it rains too much. We rely less on trumpet-blowing and more on tactical weapons and economic sanctions to bring down walls and destroy our enemies.

Thou shalt not kill, however, is timeless. It's good, sound advice. It's like "Turn the other cheek," and the Golden Rule, "Do unto others as you would have others do unto you." It's a common-sense way to live in the world, a philosophy found in every religion, including Judaism, Catholicism, Protestantism, Buddhism and Islam.

The need to punish and extract revenge remains a real and understandable human emotion, but succumbing to these emotions is as pointless as it is base. How much, for example, can we pay the guards who strap down the arms and legs of the condemned to the table? How much can we pay the nurses who put in the needles, and the men who push the buttons that start the poisons flowing down the tubes? How much does it cost for us to turn them into murderers so we can feel validated and sleep at night?

Isn't a lifetime in prison punishment and revenge enough?

But, OK, maybe I'm wrong. Maybe it's good to kill. Then what are the guidelines? How do we rewrite Exodus to eliminate our collective guilt?

Thou shalt not kill unless it's in self-defense? Thou shalt not kill unless that person is diddling his daughter? Thou shalt not kill unless that person has killed someone else, been tried and convicted, and is probably poor and black anyway? Thou shalt not kill unless they're gooks, communists or from Iraq? Thou shalt not kill unless you really need those Nikes? Thou shalt not kill unless you are running to be president of the United States?

I'm sorry, but in the wake of McVeigh's execution, I can only say one thing: dead country walking.

~ ~ ~

November 8, 2001

THE AFGHAN WOMAN

(This was written after the United States began its attack on Afghanistan.)

In a warm and tender moment, my husband wraps his arms around me and holds me tight against his heart.

I close my eyes and see the Afghan woman. She, too, is in the arms of her husband. They are a handsome pair, these two — young, dark-haired, dark-eyed, as much in love as we are. And like us, all they want is to live their life together. But they have not eaten for days, their home has been demolished, and they are crouching for cover behind a rock.

It is a slow Sunday, and I idly leaf through the Christmas catalogs that are forming piles on my nightstand. Eddie Bauer, J. Jill, Smith & Hawken, The Company Store, Sierra Designs. I am a writer, so I am poor, but if I had money there would be many interesting things to buy.

Then I close my eyes and see the Afghan woman. Her clothing is in shreds — they flutter in the cruel wind. There is nothing for her to buy, and if there was, she would not have money.

On Monday mornings I weigh myself, then promise to diet. But in my mind the Afghan woman and her husband are thin and weak with starvation.

It is growing cold now in Vermont, so I put flannel sheets on the bed and poke at the wood stove. I add a log and the coals spring into flames.

Then I close my eyes and find myself looking into the wild frightened eyes of the Afghan woman. Winter has come early to Afghanistan this year. She has no bed, no sheets, no stove. There is no wood for her husband to cut, and if there were, there would be no matches to light a fire. Their only heat comes from their two bodies pressed together, and all they want is to survive.

I walk with a friend. Since Sept. 11, she tells me, she has not felt threatened. She knows that if something bad happens, she and her family can flee north to Canada. "I have the strength and the will to live in the woods and to hunt to feed my family," she says.

And I see the Afghan woman has no place to run. She is brave; she would hunt if there were something to hunt. But everything that moves or grows was eaten long ago, or else it dried up and blew away in the drought.

I read a magazine story about women's relationships with their fathers. The writer offers insights about young girls who seek their fathers' approval, and as a result, end up in careers that might not fulfill their deepest needs.

Usually, I enjoy insights about how my childhood might have affected my life. But now I think about the Afghan woman; for her, just now, self-actualization is not an burning problem.

A plane flies overhead as I walk down Kipling Road. It could be a cropduster, I think idly, and try to find it in the sky. It turns out to be just a small plane, a needle darning the clouds, in and out, in and out.

We are carpet-bombing Afghanistan today, dropping bombs the size of Volkswagens. When the Afghan woman looks up, it is not out of idle curiosity, and why do I feel the same terror that her heart feels as it beats against her chest?

I am haunted by this Afghan woman, whom I have never met, and who has done nothing to deserve her awful life. I am as haunted by her as I am by the thousands of people who lost their lives on Sept. 11.

The world has gone mad. First, psychotic, angry, hate-filled men inflict pain, terror and destruction on my country.

Then, in retaliation, my country bombs a people we openly call "innocent."

The bombs we drop are yellow, the same color as the food packages we drop. According to humanitarian aid workers, the food is only 1 percent of what is needed in Afghanistan right now. We hear that seven million people might starve there this winter.

We are using high-flying planes to catch a man who hides in caves.

We may be sending trained but unseasoned young men to fight against warriors who have defeated every invader since Alexander the Great.

In many ways, our allies are as evil as our enemies.

Thousands of would-be fighters are flocking to Pakistan; they would join the Taliban if they were allowed to. We are inflaming with hatred a Muslim world armed with nuclear weapons.

No one hates the Sept. 11 terrorists more than I do. I hate them for destroying so many unfinished lives, for hurting so many families, for ruining lower Manhattan, for hating women, and most of all, for their ghastly arrogance, which has ruined so much that was beautiful and alive.

But surely we are intelligent and creative enough to find a way to bring these criminals to justice without all this wanton and irrelevant bombing. And to bring to justice the home-grown terrorists who are, I am convinced, behind the anthrax scare.

As I watch the world go raving mad, I am torn between empathy and fear.

Although she is younger, darker and more beautiful than I am, I am that Afghan woman.

~ ~ ~

November 15, 2001

UPSTREAM FROM THE HERD

The Japanese have a saying that the nail which sticks up attracts the hammer. In America since Sept. 11, we have seen that fear of hammers throw almost the entire American media into a paroxysm of censorship and self-censorship.

Look at the evidence. Columnists have been fired for questioning the evasive actions of President George W. Bush in the hours after the attacks. The U.S. State Department killed an exclusive Voice of America interview with the Taliban leader, Mullah Mohammad Omar. (After some protest, the interview was partially aired. The acting director of VOA has since been replaced.)

CNN reporters have been ordered to balance images of civilian casualties and devastation in Afghanistan with reminders about the World Trade Center. The comic strip "Boondocks" was pulled from more than one newspaper because of its dissenting politics. TV host Bill Maher lost advertisers when he referred to past U.S. military actions as cowardly (Grenada and Panama come to mind). The editor of The New Republic ruled that "domestic political dissent is immoral without a prior statement of national solidarity, a choosing of sides."

Late last month, ABC News President David Westin was at a Columbia University journalism school forum — where you'd think you could speak your mind freely — and was asked whether "the Pentagon was a legitimate military target."

"I actually don't have an opinion on that," he said, "and it's important I not have an opinion on that as I sit here in my capacity right now." He later had to apologize for trying to make a point about journalistic objectivity. "I was wrong," he said. "Under any interpretation, the attack on the Pentagon was criminal and entirely without justification."

Newspapers have been branded "terrorists" when they draw attention to the vulnerability of our nuclear power plants. As if terrorists who understand complicated airline schedules and shop at Wal-Mart couldn't figure that out for themselves.

"Wouldn't it have been wonderful," said I. Michael Greenberger, a counterterrorism expert in the Clinton administration who is now at the University of Maryland law school, "if at the end of August someone had written about the vulnerability of the World Trade Center to hijacked planes? Maybe we could or would have taken steps to prevent the attacks. I can understand people's anxiety, but my bottom line is the greater danger is not being aware of our vulnerabilities."

Not even pop music has escaped. In September, Clear Channel Communications, a company that owns and programs 1,000 U.S. radio stations, sent out an e-mail hit list of songs with "questionable lyrics" that should not be played. The list ran to several pages and included John Lennon's "Imagine" as well as AC/DC's "Shot Down in Flames," Van Halen's "Jump," Talking Heads' "Burning Down the House," Pink Floyd's "Run Like Hell," and, of all things, the Bangles' "Walk Like An Egyptian." I could make an argument for not playing Jerry Lee Lewis' immortal "Great Balls of Fire" right after the attacks, but why Cat Stevens' "Peace Train?"

Later, Clear Channel denied the existence of the list, which was published in full by Eliza Truitt in her Slate column of Sept. 17. Her piece was called, "It's the End of the World As Clear Channel Knows It," and yes, that REM song was also on the list.

But the most insulting censorship of all, however, has come from the Bush Administration, which warned television news to stop showing taped interviews of Osama bin Laden. And television news agreed to stop!

In disgust, Mark Bowden wrote in The Philadelphia Inquirer, "I'd like to see a cable channel devoted to him — all Osama, all day, seven days a week. Every new tape provides clues to his whereabouts and intentions. Every new appearance further demystifies him. Much has been written about the man's supposed charisma and public relations genius. I don't see it. Granted I'm viewing him from across a great cultural divide, but to me he looks like ZZ Top in army surplus."

Bowden points out that despite bin Laden's frequent calls to all Arab nations to join him in jihad, none have.

"The more Osama bin Laden and his band of so-called holy warriors preach... the more they inevitably isolate themselves," Bowden wrote. "The vast majority of Arabs and Muslims have no desire to return to the seventh century, to forbid education to women, to deny freedom of speech or worship, or to crash themselves into tall buildings. Their aspirations are not unlike our own."

The American media, suddenly afraid of its own shadow, is walking in lockstep into an abyss and taking us with it. Dissent is seen as disloyalty. Honest disagreements are seen as unpatriotic.

This is a time when we need as much news and information as possible. Love of country means being honest about its strengths and shortcomings. If you don't see what's wrong, you can't fix it. If you don't admit to making mistakes, you can't learn from them.

America is not — yet — a totalitarian state, where anyone who deviates from the party line can be imprisoned. Yet, "If you're not with us, you're against us," remains the Bush Doctrine.

"Implicit in their denunciation is a demand for uncritical support, for a love of government more consonant with the codes of tsarist Russia than with the ideals upon which the United States was founded" wrote George Monbiot in the Guardian of London. "The charge of 'anti-Americanism' is itself profoundly anti-American... If we are to preserve the progress, pluralism, tolerance and freedom of thought which President Bush claims to be defending, then we must question everything we see and hear."

America is about freedom and tolerance and diversity. These ideals aren't always upheld, but they are what makes us different from, say, the Taliban and Osama bin Laden. Theirs is a world where you think as they do or you die.

British essayist G.K. Chesterton once said: "'My country, right or wrong' is a thing that no patriot would think of saying except in a desperate case. It's like saying, 'My mother, drunk or sober.'"

The media could learn something from Texas journalist Jim Hightower, who says, "Always drink upstream from the herd."

~ ~ ~

December 12, 2001

DEATH MAKES A HOLIDAY

On the day after George Harrison died, I strolled over to Strawberry Fields, the memorial in New York City's Central Park that Yoko Ono built for her husband, John Lennon, after he was gunned down in front of their home across the street.

More than a thousand people were jammed into the small park-within-a-park. The "Imagine" mosaic at the center was heaped with bouquets of flowers, burning candles, and pictures of John and George. Groups gathered around guitarists singing George Harrison and Beatles songs — "Give me love, give me love, give me peace on earth," and "Hey

Jude." Behind me, a man selling bottled water was singing, "Hey dude, don't make me dry."

I happened to be visiting New York on a different but equally death-related matter — an ongoing quest to understand the events of Sept. 11 and the disappearance of the World Trade Center and over 3,000 people.

Death takes many forms, and George Harrison's was quite different from, say, that of a Cantor Fitzgerald trader. But there is one striking similarity. Whether we like the idea or not, today death is a major tourist attraction.

We like to think of tourism as a way of relaxing — us on a tropical beach somewhere, maybe, with a waiter bringing us a tall, cool, fruit-laden drink. We don't, as a rule, connect tourism and death.

But when you think about it, people have always been attracted to sites where important or mass deaths have occurred. The early pilgrimages were to sites of religious deaths. The Via Dolorosa, the route followed by Jesus when he was crucified, is only one of many early examples.

The Tombs of the Pharaohs in Egypt and the Coliseum in Rome are major tourist attractions. So is the Tower of London, where historically important figures were beheaded. After the Battle of Waterloo in 1815, hotels and restaurants sprang up around the Belgian battlefield and changed the route of the 19th century British Grand Tour forever.

Academics, who study this kind of travel, have invented an awkward word for it. They call it thanatourism. Sometimes it's also called dark tourism.

Thanatourism seems to be the dirty little secret of the tourism industry. It thrives at the Texas School Book Depository and the "grassy knoll" in Dallas, where you can buy a coffee mug decorated with crosshair rifle-sights, at Auschwitz and in Holocaust museums around the world, in cemeteries where celebrities are buried, and at the site of Princess Diana's tragic car crash in Paris.

Tourists visit places of public execution, like the Place De La Guillotine, sites of mass death like Pompeii and Dachau, places associated with celebrity deaths like Graceland, museums and memorials like the Vietnam War Memorial in Washington, and battlefields like ancient Troy, Gettysburg, Pearl Harbor and Omaha Beach.

Does it sound crazy to think of death as a niche market? Then what do you make of the "Titanic cruises" offered by charter companies, where tourists eat meals identical to those served on the ship and hear music identical to the music played on the ship, as they travel to the precise spot where the ship lies at the bottom of the ocean?

Manhattan's Ground Zero, with its hawkers of American flag pins, World Trade Center pictures, gourmet food and various flavors of religion, is well on its way to becoming a classic example of the genre.

The topic of thanatourism is filled with moral ambiguities. The most agonizing is whether one can learn deep and sometimes ugly truths about human nature while, at the same time, wearing shorts, eating a hot dog and reading a guide book. In 1999, two Scottish professors, John Lennon (a different one) and Malcolm Foley, wrote a book on thanatourism, "Dark Tourism," and described their visit to Auschwitz-Birkenau:

"Groups of schoolchildren were taking photographs of each other, parents were photographing their children at the gates of Birkenau, and indeed, school parties were sitting on the ruins of the crematorium eating sandwiches."

That reminded me of a sign I saw at Ground Zero that read, "All of you taking photos .... you've forgotten this is a tragedy site, not a tourist attraction." Unfortunately, in a world where images of crisis and disaster can be instantly broadcast around the world, a strange combination of empathy and excitement easily turns tragedy sites into tourist attractions.

Developers of thanatourist attractions are painfully aware of the inherent conflict in what they do. A sign at a concentration camp in the Czech Republic says, in four languages, "You are entering a place of exceptional horror and tragedy. Please show your respect for those who suffered and died here, behaving in a manner suitable to the dignity of their memorial."

What are the alternatives? Destroy these places? That's the argument taking place in New York right now — is the World Trade Center site a graveyard, consecrated ground, or is it real estate ripe for new development, with maybe a memorial on the side? As J. Baudrilliard wrote about the Holocaust in 1988, "Forgetting the extermination is part of the extermination itself."

Thanatoursim raises many fascinating questions. Is it a spontaneous outpouring of love and respect, as it was that day for George Harrison? Or does thanatourism turn death into a commodity? Is it exploitative? Is it macabre? Is it a deeply and intensely human need? Is it a way to comprehend great tragedy? Is it a way to understand ourselves and the human condition? Is it a way to put ourselves into extreme circumstances in order to figure out what we would do? Is it a way to acknowledge the depths and heights of human behavior? Is it a way to pay our respects? Is it a cheap thrill? Is it tacky and sensational? Is it all of the above?

One thing, however, is certain. As long as tourists come, developers will build hotels, chefs will open restaurants, buses and taxis and tour guides will congregate, and vendors will sell film, hot dogs, postcards and bottled water.

~   ~   ~

March 7, 2002

THE ILLUSION OF SAFETY

Why does American culture spend its vast energy and emotional and economic capital on creating and maintaining two illusions worthy of professional magicians: first, that the world can be made safe, and second, that life can be made pain-free?

Think about it. Mandatory seat belt laws. No smoking in restaurants and offices. No cigarette and alcohol sales to minors (as if that stops them from smoking or drinking). Displacing wolves, bears and other predators from their natural habitats. Creating and supporting fast food chains to take all the surprise and discovery out of dining. Anti-depression drugs. Public service announcements where overpaid television stars tell us to be better parents. We won't even let a pregnant woman drink a glass of wine without making our disapproval known. The list is endless.

And now, of course, post-Sept. 11, we have to deal with the mindless madness of airline security. Talk about slamming the barn door shut after the horse!

On a trip to Florida last month, after the security guard looked into my shoes, she went through my purse and confiscated my cuticle clippers. She actually said, "These are sharp; you can hurt somebody." (Yes, I could stab my finger; it might bleed. Arrest me.) Then she took my cheap nail clipper, extended a little flap of metal on it that I didn't know was there, broke it off, and handed the rest of the gizmo back to me. She had the grace to look ashamed.

Safety is an illusion; you would have thought that if nothing else, Sept. 11 taught us that.

But it didn't, really. Since then, we've been in a paroxysm of American denial. We seem to be thinking that if we just think of everything that can possibly hurt us or go wrong, and stop it or make it go away, then we'll be safe. No matter what the cost.

Are we naive? Are we a nation of cowards? After all, Justice Antonin Scalia recently said that the safest places in the world are totalitarian dictatorships. Is that what we want?

I think Americans' frantic need for the illusion of security, our denial of danger, comes partly from the fact that we live so much of our lives vicariously through television and movie screens. Volcanoes can erupt, ships can sink, wars can happen, but we feel and experience it all second-hand — we have become passive viewers of the pain of the world.

Also, we may be starting to believe that what we see on the screen — those illusions on which enormous amounts of money are spent — is real. Do people really think that Hong Kong action stars can fly up the side of a building? In skirts?

I read about a family on vacation in Yellowstone National Park. They wanted to take a picture of their daughter with a bear that had just ambled by. So they put the girl next to the animal and poured a jar of honey over her hand. Then, through the viewfinder, they watched the bear maul the child.

I puzzled over that story for a long time. Were they simply a family of imbeciles? Now I think that maybe, having seen bears in endless cartoons on television, and having received many so lectures about wildfires from Smokey the Bear, they really thought that bears were friendly. Hey, Boo Boo!

An additional problem is that Americans are now the masters of the ersatz universe. We easily control our indoor environment. We use plastic surgery to redesign our bodies and improve on God. We divert rivers and streams. We rip the tops off mountains to mine their minerals. We can actually move mountains. We don't have to go to Europe, where we might make fools of ourselves because we don't speak the language.

We have the Epcot Center and Las Vegas, where the experience of foreignness is feigned for our enjoyment.

Americans who have lived outside the country have a special appreciation for the fact that American culture is only one of many cultures, and that many other people have equally reasonable responses to the world's stimuli. They also have a better understanding that we're all traveling on one planet, that we're all in it together.

Sometimes I wish that we could mandate cross-cultural experience for everyone in America. It might make the world a better — and safer — place.

~ ~ ~

January 23, 2003

FAST FOOD FASCISM

McDonald's is under attack these days, but for all the wrong reasons. Yes, the fast food industry sells unhealthy food. Yes, it induces people to overeat for profit. Yes, ranchers cut down rain forests to supply it with cattle. Yes, that reduces the world's oxygen supply. But the real crime of McDonald's — supposedly the shining symbol of American capitalism — is that it is truly and deeply anti-American.

The fast food industry stands against the personal values that made this country great: rugged individualism, originality, creativity, a sense of adventure, non-conformity, and above all, total fearlessness.

In an effort to standardize products and maximize profits, the fast food industry has infected America with an insidious creeping fascism that was never political in itself, but which has had deeply political consequences.

Sit in a McDonald's for a half hour with a critical eye. The lights are glaring; there's no relaxation or goodwill to go along with the food. The chairs and tables are bolted to the ground. You can't draw up a chair to another table, for example, to join a larger group. Even if the chair is uncomfortably close to the table, there is nothing you can do but accept the discomfort. It's like a prison cafeteria; shut up and eat.

The foliage, furniture, plates, utensils and cups are plastic. You are completely disconnected from the natural world. All the decoration is advertisement. It's no wonder that so many people wear corporate logos on their clothes and think it's right to put advertisements in schools; they're completely desensitized; life doesn't exist outside of commercials.

Fast food restaurants create a false sense of abundance. They offer access to a ready supply of condiments, sugar packets, straws, napkins and coffee cream — things that cost the restaurant almost nothing and have no real value.

They also offer a false sense of control. You appear to have many choices — a Big Mac, a cheeseburger, a quarter pounder, a double quarter pounder or a "Big 'N' Tasty" — but they're all pre-packaged, frozen hamburger. If you want to be radical, have fried chicken, fried fish pieces, even flatbread sandwiches. But you have no control over portion size, or the way your meal is cooked. Or what it is cooked in. After a while, you don't even think you *should* have control.

One of the ways we learn who we are is by the choices we make. Being given free reign to make meaningless choices, as at a fast food restaurant, translates directly into the political arena, where we are asked to make empty choices between multi-millionaires and the almost identical political parties which own them.

The overworked and over-managed young food zombies in fast food restaurants are being trained to accept a lifetime of deadening and unfulfilling jobs. They learn early that making suggestions and demands — don't even think union! — will get them fired. Fear plays a large part in this kind of work; I once took out a notebook to write something down in a McDonald's and the young manager looked panic-stricken. He was probably afraid of his own managers.

In order to navigate the world intelligently, our language must be clear and well-grounded. McDonald's corrupts language. What on earth is a "McSalad"? A "Happy Meal?" A "Mighty Kids Meal?"

Many books have been written about the frighteningly poor quality of fast food. Eric Schlosser's "Fast Food Nation: The Dark Side of the All-American Meal" is a revelation. A new book by Greg Critser, "Fat Land: How Americans Became the Fattest People in the World," reveals how the fast food industry discovered that Americans are so ashamed of appearing gluttonous that they wouldn't order two orders of fries. In response, the industry created "supersized" portions and along with it, a nation of supersized people.

Once you have accepted standardization in fast food restaurants, you may be unquestioning about it in other places. In my supermarket, all the pork is now pre-packaged by a company called Smithfield. The packaging offers a list of ingredients: pork broth, potassium lactate, salt, sodium phosphates, and natural flavorings; shouldn't the only ingredient in a pork roast be pork?

The fast food industry is now under attack from many sides. McDonald's stock has lost half its market value in the last two years; it has closed more than 100 restaurants and fired its CEO. Its arch enemy, Burger King, was on the market for two years without finding a buyer; it recently sold at a discounted price that dropped from $2.3 billion to $1.5 billion in just six months.

Obese people are suing fast food restaurants here, while abroad, they are being attacked for corporate imperialism. McDonald's, with 23,000 restaurants in about 121 countries, has been attacked in China, Denmark, France, Bangalore, Colombia, Russia, Argentina, Belgium, South Africa and Great Britain.

My own private rebellion against fast food restaurants dates back 30 years, as I watched juicy fresh hamburgers and fried chicken disappear all across the country, along with the small, quirky family-owned restaurants that served them.

Why, I wondered, as Americans grew wealthier, did they also grow so timid? Why did they reject the adventure of discovery, of making choices, of exploring the world? Why were they willing to sacrifice flavor, freshness, variety and a strong connection to the natural world for safe, predictable, boring and homogenized food? I can't blame the fast food industry for being so eager to oblige them.

I may be leaving myself open to a charge of elitism here, but no, I don't want to become a vegetarian, and no, I don't think that wanting restaurants to serve the kind of fresh, tasty, wholesome and inexpensive food that I remember from my childhood makes me a snob.

By unquestionably accepting the corruption of their food, Americans have come to accept the corruption of just about everything else — low pay, out-of-reach health care, corporate corruption, irrational wars, tax breaks for the rich, and McPresidents of the United States.

Today there are thousands of fast food restaurants and millions of people who actually believe this is the way food should be. Is it such a great step to thinking that Americans will also accept a degraded form of something as complex, difficult and demanding as real democracy?

(About a year after I wrote this piece, Morgan Spurlock's wonderful "Super Size Me," in which he almost kills himself with his self-designed campaign of eating at McDonald's, and only at McDonald's — breakfast, lunch and supper — became the sixth largest grossing documentary of all time.)

∼ ∼ ∼

February 20, 2003

Peace And Poetry On Earth

"I would like to thank Mrs. Bush for being so thin-skinned," said the writer Jamaica Kincaid on a cold and clear Sunday afternoon in Manchester, Vt. "To think that a woman who lies down at night and has dinner across from a man who is the lord and master of weapons of mass destruction, and plans to use them could not listen to the words of some poets who disagree with him!"

The 500 people gathered at the First Congregational Church that afternoon to hear 11 great American poets "honor the right of protest as a patriotic and historical American tradition" could not have agreed with Kincaid more. They cheered.

The reading, organized by the Northshire Bookstore in Manchester, was inspired by our revered yet endangered First Amendment: "Congress shall make no law respecting an establishment of religion, or prohibiting the free exercise thereof; or the freedom of speech, or of the press; or the right of the people peaceably to assemble, and to petition the Government for a redress of grievances."

The reading was one of many held across the country last weekend after First Lady Laura Bush canceled a White House gathering in honor of Emily Dickinson, Langston Hughes and Walt Whitman because she was afraid that the invited poets might express anti-war sentiments.

Poets against war — imagine that! I suppose that when she conceived of the forum, Mrs. Bush could not imagine that.

The gathering in Manchester was remarkable for the number of distinguished men and women who came to read, most of them with strong connections to Vermont. Grace Paley, Vermont's new state poet, read, as did Galway Kinnell, a former Vermont poet laureate and a National Book Award and Pulitzer Prize winner. Donald Hall, from bordering New Hampshire, has a National Book Critics Circle Award. Julia Alvarez, a writer in residence at Middlebury College, has published many books. So have Jay Parini of Weybridge and the Irishman Greg Delanty, who teaches at St. Michael's College. Ruth Stone of Goshen won the 2002 National Book Award. David Budbill is a musician and poet from Wolcott.

Jody Gladding, a young poet from East Calais, displayed a wicked sense of humor; she chided the wealthy golfing class — our "forefathers" — for being devoted to "trying to get their little white balls into all 18 holes."

William O'Daly, co-founder of Copper Canyon Press, was the foreigner. He came all the way from California on an airline ticket paid for, he announced, by a Republican. He read his own poem, "To the 43rd President of the United States."

"What if Kuwait grew carrots?" he read. "What if Iraq's main exports were chick peas and cotton shawls... It appears the one thing we cherish more than petroleum or our children is the greased machinery of destruction."

O'Daly received wild applause, especially from the many war protestors in the audience who were fresh from marching in Washington and New York the day before; some were wearing green t-shirts that said, "Why should Vermonters die for Texas billionaires?"

It seems especially odd that Mrs. Bush would honor Whitman, a born rebel. In "To the States," Whitman wrote that there can be no safety for America "without free tongues, and ears willing to hear the tongues." And he advised states to "resist much, obey little. Once fully enslaved, no nation, state, city of this earth, ever afterward resumes its liberty."

Whitman "loved America, so much he was continually disappointed," said Kinnell, who also read Pablo Neruda on the Spanish Civil War. "...And from then on blood," Neruda wrote. "Come and see the blood in the streets."

Throughout the ages, the image of blood in the streets has inspired poets to write passionately against war. Does Mrs. Bush know of any poets who have written enthusiastically in favor of it?

These are dark days for our democracy. Our government is currently asking for the power to strip people of their citizenship so they can be held without trial and possibly be "disappeared." Last week the Justice Department filed an amicus brief in federal court supporting Mayor Bloomberg's decision to prohibit demonstrators from marching in New York City. The First Amendment is very much in peril.

W.H. Auden once said famously that "Poetry makes nothing happen," and no one in Manchester believed that President Bush would slap his forehead and say, "Oh my God, I'm making a mistake if all these great minds are arrayed against me." Certainly not after he so easily dismissed the voices of millions of anti-war protesters who had gathered in 602 cities around the world the day before.

The poetry reading and President Bush's casual dismissal of the anti-war protests brought to my mind Shelley's poem, "Ozymandias of Egypt," about an ancient statue found in pieces in a lonely desert.

When Shelley describes the ancient despot's "wrinkled lips and sneer of cold command," it was not too great a mental leap to the arrogance of President Bush. "I am Ozymandias, king of kings. Look on my works, ye mighty, and despair," the despot says. But, as Shelley points out, nothing beside the ruins remains.

Despots die and their wars are read about in history books; we cluck our tongues, shake our heads and wonder at their evil. But poets always have the last word, as Mrs. Bush, herself an avowed avid reader, should know. As Auden says, time "worships language and forgives, everyone by whom it lives."

Words live. Poetry lives.

Alvarez chided Mrs. Bush in her poem, "The White House Has Disinvited the Poets." "No poetry until further notice," she said. "Why be afraid of us, Mrs. Bush, when you're married to a scarier fellow? We bring you tidings of great joy — not only peace, but poetry on earth."

March 20, 2003

MASTERS OF WAR

I still turn to Bob Dylan's early masterpiece, "Masters of War," whenever my beloved America makes the mistake of choosing might over right.

As Dylan wrote for all time, "Like Judas of old/You lie and deceive/ A world war can be won/You want me to believe... You fasten the triggers/For the others to fire/Then you set back and watch/When the death count gets higher/You hide in your mansion/As young people's blood/Flows out of their bodies/And into the mud."

We are the most powerful country on the planet and we should be leading the world with grace. Instead our leaders have chosen to lead it with sanctimony, lies and war. No matter how evil Saddam Hussein might be, he is weak and isolated. We can only look like sandbox bullies to the world, and in truth, we are acting like sandbox bullies in the world.

Which is why I spent the hours leading up to President Bush's "Moment of Truth" speech Monday night trembling with fear. In truth, I couldn't fear that man any more than if I was an Iraqi mother living in Baghdad.

I couldn't even look at Bush's pinched, self-righteous face on the television screen without cradling a large bag of Hershey's kisses in my arms. I'm starting to think of the American attack on Iraq as the "Chocolate War" because it's going to take a lot of chocolate to comfort me through this one.

Although people berate the news media for giving Bush and his henchmen a free ride, we know, thanks to the efforts of many serious journalists, far too much about this man and his plans.

We know, for example, that "The Bush Doctrine" calls for unilateral American global hegemony. This Hitleresque doctrine was created by Deputy Secretary of Defense Paul Wolfowitz and other neoconservatives during the 1990s, long before the terrorist attacks of 9-11.

Their plan calls for the United States to indefinitely dominate Europe, East Asia and the Middle East and to prevent Western European countries from developing the ability to challenge us or to defend themselves without us.

That is why the right-wingers were frothing at the mouth when Bill Clinton took the presidency away from them and stalled America's domination of the world for eight long years. It was never about oral sex in the Oval Office. You can almost hear them screaming, "It's about making war, not love, you fool!"

The war against Iraq is only the first stop on the train of bloodlust and madness that is now pulling out of the station of rational thought. We know that Iran, Syria and North Korea are on the list. We already have soldiers fighting in the Philippines. We can only pray for the Palestinians.

Speaking of prayer, these wars are being cloaked in a perverted form of Christianity that gives new meaning to the expression "killing them with kindness." Dylan was right on the money when he wrote, "Even Jesus would never forgive what you do."

One of the "justifications" for this war is that Saddam Hussein is so evil that he has stockpiles of chemical weapons. We know this is true, mainly because American companies were the ones who sold them to him — all the gases, the seed stock for anthrax germs, and the chemicals to make the nerve gas sarin.

"The United States, the world's leading arms supplier, is taking the world to war to stop arms proliferation in the very country to which it shipped chemicals, biological seed stock and weapons for more than 10 years," writes Paul Rockwell in the San Francisco Chronicle.

The fact that these terrible weapons may now be turned on American soldiers can only drive us to despair. We also despair for the people of Iraq, who have been living in fear under one dictator and now might have to die so he can be replaced with another who will allow America to suck dry the country's oil resources.

Bush's mastery of propaganda has convinced 43 percent of Americans that Iraq was involved in the terrorist attacks, and millions of others that dissent is treasonous.

"There is a case for getting tough with Iraq," writes Paul Krugman in The New York Times. "But it's not a case the Bush Administration ever made... So now the administration knows that it can make unsubstantiated claims, without paying a price when those claims prove false, and that saber rattling gains it votes and silences opposition."

Is it any wonder that so many of us are afraid?

Millions of people around the world have demonstrated against Bush and this war, but their protests fall on deaf ears. Not to make fun of the seriousness of the situation, but comedian Bill Maher was right when he said, "How bad do you have to suck to lose a popularity contest with Saddam Hussein?"

Being among the millions who chose to light a candle rather than curse the darkness, my husband and I went to a peace vigil on Sunday night. We were deeply moved, but in my heart I knew we were there less to pray for peace than to mourn for the many, many coming dead.

The only way to defeat a bully is to stand up to him. Despite the odds we must continue to fight against Bush, so wrong and yet so full of moral certainty, and his destructive policies abroad and at home.

It seems that Dylan was talking across the years to Bush when he wrote, "Is your money that good/Will it buy you forgiveness/Do you think that it could/I think you will find, when your death takes its toll/All the money you made/Will never buy back your soul."

~ ~ ~

April 17, 2003

For Lack Of A Beautiful Mind

(During the run-up to the Iraq invasion, in March of 2003, Barbara Bush, wife of former president George H.W. Bush and mother of President George W. Bush, appeared on ABC-TV's "Good Morning America." She was asked if she and her husband watched television news. She said they did not pay attention to it.

"But why should we hear about body bags and deaths and how many, what day it's going to happen, and how many this or what do you suppose?" she said. "Oh, I mean, it's not relevant. So why should I waste my beautiful mind on something like that?")

For lack of a beautiful mind, I care about the Iraqi dead and wounded. I care about the looting and destruction. I care about the lies and hypocrisy of my government and what comes next: the profiteering.

For lack of a beautiful mind, I can not be like Barbara Bush, the queen mother, our lady of the white hair and pearls, who believes that her son the president was called upon by God to lead this nation.

"Why should we hear about body bags and deaths...?" she said on television just before the war. "Oh, I mean, it's not relevant. So why should I waste my beautiful mind on something like that?"

For lack of a beautiful mind, I care about Bubbling Bob.

"Dozens of corpses lay rotting by roadsides or in cars blown up by U.S. forces as they captured Baghdad," reported David Fox of Reuters. "Nearby, the corpse of an airport worker rolled around in the current of a pool... 'That's 'Bubbling Bob', said one soldier. 'Been there a while. I ain't gonna fish him out. Let the Iraqis do it.'"

For lack of a beautiful mind, I am condemned by conservatives like Cal Thomas, who is syndicated in 540 papers. He wants me, among many others, to stand trial in a "cultural war crimes tribunal" for being "wrong" about the war in Iraq, as if might makes right.

For lack of a beautiful mind, anti-war protesters like myself "have proven themselves irrelevant of today's reality, which includes a freed Iraqi people for whom the operative conjunctive phrase isn't 'yes but' but 'yes and,'" crowed Kathleen Parker, whose column is syndicated in 300 newspapers.

Yes and let's loot? Yes and let's destroy 8,000 years of mankind's history by smashing every precious artifact in our own museum? Yes and let's burn the priceless documents in the National Library and Archives? Yes and let's take revenge and yes for what? Yes and let's steal the hospital beds out from under the wounded? Yes and let's protest the installation of a puppet government and be shot by American troops? Yes and let's let anarchy and chaos reign.

For lack of a beautiful mind, I cannot be like Defense Secretary Donald Rumsfeld, who said about the looting, "Freedom's untidy. And a free people are free to make mistakes and commit crimes."

"Is this your liberation?" a frustrated shopkeeper screamed at a US tank crew as they watched a gang of young men steal everything in his hardware store and cart it off in one of his own wheelbarrows.

"Hell, it ain't my job to stop them," drawled one young marine, lighting a cigarette as he looked on, according to Fox News. "Goddamn Iraqis will steal anything if you let them. Look at them."

For lack of a beautiful mind, I have a hard time understanding soldiers like Sgt. Michael Sprague of White Sulphur Springs, W. Va., who told British reporter James Meek, "I've been all the way through this desert from Basra to here and I ain't seen one shopping mall or fast food restaurant. These people got nothing. Even in a little town like ours of twenty five hundred people you got a McDonald's at one end and a Hardees at the other."

For lack of a beautiful mind, I am repelled by the words of Sgt. Eric Schrumpf, 28, who, while explaining to New York Times reporter Dexter Filkens how frustrating it is when Iraqi soldiers use civilians as human shields, said he had deliberately killed an Iraqi woman. "I'm sorry, but the chick was in the way."

For lack of a beautiful mind, I agree with the Iraqi man who told a U.S. Marine, "I'm going to exercise my right of free speech for the first time in my life — we want you out of here as soon as possible."

For lack of a beautiful mind, I noticed right away that there were only a few people in Fardus Square when the Americans toppled that large statue of Saddam Hussein. Granted, it was a beautiful piece of symbolic video footage, but why didn't our corrupt media report that the square had been blocked off by U.S. soldiers, that the few Iraqis allowed inside were exiles who had been flown into the country a few days before, and that the entire production had been staged for the cameras?

For lack of a beautiful mind, even though North Korea, Iran and Syria are now making conciliatory overtures to the U.S., I believe that the theory behind this war, that America will be safer when the Middle East is a series of "Americanized" democracies — because "democracies don't make unprovoked attacks on other countries" — is corrupt. As David Olive wrote in The Toronto Star, "When the world's most powerful democracy launched its invasion of Iraq last month, that theory failed its first test."

For lack of a beautiful mind, I am repelled that Bush's Republican party contributors are lining up for contracts: Halliburton, SteveDoring Services of America, Bechtel, International Resources Group, Exxon.

For lack of a beautiful mind, I am disgusted that the Rev. Franklin Graham, Billy Graham's son, who said after Sept. 11 that "The God of Islam ... is a different God, and I believe it is a very evil and wicked religion," is planning to participate in the rebuilding of Iraq, along with other Christian fundamentalist groups.

"We are there to reach out to love them and to save them, and as a Christian I do this in the name of Jesus Christ," Graham said.

For lack of a beautiful mind, I believe that George Monbiot of The Guardian told the truth when he said, "They have unlocked the spirit of war, and it could be unwilling to return to its casket until it has traversed the world."

July 17, 2003

EVERY STEP YOU TAKE

My dentist was preparing to make a mold of my teeth the other day when he made a little joke.

"Now I'm going to register your bite," he said in dentist-speak. "Has your bite ever been in the national register before?"

And for a moment — just a moment — I actually thought he meant it. Yes, I thought that Attorney General John Ashcroft, having already lost his mind, was requiring all American dentists to register their patients' teeth with the Justice Department as part of, say, the Patriot Act.

That's just another sign of how bad it's gotten in our so-called "land of the free." We are now prey being hunted by the raptors of both government and industry.

The Associated Press, for example, recently revealed that corporations are readying a technology that will replace bar codes on household products with pinpoint-sized computer chips and tiny antennae.

The transmitters will tell grocers when milk has passed its expiration date, for example, as if they don't already know. Which grocery store or supermarket do you know that doesn't put the freshest milk in the back so the older milk will be bought first?

No one would care if this future technology was meant to help with inventory, but the real idea — get this — is to keep the antennas transmitting after we take the products home.

That's right, Procter & Gamble and The Gillette Co. want to send their products into our homes to spy on us.

"Homes equipped with receiver-readers could alert consumers when they are running low on orange juice or their prescription for heart medicine is about to expire," said the AP, once again displaying its remarkable ability to print even the most outrageous lies, excuses and bald-faced scams with a straight face. "Hooked up to a national network like the Internet, the at-home devices could also provide details to marketers about a family's eating and hygienic habits."

When Sting sang "Every Breath You Take" with the aptly-named band The Police, he probably wasn't thinking about his dental floss reporting directly back to the manufacturer. But this AP story certainly gives new meaning to the chorus, "I'll be watching you." And talk about splitting your loyalty. Shouldn't that floss owe its allegiance to the man who bought it and owns it now, rather than its manufacturer?

Long ago and far away, I felt relatively safe from corporate marketing. I won't wear anything with a designer logo unless the manufacturer pays me, for example, and that's never happened. Television ads go by me in a blur — I've never bought something because it was advertised. I go into stores when I need something — shopping is not my idea of entertainment.

But I should have known that corporate America would get me anyway. Recently, I had to take the time to register my name and phone number with the National Do Not Call Registry in an attempt to put an end to infuriating telemarketing calls. Registering won't end charity or political telemarketing, and it will only block the calls for five years, but it feels good to be doing something to fight back. (Register on-line at donotcall.gov or by phone at 1-888-382-1222.)

In case you think I'm just an old grump, more than 23 million people have already registered. According to The New York Times, "it's as if one-fifth of all American households suddenly put 'no soliciting' signs on their front doors."

Now telemarketing companies are complaining that two million people will lose their jobs — in a bad economy. Well, what does it say about our economy when people have to lie over the phone to strangers just to pay their rent?

In an attempt to get my name off corporate mailing lists, I've had to register with companies I've never heard of before — Experian, Equifax, Innovis and Trans Union. (To do the same, write to them at Opt-Out Dept., PO Box 24025, Seattle, WA 98124-0025; then try to figure out when you agreed to Opt In.)

Being under attack by corporate America is nothing, of course, when you compare it to being under attack by our own government. From The American Conservative to The Village Voice, all sides of the political debate are uniting in outrage over the endless surveillance now being inflicted on us in the name of "fighting terrorism." Last October, then-House Majority Leader Dick Armey branded our own Justice Department "the biggest threat to personal liberty in the country."

It's no secret now that our cities, roads and highways have cameras tracking our movements. A New York City guerrilla theater group, The New York Surveillance Camera Players, which was formed long before Sept. 11, 2001, puts on shows just for the New York City cameras. You know that weird pyramid with the eye that you see on the back of the dollar, they ask? The Great Seal of the United States? Welcome to our lives, they say.

In the Eisenhower years people used to say, "What's good for General Motors is good for the country." At least, back then, they recognized that corporations and the country were two separate things. Now General Motors, along with the rest of corporate America, owns the country, plus all the politicians who are running it into the ground.

So I won't be too surprised when, sometime soon, a small voice comes out of my underwear drawer and says, "Joyce, we're getting a little frayed in here. It's time to go to Wal-Mart." Or that it's speaking in John Ashcroft's voice.

~ ~ ~

October 30, 2003

FUN WHILE IT LASTED

If Darwin was right, then America is doomed.

In its 20th annual State of the World report, issued last January, the Washington-based Worldwatch Institute concluded that the human race may have only one generation to save itself from ecological collapse.

The statistics from the report are sobering.

- One-fifth of the world's population — about 1.2 billion people — are in absolute poverty and are trying to live on less than a $1 a day.
- 420 million people live in countries which no longer have enough crop land to grow their own food.
- One-quarter of the developing world's crop land is too degraded to till, and 500 million people live in regions prone to drought. By 2025, that number could increase fivefold to about 3 billion.

- About 30 percent of the world's surviving forests are seriously degraded and they are being cut down at the rate of 50,000 square miles a year.
- Wetlands have been reduced by 50 percent over the last century.
- A quarter of the world's mammal species and 12 percent of the birds are in danger of extinction.
- Carbon dioxide levels — a key contributor to global warming — are the highest they've been in hundreds of thousands of years.
- Global production of toxic waste has reached 300 million tons a year.

Capitalism is built upon the idea of never-ending growth. We have been led to believe that all consumption is good and that the more we consume, the better off we are. But the notion of limitless consumption without consequences is starting to bump up against the very real limits of our planet's natural capital.

For example, it's estimated that global consumption of oil will start outstripping supply within a decade, and that there may be only 80 years or so left of reserves of phosphates — the key ingredient in the fertilizers that have become central to growing our food as the world's topsoil gets more and more depleted. Forty percent of the world's food relies upon irrigation to grow, but water is increasingly scarce.

That's why many believe that the wars of the future will be fought over resources. The U.S. invasion of Iraq is a good example of this. The U.S. currently imports about 55 percent of its oil and that figure may rise to 75 percent by 2025. With no signs that the U.S. lifestyle is going to change — in other words, without a summoning of the national will to embark on a Manhattan Project-level program to wean the nation off fossil fuels — the U.S. will have to keep invading other oil-producing nations to maintain the current American standard of living.

That is not a sustainable strategy.

"The US is in denial about what is, beyond any question, its most dangerous enemy," wrote Matthew Engel in The Guardian last week. "While millions of words have been written every day for the past two years about the threat from vengeful Islamic terrorists, the threat from a vengeful Nature has been almost wholly ignored. Yet the likelihood of multiple attacks in the future is far more certain."

Hypothesizing about why America might have this great, SUV-driven death wish, Engel reminds his readers that Europe "was developed on a coalition — uneasy but understood — between humanity and its surroundings."

Anyone familiar with the Brothers Grimm understands in their bones this "uneasy coalition" — think of Red Riding Hood, the path to grandma's house, and the danger of the wolf, for example.

"The settlement of the US was based on conquest, not just of the indigenous peoples, but also of the terrain," Engel continues. "It appears to be, thus far, one of the great success stories of modern history."

And that's true. It appears to be a wild success. We were blessed with such a beautiful and bountiful continent that we could seemingly take, take, and take some more, without ever giving back. Then we started running out of things and began rampaging around the world.

"It's the American belief that with enough hard work and perseverance anything — be it a force of nature, a country or a disease — can be vanquished," Phil Clapp of the National Environmental Trust told Engel. "It's a country founded on the idea of no limits. The essence of environmentalism is that there are indeed limits."

Well, as many of us — but not George W. Bush — have seen, there are limits. We cannot control nature and the wild, what little of it we have left; sometimes it's just a tiger in a Harlem apartment or in a Las Vegas strip show. Look at the fires ravaging southern California right now. Or the way Hurricane Isabel trashed the Outer Banks. Or the way the warmest years in the last 1,000 have come in the last decade. Or the way the sea level is rising around the world.

All this would be daunting enough. But in America's mad dash to cut down and pave over everything of beauty, pollute the very air it breathes and the water it drinks, eliminate the freedom of the wild and consume as much of everything as it possibly can, it is only carving out a path towards environmental destruction that others are happily following.

In the next 10 years, China and India will be burning fossil fuels as fast as we do in their rush to join the ranks of First World nations; their billions, understandably, want to experience the frenzy-of-delight lifestyle that America enjoys today. The economies of China and India, by the way, are growing stronger every day with jobs, factories and technological advancement that once were ours.

How can we go to China and India and say, "Hey, we've polluted the planet and stripped it of most of its resources, so now you have to be responsible and not destroy the rest of it. And by the way, give us a cut."

In fact, if there's any ray of sunshine here, it's that in the end, America will not be the only one to blame. And I don't even want to contemplate what "the end" might look like. Do you?

So if Darwin was right about the survival of the fittest, then it doesn't really help to say, "Hey, it was fun while it lasted."

(Note that this was written well before the Asian tsunami and Hurricanes Ivan, Katrina and Rita. Also note that the year 2005 was the hottest year on record — world-wide.)

~　~　~

March 25, 2004

THE ISRAELI PILOT (FICTION FOR NOW)

(I read that within 10 years, Palestinian Israelis will outnumber Jews in Israel, even without the "right of return." Soon after, I was walking in the woods when this piece of futuristic fiction, line by line and scene by scene, came into my head.

One hopes, of course, desperately hopes, that a humane solution can still be found to the Israeli-Palestinian conflict, one where both sides can live in peace and flourish. But it's hard to see an ending that does not make you shudder.

I should note that this piece was spiked by the then-editor of the Reformer and never appeared there. Maybe it was the sex scene. But it so moved the editor of The American Reporter that he read it on his Florida radio show.)

It was 7:30 in the morning and Rafael was just starting on his second cup of coffee. He had already dressed the children, kissed them good-bye and sent them off to school. And since he didn't have to report for duty until 9 a.m., he considered slipping back into bed next to his wife, Rutie, who was still asleep.

Then there was a knock on the door. He was not surprised to see two high-ranking military officers in plainclothes standing there. Messengers, he called them.

"Good morning, Colonel," said one. "Sorry to disturb you so early in the morning."

"Good morning," Rafi said, curious and yet not.

"May we come in?"

"Of course."

Rafi stepped away from the door.

"Please, would you like some coffee?"

"No, thank you, Colonel. We would appreciate it if you would come with us."

"Of course."

"Please wear your full dress uniform. Pack casual clothing. Pack a few books, if you are a reading man. You may be staying away for a few days. Maybe longer."

"Right away," Rafi said.

Rutie, naked in the bed, was just waking up. She was Yemeni, slender, with golden skin and long black hair that was tangled over her face from sleep.

She brushed her hair back with her fingers as she stirred.

"I heard voices."

"I have to go," Rafi said, starting to pack.

Rutie shivered and reached for a sheet to cover herself.

"No. Please. Don't," Rafi said. His eyes swept over her body. "Please."

He showered quickly, shaved, and put on his full dress uniform.

When he was ready, Rutie, still naked, came into his arms. He caressed the curves of her body. They kissed passionately.

He had been on secret missions before. They had said passionate good-byes before. He had always come back. This time they kissed as if they knew they would never meet again.

Israel was moments away from brutal all-out war. Twenty years ago the state had chosen to use guns and tanks instead of human kindness to deal with the Palestinians, who had chosen a more subtle way. They had had children. Many, many children.

Now, generations of Palestinians were ready to spill out of the refugee enclaves — enraged, oppressed, hungry, thirsty, poor. So many of them were living there, in such pitiful conditions, that photographs taken in the camps shocked the world.

Any day now the sheer number of angry men and women would push the Israeli army beyond its ability to control them. Fighting would spread across the desert towns and into the streets of the cities. It would be a bloodbath. Everyone knew it.

"You know where the insurance papers are, and the keys to the safe deposit box," Rafi whispered. "You will be taken care of, my love, you and the children will always be taken care of."

"I love you so much. Please be careful."

"I love you so much too."

Rafi picked up his bag and went back into the kitchen. The messengers were standing quietly, waiting. They went down the stairs into the street, where a car was idling. They sped away.

The messengers delivered Rafi to the highest office in the land.

Inside, the commander of the armed forces and the Prime Minister were waiting, both of them with dark circles under their solemn eyes.

"Do not sit down, Colonel," the Prime Minister said, and in a few short sentences, he told Rafi what his mission would be. Rafi was shocked.

"You can accept this mission or you can not," the Prime Minister said. "But I must warn you. If you do not believe you can carry it out, you will not be allowed to leave. You understand why?"

Rafi nodded.

"Take some time to decide, but not too much time," the Prime Minister said, and he and the general left the room.

When they came back, no words were needed. Rafi nodded, and the Prime Minister shook his hand.

"You are the best flyer we have," he said. "It could only be you."

He pressed a button on his desk. An older officer entered the room.

"This is Col. Avram," the Prime Minister said. "He is assigned to help you in every way."

The two men shook hands.

"An honor, Colonel."

"Sir."

Rafi looked at the Prime Minister and the commander.

"Is there any chance...," he said. "Any hope that the mission will not be necessary?"

"There is always hope," the Prime Minister said.

~

Col. Avram put Rafi in a Jeep and drove him over to the base. A small plane was waiting. When they were aboard, the colonel gave Rafi his flight plan and he took off towards the Mediterranean.

They landed a half hour later on an island Rafi had not known existed. It was uninhabited. A landing field, a large hangar and a small house were clustered together.

Rafi taxied the plane up to the hanger. He was not surprised to see what waited for him inside. It was the air force's most sophisticated, American-made fighter plane — fast, furious, far-ranging, and capable of dropping a payload of six bombs in a very short time.

He knew the plane would be armed. He said nothing, but he taxied the small plane next to it. In the house, he found everything they would need. The refrigerator and freezer were stocked with food. There was wine and beer and fine Scotch. There were two bedrooms, and two bathrooms stocked with soap, toothpaste, towels and toilet paper. There were magazines and books. There was a satellite television, radio and radar communications.

The two men settled in and waited.

~

As they could see from their television, in Israel things grew worse and worse.

"Now we will drive them into the sea," snarled the Palestinian leader, thrusting his angry face into news cameras. "We will drive them into the sea now."

There was fighting everywhere, even in Rafi's neighborhood in Tel Aviv. He worried constantly about the safety of Rutie and the children, but he was not allowed any communication with his family.

And then came the day Rafi dreaded. The television cameras were escorted into the office of the Prime Minister, who could be clearly seen, standing straight and tall, as the Palestinian leader held a gun to his head. The man shook the Prime Minister and said, "Now, Jew dog, you have oppressed my people long enough. Now what have you got to say?"

The Prime Minister looked into the cameras and said, "Now there is no hope at all."

The gun went off, and the Prime Minister crumpled to the floor.

～

Rafi and Avram looked at each other and nodded. "No hope" were the code words for their mission. They were both very quiet as they went into their respective bathrooms to shower and shave. They took their time putting on their dress uniforms, making sure every crease was razor-sharp.

They opened the hangar door and mounted the steps to the cockpit of the fighter jet. Rafi started the engines and taxied to the end of the runway. They took off into a brilliant blue sky with the sun shining brightly on the water beneath them.

～

They passed first over Tel Aviv. They were flying high, knowing the Palestinians had no anti-aircraft weapons that could reach them. Rafi positioned the plane over his own neighborhood, where his wife and children were either dead or facing certain slaughter. He opened the first bomb door, and dropped a nuclear device on the city he loved.

Without looking down or back, they were over the Holy City in minutes. There they dropped another bomb. Then they flew to Amman in Jordan. They dropped a bomb there, and flew on to Damascus. Then to Baghdad, then to Riyadh.

They were not stopped because they had left unimaginable devastation and confusion behind them.

Rafi then turned the plane south, toward the Arabian Sea. He thought about the Islamic fundamentalist Mohammed Atta, who had flown a plane into the World Trade Towers in New York City, one of the earlier blows of this seemingly endless conflict. He imagined the thrill, the rush, the intense excitement of the hatred that Atta felt as he saw the towers coming up at him. He imagined the bloodcurdling shriek of joy he must have given just before he died.

In contrast, Rafi felt dead inside. He looked at Avram, who was openly weeping. He felt his own face and it was wet with tears. They had bombed the Arab world in revenge. But there was no emotion in it.

As the sea came up under them, Rafi looked for and found a ray from the sun. Then he angled his plane so it followed the ray of brilliant light down until it crashed into the water.

~ ~ ~

April 8, 2004

IRAQ: OUR HAND IS IN THE FIRE NOW

As Iraq burns, how can I not ask: if I knew way back then, why didn't they?

As a rule, the CIA hardly ever gets to Dummerston to brief me. It's not as if I'm a personal friend of George Tenant, or even George Bush. I'm just a writer living on top of a mountain in Vermont.

Yet when the Bush Administration began selling America on a war with Iraq, I knew it was all a shuck. And when millions of people around the world took to the streets in protest, it was clear that I wasn't alone in the knowing.

How did I know? Simple. The Bush Administration wasn't making any sense.

First of all, we all knew by then that on 9/11, Bush was flying around in Air Force One like a frightened little chicken. Then, we never heard any discussion, much less saw any proof, that 9/11 was actually caused by Osama bin Laden or his al-Qaida.

In fact, it was nothing short of miraculous how bin Laden suddenly became a full-scale bogey-man in the American press while most of us were still scratching our heads and wondering, "How does the government know so quickly who is behind the attacks?" And, "If they know that quickly, doesn't it mean that they knew about these people before?" And,

"So then, why didn't they do something to stop them?" And then, "Who the hell are these people and why do they hate us so much?"

Then we went to war against the Taliban — which had been our ally only a short time before. Everything was happening so quickly. America was making momentous moves without taking any time for people to discuss them or think them through. Most of us spend more time trying to decide whether to buy or lease a car than Bush did deciding to invade Iraq.

Soon we were hearing about "weapons of mass destruction" so often that they became an acronym, "WMD." We were told that Saddam was a monster, but we knew that already. After all, we had helped him stay in power. He had biological and chemical weapons. No big surprise, we sold them to him. He was an evil dictator. But there are many evil dictators in power today, many of them friends of ours. Why is it our job to remove them? Of what concern was Saddam to us? Saddam's son-in-law, when he defected, told American intelligence that Iraq's missiles had long ago been destroyed. Saddam knew this; he invited UN weapons inspectors to search his country. They found nothing.

Iraq, Iraq, Iraq. It didn't make any sense. There were no Iraqi 9/11 terrorists. Why weren't we talking about Saudi Arabia? Most of the 9/11 terrorists were Saudis. That's where a significant amount of al-Qaida financing comes from.

Those of us who argued against the war warned that America knew nothing about Iraq, its language and its culture. We were getting ourselves into another Vietnam quagmire, we said. We would inflame the passions of the entire Middle East, we said. We need to devote our resources to eliminating terrorism, we said. It defies common sense to concentrate on Iraq when there is so much real danger in the world, we said.

No one listened, we were scorned, and look what we have now.

Bush tells his supporters, "They hate freedom and we love freedom," and at the same time his Administration closes down a Iraqi weekly newspaper — so much for democracy and freedom of speech — because it doesn't like what it says. The newspaper is owned by a radical cleric, Muqtada al-Sadr. By shutting his paper we inflame him and his supporters. A dozen American Marines are killed overnight. We deliberately bomb a mosque and kill over 40 Iraqis. We have started a religious war.

In another part of the country, in Fallujah, underpaid, overworked and over-stressed American soldiers are dying to avenge the deaths of the overpaid American mercenaries whose charred bodies were barbarically hung from the girders of a bridge. We attack the town. We start a tribal war.

All told, we have lost 600-plus Americans and counting; thousands of Americans are now missing arms or legs or eyes; we don't even keep a count of the dead and wounded Iraqis.

We create new terrorists every day. "Iraq is currently serving as a focal point for foreign jihadist fighters, who are united in a common goal with former regime elements, criminals, and more established foreign terrorist organization members to conduct attacks against coalition and Iraqi civilian targets," the State Department's counter-terrorism coordinator, J. Cofer Black, told Congress recently, according to The New York Times. "These jihadists view Iraq as a new training ground."

George Bush, Dick Cheney, Donald Rumsfeld, Colin Powell and Condoleezza Rice were monumentally stupid to start this war. They owe the American people an explanation, and there is none.

Oil? Then explain why American gas prices are climbing to record rates, why the dollar is sinking because of the national debt and why OPEC is slowing its production because it is losing money due to the failing dollar.

Because they looked like wimps when they failed to capture Saddam after the last gulf war? Well, they've caught Saddam, no one cares and still our beloved American soldiers are dying in Iraq.

Because Saddam put a hit on Bush's father? If Bush is using the bodies of American soldiers to settle a family feud then he should be arrested and tried for treason.

Because even though Saddam couldn't threaten us, he could threaten Israel? Is this a proxy war?

If your son was playing too near the stove, wouldn't you warn him about putting his hand in the flame? And if he did it anyway, wouldn't you be frustrated and upset? Here, a child is deliberately holding a hand in the flame and watching it burn. And it isn't his hand, it's ours. I listen to the news every day, it turns my stomach, and I scream, No! And if I knew way back then, why didn't they?

HER BEAUTIFUL MIND

What could be behind the Bush Administration's decision to censor the photographs of flag-draped coffins returning from Iraq? Could it really be, as the government says, to respect "the privacy of the families?" Or is it to hide the realities of war for political reasons? Or is it to protect the delicate sensitivities of the ruling class as Americans die to build them an empire?

As the argument over this censorship continues, I hope people remember a widely-quoted remark made by the president's mother, Barbara Bush, last year during the build-up of the war — the lying time.

"Why should we hear about body bags and deaths," Barbara Bush said on ABC's "Good Morning America" on March 18, 2003. "Oh, I mean, it's not relevant. So why should I waste my beautiful mind on something like that?"

We know this particular censorship can't be about privacy. Since the photos were made public last week, many family members have praised their publication. And since the coffins are anonymous, what privacy is protected?

Were the pictures censored to prevent Americans from having a visceral understanding of the price we must pay for our aggressions overseas? Does "out of sight, out of mind" mean we will not hesitate to "stay the course"?

This kind of thinking dates back to the Vietnam War, when some conservatives decided that the war was "lost" because of television. But those televised images were in our living rooms for years before the final fruitlessness of the effort brought the war to a close.

Most of us know that over 700 American soldiers have died in Iraq so far — and we're still counting. That means 700 extended families in mourning, 700 pictures of funerals and crying parents on the front pages of hometown newspapers, and 700 communities paying their hushed last respects. The number of people personally touched by the deaths of Americans in Iraq is growing exponentially.

Until last week, most of us didn't personally know anyone killed in Iraq. But the need to know was a force that started hitting critical mass:

- First, newspapers and magazines began to do stories about soldiers in rehabilitation — men and women learning to live without arms and legs. From Iraq, as of this writing, there have been 2,470 Americans wounded so badly they could not return to their duty. (Another 1,394 were able to return after being hurt, according to several Web sites which track the numbers.)
- The coffin photographs started leaking out.
- Garry Trudeau courageously allowed his "Doonesbury" character, B.D., to have his leg shot off, which brought the war home to the funny pages.
- NFL football star Pat Tillman's death in Afghanistan put an even more personal face on war.

The American people, to their eternal credit, want to know the truth. The Seattle Times ran the first coffin picture, taken by a contract cargo worker in Kuwait who wanted to show the parents back home how respectfully their children's bodies were being treated. (She and her husband, who was also working in Kuwait, were fired.)

The Times' editor reported that almost 100 percent of the feedback on the first day was favorable. The next day, favorable comments were running 50-to-1, and the day after 30- or 40-to-1. (Many more pictures, taken by the government and released through the Freedom of Information Act, are available on-line at www.thememoryhole.com).

To bring home the deaths even more, on tomorrow night's "Nightline," Ted Koppel will devote the entire hour to showing photographs and reading the names of the soldiers killed in Iraq.

You can argue both ways about the long-term impact of these images. Those who believe we need to be in Iraq will accept the deaths as the price we pay for "liberating" the country. Those who are adamantly opposed to the war will see it as the cost of occupation and empire.

As the discussion over the censorship of the photos continues, I hope people remember the blood-chilling arrogance of Barbara Bush's remark. None of us have beautiful minds. We all have bloody minds now, and bloody hands. Whatever our political persuasion, the pictures should make us more aware than ever that war should be a last resort, not a first.

(A few months after I wrote this piece, we learned that Pat Tillman was accidentally killed by his own troops, and the Pentagon lied about the circumstances of his death, claiming he was bravely killed in action. His family is still fighting the Army, trying to learn what happened and why the Army lied. And as of this writing, we still are not allowed to see photographs of the bodies returning from Iraq.)

～ ～ ～

May 6, 2004

A Grin To Destroy The World

"Men heap together all the mistakes of their lives and create a monster called Destiny," Oliver Wendell Holmes once wrote, and now Destiny has arrived at the door of the United States.

Ugly she is, and grinning.

What sense can we make of the hideous photographs that have come out of Saddam Hussein's prison in Iraq? I don't think we will ever understand them, as we will never understand the minds of mass murderers and torturers. But how can we live with them? How can we adapt them to our reality? How can we move past them when the mass murderers and torturers are us ?

The truth is, we can never move past them.

What can we make, for example, of the young grinning female soldier — identified as Sabrina Harman, 26 years old, from Alexandria, Virginia — crouched behind a pyramid of alive, hooded, naked Iraqi males. As she poses for the camera, a male soldier stands behind her, his arms crossed, also grinning.(The photos can be seen on-line at The New Yorker site — newyorker.com).

This is a picture that chills me to the bone. As a symbol, it supplants several years of tragic symbols, beginning with that twisted piece of architectural geometry left standing after the World Trade Center towers fell. It supplants even the immediately-iconic photograph of the hooded Iraqi wearing only a poncho made of a striped blanket, standing barefoot on a little box with electrodes attached to his hands and genitals.

President Bush can try to pump us up with staged photographs of American soldiers pulling down a statue of Saddam, or himself, dressed in a flight uniform with a padded crotch, stepping onto the deck of an aircraft carrier while a banner made at the White House claims "Mission Accomplished."

But how do we accept the photographic reality of ourselves as revealed in those pictures from Abu Ghraib prison? That we demonized these people? That we tortured them? That we humiliated them? That we stripped them of their humanity, sexually abused them, shamed them in the eyes of their God and shamed ourselves in the eyes of the world?

For the millions in the Arab world who already believe that women should have no civil rights, what could be more devastating than that grinning female soldier? She revels in her ultimate power over these men. Instead of bringing the ideals of democracy — with its lovely strands of feminism — to the Arab world, we've given them a million years of reasons to keep women in burqas and maybe start binding their feet.

The backlash will be horrendous. In a people who think that holding a grudge for a millennium is the natural way of things, and who already dislike and distrust Americans, we have created a passionate hatred that will last for generations. We have bequeathed endless war to our grandchildren and to their grandchildren. These Iraqis — we call them prisoners. We are "softening" them for "interrogation." What could possibly be their crimes? Working for Saddam? But until Bush unilaterally and for no good reason invaded their country, what they did was perfectly legal. For fighting against Americans? Why is that a crime, when the Americans are the invaders of their country?

Although I try, I fail to understand it in terms of role reversal. What if, for no real reason other than their leader's hatred for our leader, their army arrived here? What if their army were — and this is difficult to imagine — successful?

Say they take Washington. Say they find Bush hiding in a rat hole. They can take him to the Netherlands, or to a court in their country or ours. They can try him for war crimes. Would they have the right to put all the people working in the West Wing into prison? Criminalize Donald Rumsfeld, Condi Rice, Dick Cheney, Karl Rove and Colin Powell? Put their pictures on playing cards? Throw them into jail? Strip them naked? Sodomize them? Take photographs of the torture? And grin?

The Bush Administration does not think like this. These people do not believe they are doing anything wrong. They remind me of a poem I recently came across, one by Polish Nobel Prize winner Wislawa Szymborska called "In Praise of Feeling Bad About Yourself": "The buzzard never says it is to blame/The panther wouldn't know what scruples mean/When the piranha strikes it feels no shame/If snakes had hands they'd claim their hands were clean... On this third planet of the sun/Among the signs of bestiality/A clear conscience is Number One."

We claimed we were bringing peace and freedom and democracy. Instead we brought the other side of America, our trailer trash minds, our racism, our misguided sense of superiority, our ignorance of other cultures, our greed and our stupidity. We brought everything that threatens to destroy civilization — ours and everyone else's — not to further in its creation.

The Armed Forces can court martial, "discipline" and fire as many soldiers, intelligence operatives and mercenaries as they can. The president can go on Arab television, wave his fist and denounce whomever he wants. The damage is done.

Just after the war in Iraq began, I quoted George Monbiot of the UK's The Guardian, who said, "They have unlocked the spirit of war, and it could be unwilling to return to its casket until it has traversed the world." I think we have to face the fact that he was right.

~ ~ ~

May 13, 2004

WHICH SIDE ARE YOU ON?

Say it's 1770 in the Colonies. Tempers are starting to boil over about land ownership, taxes and debt-collecting. Yet many are thriving under the rule of the English king, George III. It's treason and heresy to publicly damn him. Are you a Whig or a Tory? Which side are you on?

That's what I was thinking when I saw "The Equivalent Lands," last weekend. The play, by Joe Greenhoe, was put on in Dummerston, Vt., by the Vermont Theater Company. It was sponsored by the Dummerston and Putney Historical Societies.

The play tells the story of Lt. Leonard Spaulding, who bought land on the western bank of the Connecticut River from the governor of New Hampshire. He cleared the land, built a home on it, brought his family there, and began working it, only to have it taken away by the state of New York during a land grant dispute. Spaulding eventually led a rebellion against the king that some consider the first volley in the Revolutionary War.

History is written by the winners, so from our view, the Revolutionary War looks like a fait accompli, a dead cert from the start. It was fought and won by patriots and heroes and for all the right reasons: independence, self-determination, taxation with representation. "We hold these truths to be self-evident, that all men are created equal." Good stuff, all of it. But the truth is that progressive or conservative beliefs and politics are not new creations; they have been deeply held convictions since the dawn of time. During the Revolutionary era, neighbor was pitted against neighbor. Many supported the king.

It takes a lot of courage to challenge the status quo, especially when the costs are high. Back then, the status quo was George III. I couldn't help wondering if I would have had the courage to damn the king and possibly die for my beliefs. Would I have risked "Our lives, our fortunes and our sacred honor," as the Revolutionary soldiers did, according to the Declaration of Independence?

Which side will you be on?

Or say it's 1950, and for a while you really believed in the ideals of brotherhood and socialism — before the realities of Soviet-style Communism made a mockery of them. Now Sen. Joseph McCarthy is holding hearings in Washington, and you're trembling in fear. Will they call you to testify? Will you lose your job and your standing in your community? If you are called, will you name names? Or will you have the courage of your convictions and be blacklisted for life?

Which side will you be on?

We've been brainwashed by our entertainment industry. We always identify with the victorious —with the heroes, the beautiful people, the leading actors and actresses of any play or movie or show on television. No matter what we look like, while they are on the screen, we are them.

In our national life, this translates into thinking of ourselves as "the greatest country on earth," and "the good guys." The other guys are the villains, or, in the language of our president, "the evil-doers."

Now which side are you on?

After 9/11, several columnists lost their jobs for pointing out that Pres. George W. Bush hid in a bunker on the day of the attacks. The Dixie Chicks' records were burned. Censorship was everywhere.

Americans, suddenly aware of their vulnerability, desperately wanted to believe they had a leader who could keep them safe. Playing on that, the right-wing Republicans erected an impermeable wall around Bush and Vice President Dick Cheney: no press conferences; no public appearances that weren't scripted; lies and evasions from the press secretary to a cowed and imprisoned White House press corps. Speaking against Bush was called treason. People were denounced for it. The wall helped maintain the illusion that the government was on our side, working to protect us. God save the King!

Now the wall has been shattered. First came the immensely touching photographs of flag-draped coffins. Then ABC's "Nightline" showed us the names and faces of 721 Americans who have died in Iraq. Then came the Abu Ghraib torture photos and videos. Then came the even more shocking information that "contractors" (read mercenaries), not American soldiers, are running that show. Now we have the revenge beheading of an American businessman.

Meanwhile, the conservatives — Who are these people? How deeply can one person dig his or her head in the sand and still be able to breathe? — are doing their best to regain control of the images. They already have control over the war.

Secretary of Defense (we attacked Iraq without provocation — shouldn't the name of his department be changed to the Department of Offense?) Donald Rumsfeld has taken "full responsibility" and apologized, as if that means anything more than a Britney Spears song: Oops! We did it again! Sinclair Broadcast Group and Piedmont Television, — companies which own ABC stations — censored the "Nightline" show as "a blatant political act to undermine support for President Bush and the war." Rush Limbaugh said our soldiers in Abu Ghraib were just "letting off steam" and their interrogation techniques were no more serious than a college hazing. (That kind of hazing has been outlawed for a long time now, Rush.)

Meanwhile, the Administration, which is supposed to keep us safe in the wake of 9/11, is minting new Middle Eastern terrorists as if they were golden nuggets, while at the same time bankrupting our country with the cost of war. (The woman who took the coffin photos was fired from a $100,000 contract job. Is anyone in the United States making $100,000 a year loading cargo planes?)

Which side are you on, America? Why aren't you in the streets, demanding that Bush resign? Why aren't you demanding that he be tried as a war criminal? Why aren't you demanding the withdrawal of American troops from Iraq, where we have no right to be? How much more truth do you need slammed down your throats?

Now think back to those Revolutionary War days. Those of you who were right-wing conservatives then — the Tories — backed the king and lost. And you're still backing the wrong horse.

I know it's hard to admit you are wrong. No one wants to believe their king or their president is a liar and a jackass. No one wants to believe that everything they are told, everything they believe in, is a lie.

George Orwell said, "Speaking the truth in times of universal deceit is a revolutionary act." After a year in Iraq, Americans know the truth. When do they become revolutionary? When do they say, "Enough. No more. We don't want to be the biggest bully the world has ever seen."

Which side are you on?

I believe what the great essayist E. B. White wrote in December of 1941, just as America entered World War II: "To hold America in one's thoughts is like holding a love letter in one's hand — it has so special a meaning... (But) who is there big enough to love the whole planet? We must find such people for the next society."

~ ~ ~

May 27, 2004

WHO DO YOU LOVE? HOW DO YOU LOVE?

Here's a rock-solid truth that our culture likes to deny: we don't choose the people we love.

Despite what we're shown on television shows like HBO's "Sex and the City," UPN's "Girlfriends" and NBC's "Friends" — an endless series of picky dating rituals designed to help us find "the right one," — much less the angry signs homophobes carry in the streets, the truth is that few of us can explain how we ended up loving the one we're with.

We may pine for the tall, dark and good-looking investment banker (of either sex) who drives the splashy car, we may chase after free love until we discover how expensive it really is, but who we end up loving is usually a big surprise.

We have no power over love. As Bob Dylan recognized, "it falls on strangers, travels free." Love chooses us. And woe to those who mess with it — that's when they learn love's real power.

Families know this truth. We don't pick our parents, as any disgruntled teenager can tell you. And reasonably good parents can be horrified by their children's actions — Columbine comes to mind. We love our families for the same reason that they drive us crazy — because they're our families, and that's all there is to it.

Adoptive families know this truth. A couple fills out forms, writes checks, answers endless questions, often travels to a foreign country and — lo and behold — unto them a child is given. And they love this child instantly, completely, protectively and forever.

Friends know this truth. We don't really choose them. They're usually people who were kind to us when we needed a hand, or who sat next to us in class and shared their notes, or who lived down the road and offered us a lift when our car broke down.

Same-sex couples know this truth. How many are born masochistic enough to "choose" homosexuality — to be preached against, humiliated, ostracized, beaten up, occasionally murdered and, on the up side, getting a job making straight people attractive — these are life goals? Sometimes men fall in love with men. Sometimes, after that, they fall in love with women. Sometimes women fall in love with women. Sometimes women fall in love with women but eventually marry — and love — men. It's all one great big love stew.

Given this basic truth, why are so many people outraged by gay marriage? How could it "change marriage as we know it?" What are these fools thinking?

Myra Marx Ferree, a professor of sociology at the University of Wisconsin-Madison, has a chilling answer. Writing in Sunday's Newsday, Ferree argues that right-wing Christian opposition to gay marriage is an attack on all marriages, and that a constitutional amendment to define marriage as a union strictly between a man and a woman could have the power to destroy heterosexual marriage as we know it today.

The amendment, she points out, is based on a simple and false premise: that marriage has always been the same — the Biblical model, if you will. But marriage has taken many forms over the centuries, and Ferree describes three American models.

The first is pre-Industrial Age patriarchy. "It assumes men are heads of households and women are property the husband owns, lacking any rights to earn an income, own property or even have custody of children," she said.

Then comes industrialization, taking such things as production of food, clothing, medicine and soap out of the home, putting them in offices and factories. Along with this came the struggle for women's emancipation.

Social conservatives of the time argued that if women had the right to vote, inherit property, earn money and have opinions different from their husbands, they would leave their husbands and it would be the end of marriage. (They had either low self-images or high levels of guilt about the way they enslaved their wives, sisters and daughters.)

Marriage didn't end, however. It changed. In general, men took up the role of "provider," leaving home every day to earn a paycheck. Women became "homemakers," — "specialists in raising children and providing domestic comforts."

This was better, but not the best. Wives legally owed domestic support to their husbands and could not be paid for their work at home. Husbands owed their wives financial support; they had to pay alimony if the marriage broke up. The husband had the right to his wife's sexual favors, so there could be no such thing as marital rape, while the woman had the right of custody of the children, so there could be no such thing as joint custody.

In the modern world, marriages are partnerships. Women and men both work — and are paid equally (under law, if not always in the real world). They both vote, have bank accounts and credit, and share in child-raising and child custody.

Contemporary marriage, like a Cantonese restaurant menu, allows couples to chose their own style: backward to the patriarchal, staying with the provider/homemaker model, or entering into a working partnership.

"Employers or states no longer can enforce such assumptions on all couples," Ferree said. "Since there are no legally specified differences in what men and women must contribute to a marriage or what they can hope to get out of it, there is no legal need for a partner marriage to be between a man and a woman. The assertion that a legal marriage needs one of each opens a door to laws that would again give different rights to husbands than wives."

If religious conservatives win their fight to define marriage as between a man and a woman, Ferree warns, they might not stop there.

We find ourselves now in a strange period of what might be called an attempt at Christian Fascism. Our president believes God has called him to the White House (it certainly wasn't the popular vote). Empowered by Bush, evangelical Christians are pushing for a rollback of Darwin, the end of scientific experimentation, and the coming of Armageddon. The hallowed American separation of church and state has never been more under attack. The goal is the creation of a Christian nation — and later a Christian world — under Biblical law.

So after a constitutional amendment, the next logical step would be defining the roles of men and women in heterosexual marriages according to Biblical standards. Can't you hear the patriarchy calling?

We don't choose who we love, and that's the truth. But most of us do love, and we can choose how we love.

If we don't want to see women forced to walk two steps behind their husbands, if we don't want to see them lose the right to vote, to work, to have credit and to own property, if we don't want to live in an anti-democratic and insanely fundamentalist country, then we must all fight for the right of homosexuals to marry.

~ ~ ~

July 22, 2004

AT WAR WITH SUMMER

Honeysuckle, climbing roses, day lilies, bee balm, lavender, flowering clematis, black-eyed Susans, cosmos, pansies and petunias.

Nine hundred Americans now dead in Iraq.

And so it goes, in this summer of my mad discontent. The flowers are gorgeous. The greenery couldn't be lusher. The weather couldn't be more perfect (although we could do with a bit less rain). The news couldn't be worse. There is a war going on in my head between the joys of a perfect summer in Windham County and the world.

George W. Bush believes God wants him to be president of the United States. He is a madman. Many are still afraid to say it. Yet many others believe him.

Tiger lilies — those raucous short-lived fragile orange flowers surrounded by great green skirts of leaves — have turned out to be the wildflowers of Windham County. They are everywhere, beautiful in their hundreds, standing straight up and drinking in the sun wherever our roads lead us.

At an ACLU event, New Yorker reporter Seymour Hersh reveals that our government is frantically suppressing videos of American soldiers raping young boys at Abu Ghraib — the screams are the hardest part of watching, he says.

Art is everywhere this summer. In one magical weekend recently, I went to three art shows in three different towns. I enjoyed the work of over 45 artists. Many of the pieces made me rue the fact that I'm flat out of wall space. How magical to live in a place where so many artists choose to live.

The Sydney Morning Herald, one of Australia's leading newspapers, reports that one week before the "hand-over" of Iraq, now-Prime Minister Iyad Allawi visited a Baghdad police station, encountered seven suspected insurgents lined up against a wall, drew his gun, and shot them all. Six died. We have turned Iraq over to another strongman. Meet the new boss, same as the old boss.

According to data taken from the 2000 census, Vermont ranks seventh in the nation for the total number of artists living — and earning a living — in the state. We are fourth ranked for fine artists. We lead the nation in the number of writers and authors who make their homes here. Last week in Putney, I heard Vermont poet Veranda Porche and some of her friends read their work. Veranda sang a song about letting her daughter go to explore this dangerous world. It sent chills up my spine.

Bush goes around the country repeating the Republican mantras, "America is safer now" and "The world is now more peaceful," while thousands cheer. Yet Iraq is inflamed, new terrorists are being minted at almost every corner of the globe, America is regarded as a rogue nation by the rest of the world, and our own Department of Homeland Security is issuing new threat warnings virtually every week.

Last weekend I visited with some cousins in a beautifully restored 1820s home in upstate New York. I didn't know two of them very well, but the time we spent together was seamless, as if we had been best friends all our lives. We spent two days talking, swimming, walking, cooking and drinking shots of iced Stoli. We never once mentioned politics. We saw a bobcat at the tree line. The power and importance of blood, of family, has never been clearer to me.

Michael Moore's "Fahrenheit 9/11" shows the vapidity, cupidity and stupidity of our leaders. Robert Greenwald's "Outfoxed" shows how Fox News buttresses the evil actions of our government. I was raised to believe in common courtesy. Watching Bush lie and Bill O'Reilly ridicule, censor and shout at his guests disgusted me so much that I have to turn off the television set.

On the positive side, Moore is making millions of dollars because people are flocking to hear the truth. Greenwald couldn't get his film into theaters, so he arranged for it to be shown at house parties across the country, before releasing it on DVD. At the party I went to, 130 people showed up.

The Bush Administration floats a trial balloon: can it suspend our elections if there is a "terrorist attack"? I put those words in quotes because I believe the Republicans will do anything and say anything to keep their power. I believe they might, very well, "suspend" democracy.

A few weeks ago, while walking near the campus of World Learning, Inc., I saw a moose.

The Democrats have nominated an uncreative man, John Kerry, to challenge Bush. It is hard to find enthusiasm to support him, yet he is the one thing standing between sanity, peace and four more years.

Still, Garrison Keillor writes, "This is Democratic bedrock: we don't let people lie in the ditch and drive past and pretend not to see them dying... Everybody knows this. The logical extension of this spirit is social welfare and the myriad government programs with long dry names all very uninteresting to you until you suddenly need one and then you turn into a Democrat. A liberal is a conservative who's been through treatment."

Honeysuckle, climbing roses, day lilies, bee balm, lavender, flowering clematis, black-eyed Susans, cosmos, pansies and petunias.

Nine hundred Americans now dead in Iraq.

January 6, 2005

FOR WHOM THE BELL TOLLS

Even as the death toll climbed, the bodies washed ashore, and the horror of it began to sink in, there was just one thought running through my mind: how can it be made any clearer that we are all one world, we are one world, we are one?

It may come as a revelation that the India plate can slip under the Burma plate and cause an earthquake deep in the Indian Ocean that has the power to raise two tsunamis and kill more than 150,000 people as far apart as India, Bangladesh, Thailand, Myanmar, Singapore and Indonesia. That whole islands — 42 in the Maldives alone, we hear— can disappear at once. That 94,200 people can die in under an hour in Sumatra.

But when something that happens in Thailand in Asia also affects Somalia in Africa, how can it be a revelation that we are all in this world together? The waves washed away villages of fishermen as well as exclusive resort hotels. They killed humble merchants as well as wealthy tourists from 40 countries. The water did not stop to ask if you were from Europe or Bangladesh, if you were brown or black or white, if you had gold around your neck or two babies in your arms.

It didn't matter if you were a rebel fighting for your independence or a soldier fighting against it, not in Tamil or Aceh. If you were in the path of the waves, you drowned. If you survived the waves, you helped.

People in the rest of the world, in shock, reached as one for their checkbooks. We offered every imaginable kind of empathy and assistance because every cliché had suddenly become true. "We are the world." "The family of man." "The global village." "It's a small world after all."

We — those of us who do not live near the Bay of Bengal — thought of the people we love and then of the people who were lost. We understood. We ached.

We wept for the villages that lost all their children — according to UNICEF, one-third of the victims were children, in this, 2005 , the midpoint in the U.N Decade of Peace and Non-Violence for the Children of the World. "The children were playing on the shore" became a sentence full of horror. Of course the children were playing on the shore. Where else would children play?

"Wall of water" became a nightmare phrase.

Was there a lesson for us in the news that none of the animals in Sri Lanka's Yala National Park — the elephants, buffalo and deer — seemed to die, even though floodwaters swept through the park, uprooting trees and destroying the hotel? That the animals instinctively sought out higher ground?

Was there a lesson for us in the news that none of the indigenous members of the isolated tribes in the Indian archipelago seemed to die? That they instinctively sought out higher ground?

Was there a lesson for us in the news that, as the AP reported, "scientists knew in advance that southern Asia was going to be hit by a tsunami, but attempts to raise the alarm were hampered by the absence of early-warning systems in the region"?

Now we're entering the scummy part — where we assign blame, where we hear of corrupt officials siphoning away relief money from starving orphans, where we learn of thieves and rapists who are taking advantage of the homeless and where we hear that "the possibility of anti-foreign resistance (i.e. Sri Lanka), especially in rebel occupied areas, may prevent the delivery of aid and assistance," according to the Web site Globalsecurity.org.

I guess that's being part of the human family, too.

Whether you are a multimillionaire rock star (U2 bassist Adam Clayton was vacationing in Malaysia) or little seven-year-old Dinakaran of Chinnakalapet, India, who was saved by his dog, John Donne's words in "Devotions upon Emergent Occasions" rang out loud again last week: "All mankind is of one author, and is one volume... No man is an island, entire of itself; every man is a piece of the continent, a part of the main."

Donne wrote that poem in 1623, but some of us still haven't learned the truth that we are all one. No person is above another. No person is more blessed than another. No person has the right to subjugate another. No person has the right to torture another. No person has a right to hoard — and flaunt — his wealth above another.

"Any man's death diminishes me, because I am involved in mankind," Donne wrote. "And therefore never send to know for whom the bell tolls; it tolls for thee."

February 17, 2005

DEMOCRACY IS THE LAST REFUGE OF A SCOUNDREL

Times have changed since Dr. Samuel Johnson said that patriotism is the last refuge of a scoundrel. Democracy is the last refuge now.

The First Amendment to the Constitution says that Congress shall make no law abridging the freedom of the press. But it doesn't say that the rich and powerful can't manipulate the press until it is destroyed or self-destructs.

The press is democracy's first line of defense against corruption and tyranny. Whether we get our news from the newspapers, the Internet or television, we depend on good reporting and thoughtful editing to tell us what is happening in the world.

The press may be many things — corporate-owned, profit-minded, certainly risk-averse — but every day, in our country and around the world, reporters are struggling to uncover and tell the truth. Many risk their lives in the hope that the truth will make their readers free — or, at least, a little freer. Last year 129 journalists and media employees were killed in the line of duty.

But if a party in power, such as our current Administration, does not want an informed citizenry — if, in fact, an informed citizenry is the last thing it wants — what then? Since the press is protected by the First Amendment, the only thing left is to destroy its credibility. That is what the Republican right-wingers have done, and brilliantly.

The destruction has been on-going. From the very first whining about bias in "the liberal media," to the establishment of a Republican television channel, Fox News, which spews out lies and character assassinations, to an attempt to destroy the Freedom of Information Act, to eliminating presidential press conferences, to denying government access to all but true believers, the meek and the hand-chosen, the Republican right has done a terrific job of stifling the free flow of information.

The media has been complicit in its own destruction. Afraid of the bullying of the Bush Administration; egotistic, protective of their bottom lines, caught up in conventional wisdom, in love with their high salaries, perks and access — yes, Big Media has been easy to manipulate. And the more it allows itself to be weakened, the less people trust it. In a recent Gallup poll on job ethics, journalists ranked just above car salesmen.

With the press weakened, the Bush Administration has been able to govern with big lies — weapons of mass destruction in Iraq, for example, or the current manufactured "crisis" in Social Security.

Lately, a few of this Administration's press manipulations have been revealed; in the light of day, the worms and roaches found wriggling in this West Wing aren't very pretty.

First in the spotlight was Armstrong Williams, a conservative African-American political commentator and co-founder of Graham Williams Group, a public relations firm. (The Graham, by the way, is Stedman Graham, Oprah Winfrey's long-time boyfriend.) Williams, it turned out, was paid $240,000 by the Dept. of Education to flog the president's No Child Left Behind initiative.

How crazy is that? Let me count the ways. First, federal law prohibits covert government publicity or propaganda campaigns - and this one clearly reeks of propaganda. Second, Williams was paid to lie to us with our own money. Third, Williams is a Republican shill anyway - he would do it for free. Fourth, Williams's Web site claims, (according to The New York Times), that he focuses on such issues as "the restoration of morality in today's society." Maybe Oprah could do a show about this?

Having a newspaper column — having a public voice — is an honor. In return, the public expects columnists to do their own reporting, think things through and then write their conclusions, sincerely. When they sell their columns, they stop being columnists and start being whores.

No sooner had Williams been unmasked than the conservative pro-family, stay-together-no-matter-how-bad-it-gets columnist Maggie Gallagher was caught writing pamphlets for the government. Gallagher, like most women, was paid less than the men — she only got $21,500 for selling out. Maybe that could be a new column topic for you, Maggie — equal pay for equal work?

The story grew more insidious. Last week, we learned that a fake journalist, James Guckert, writing under an assumed name, Jeff Gannon, and working for a right-wing opinion Web site posing as a news organization, Talon News, was given an all-access White House press pass to ask softball questions which the White House wanted asked during press conferences. Later, to show how the Republicans are not afraid to dirty their hands, we learned that Guckert is also a male prostitute — several gay prostitution sites show him nearly nude in come-on ads. He has ripped abs.

A free press is the hallmark of a democracy. By trying to corrupt, intimidate and manipulate it, the Bush Administration has shown us just how little respect for democracy they really have, here and in Iraq. What they care about is power and control.

After Dr. Johnson said patriotism was the last refuge of a scoundrel, the cynic Ambrose Bierce amended it with, "I beg to submit that it is the first." Then H.L. Mencken jumped in: "But there is something even worse: it is the first, last and middle range of fools."

If you substitute "democracy" for "patriotism," I beg to submit that you have the situation in America today. Whether your political views are right, left or center, your news sources are being corrupted, your mind is being manipulated and you should be outraged.

~ ~ ~

February 24, 2005

This Brave Little State Of Vermont

It may sound corny, but every time I get off the highway at Montpelier and turn my car towards the golden dome of the Statehouse, my eyes get misty.

Vermont's Statehouse is elegant in a musty, Victorian, governmental, gilded and over-decorated sort of way. But once you're inside, it feels casual, more like a high school than a government. When I mentioned that to my representative, Steve Darrow, D-Putney, he knew exactly what I meant.

"But we have a steeper learning curve, and bigger desks," he joked. "And nothing is mandatory. Someone said that to attract legislators, dangle trinkets and snacks like you would for the third and fourth grades."

I was there on Tuesday because one of my good friends, Carolyn Partridge, D-Windham, is now the House Majority Leader, and I wanted to learn more about what she does. On Tuesdays, the Democrats caucus with Carolyn as their facilitator.

But it's not as if I don't know other people at the Statehouse. I know my entire delegation — that's what's so great about Vermont. And they know me because I'm what they love to see up there — a constituent!

Carolyn was busy when I arrived, so I tagged along on a guided tour. The brilliant gold dome, the guide said, does not sit over the large House chamber, as domes do in every other statehouse in the country. It's just dropped on the top like a big gold weight. It was something about the designer not getting along with the architect, he said.

"Inside, it's just like a barn," he said. "Raw wood and nails sticking out."

The oil paintings of dignitaries were especially interesting. John A. Mead, governor from 1910 to 1912, for example, is wearing a wing collar, a formal black suit and a white tie. The next painting over is of Governor Howard Dean, 1991-2002, sitting in a canoe looking like an ad from a L. L. Bean catalog. Past the front entrance is a lovely portrait of Governor Madeleine Kunin, 1985 to 1991. She's painted sitting next to a big vase of flowers. Different years, different styles of painting, different styles of governors. Thomas Salmon, governor from 1973 to 1977, looks like a scamp. Edna Louise Beard, "The first lady member of the House" and "The first Senator of Orange County," 1921, was a babe.

The caucus was in Room 11. The last time I was in that room, the Republicans were giving a presentation on the evils of homosexuality. Scurrilous propaganda was distributed and videos of a Gay Pride parade were shown. That was during the time of the civil unions debate, when lies lost out to the truth that Vermonters think people should marry whoever they want.

Now the room was filled with serious policy wonks, and Carolyn was leading them. I was very proud.

Because I was a guest, she introduced me. The members applauded in welcome, and I felt like I'd just won an Academy Award.

Then, to lighten the atmosphere, they held a little trivia contest: which Democrat was born furthest away from Montpelier? It was Helen Head from South Burlington, who was born in Georgia.

We heard a report from Steve Howard of Rutland on the state's bridges and roadways. It was filled with phrases like "not a pretty picture" and "dire." It seems that Vermont has 846 bridges. They each have an 80-year life span, but 40 years is the point at which maintenance has to be done on a bridge "to save it from having to be totally replaced at a higher cost." We're only fixing 28 bridges a year. To fix them all, we'd need to spend $127 million a year for the next 10 years. Needless to say, that isn't going to happen, which is why he also used words like "serious need for these upgrades," "pavement also a concern," and "the infrastructure is falling apart."

When he was asked about the governor's response to this disturbing data, Steve said "No official response, but they have recognized that paving and bridges are a priority."

This was inside stuff, and I was enjoying myself. Then Bill Lippert of Hinesburg gave a report about the Judicial Retention Committee. It seems that in Vermont, judges — and even justices of the Supreme Court — have to be reappointed by a joint session of the House and Senate every six years. Misinformation abounds, Bill said.

At every judicial swearing in, an oath is taken to uphold the Constitution. Then, a bit later, the justices and judges also sign a written pledge saying the same thing. Until 1998, no one kept track of the paperwork, so several justices and judges do not have their oaths on file. This has led to some complaints that 12 judges and one justice (my guess — the most liberal ones) refused to pledge allegiance to the state's Constitution.

"But the justices and judges aren't responsible for the paperwork, and it's simply not true," Bill said. "So be prepared when your constituents ask you about it at Town Meeting."

They also discussed the federal government's attempt to play bait-and-switch with Medicaid by offering a block grant instead of a matching grant. Understanding the details requires superior wonkestry, a talent I do not possess. But I could see that the House Dems were appropriately wary.

I left the room impressed with my friend, my representatives and my state government. I wished I felt as secure about the federal government.

What made me feel especially confident was a quote from Calvin Coolidge mounted on the wall outside the room. "If the spirit of liberty should vanish in other parts of the Union and support of our institutions should languish," he said, "it could all be replenished from the generous store held by the people of this brave little state of Vermont."

April 7, 2005

A QUIVER OF FEMALE OPINION ARROWS

A few weeks ago, I got a phone call from a colleague who was furious about a local political issue — one that touched on gender. I had to write about it, she insisted, because I was a female columnist.

Until then I hadn't thought much about column-writing and gender, but her call made me angry. Was I a good columnist or a good female columnist? Was she using the word "female" as a qualifier? What did my genital organs have to do with writing, anyway?

As it turns out, this is one of the conundrums of feminism — the conflict that lies at the crossroads of experience and theory. For example, think of a women's film festival. Why should we need one in 2005? Doesn't it ghettoize women's experiences? Films tell stories about people — aren't women included in the term "people?"

This reasoning makes perfect sense until we notice that most Hollywood films are centered around men. Then we see women's festival films as rare and wonderful; we're thrilled to have the opportunity to see them.

See how easily a fine, righteous theory can get trumped?

I was still mulling over gender and column-writing when gender hell broke out in the world of big-time journalism. A female syndicated columnist publicly raked over the coals a male Op-Ed editor of a major newspaper because he wouldn't run her column. She accused him of gender bias and pointed to the huge imbalance in the number of male and female opinion writers in his — and every other large newspaper's — editorial sections.

Having a vagina and an opinion at the same time suddenly mattered. A number of powerful editors jumped into the fray, and — lo and behold — almost all of them were women.

Most started their own columns by listing the few amazing women who write widely-read opinion columns today — women like Maureen Dowd of The New York Times, Ellen Goodman of The Boston Globe, Katha Pollitt of The Nation, Barbara Ehrenreich and the ever-great Molly Ivins. Some of them even mentioned the batty right-wingers like Ann Coulter and Maggie Gallagher.

The discussion was fascinating. Zofia Smardz, editor of The Washington Post's Sunday Outlook section, explained the dearth of female columnists by saying that men are willing to jump into print while women are more careful. "Think of a man as carrying a quiverful of arrows," she said. "When he spies a target, he lets fly with the whole caboodle. Most of his arrows will miss the bulls-eye, but one is likely to hit. And that's the one people will remember — and applaud. A woman, though, proceeds slowly and considers carefully. Only when she's pretty sure she has a perfect shot does she sent off a single arrow.. And she hits the mark! Amazing! But... too bad. The guy's already walked off with the prize."

Goodman gave us the traditional view when she wrote, "In this case the question is whether fewer women jump into the pool because they fear the sharks? ... Are women more uncomfortable with confrontation? Do they prefer to mediate rather than heighten conflict?"

Anne Applebaum of The Washington Post warned that after this controversy, "every woman who gets her article accepted will have to wonder whether it was her knowledge, willingness to court controversy or just her gender that won the editor over."

In my experience, men and women can be equally opinionated. They can also be equally cautious about expressing opinions. We don't, after all, live in a society that encourages original thinking.

All of us form our world views out of our experiences: our parents and their teachings; our gender; our race; our economic status; our childhoods; our reading and education; our friends; our work; our sports; our art; our loves; our lives. In time, if we're lucky, all these experiences integrate. We become a whole, full person. We achieve some kind of wisdom.

At that point, it may seem like a step backwards to consider things from only one point of view — race, say, or gender. That's why I became angry when my colleague identified me as a "female columnist."

However, until we get the world in balance — and aren't we all, one way or another, working for that? — gender and other issues must be considered. But in journalism, as in life, they should never be the only issues we consider. We must also think about intelligence, life experience, heart and talent.

As Lakshmi Chaudhry, senior editor at the online news service AlterNet, said, "True diversity is not about getting the right mix of partisanship, or gender, or race. It's about good journalism. A newspaper staffed by different kinds of people with different life experiences can offer a vastly richer and more complex perspective on the world."

A Thousand Words or Less

SEVEN:

OBITS

(Over the years, from an emotional standpoint, obituaries have been the hardest things to write. Yet in writing terms, they seem to flow the easiest. Some of these pieces are about people I knew in passing. Some are about cultural figures who I admired from a distance. Two are very close to the bone of my personal life. And one is of a city.)

June 7, 2001

DEATH OF A JAZZMAN

It was in December of 1997, and I was sitting in a diner, waiting to interview jazz guitar master Attila Zoller. I was nervous. Attila's lifelong dream — a permanent home for his beloved Vermont Jazz Center, was coming true after 27 years. But I also knew that he was dying.

I'd seen him only a few months before, at a Sonny Rollins concert (he played with Rollins back in the '50s), and he looked fine —broad shoulders, big grin, black captain's hat pulled low over his eyes. So I wasn't prepared when he burst through the doors like a hurricane, unrecognizable except for the hat. He was a huge-eyed skeleton with waves of nervous energy racing through his body and shooting out around him like flames. His hands looked huge, his large fingers were splayed and rounded at the tips.

Attila was 70 then. He had been born into a musical family in Hungary, he told me once, and when he was about 21, already a musician in love with jazz, the Communists took over. They wouldn't let him play jazz, so he said good-bye and walked over the mountains, alone, to Austria, carrying only his guitar in a sack. Even then, he was ornery.

Attila hugged me, sat down and ordered homemade apple pie and vanilla ice cream. He ate ravenously.

"I'm supposed to eat everything I can," he said in his Hungarian-accented English. "But I can't eat. I have no appetite. So when I find something I can eat, I eat a lot of it."

I asked about his illness, and he waved his hand dismissively. "I have colon cancer," he said.

He pulled up his sweater, found a tumor and cupped it. "It's getting smaller. It goes up, it goes down, it must be the medicine."

He pinched his bicep and winced.

"I used to have muscles. Now I'm bones. But I have strength in reserve from the swimming. Every morning in the summer I swim laps in the Townshend Dam. I want my ashes to be scattered in the Townshend Dam."

For years, Attila had been well-known without being famous. From his work in Austria and Germany, where he topped the jazz guitar polls for nearly a decade, to his arrival in the United States, where he played with Benny Goodman, Chico Hamilton, Stan Getz and Herbie Mann, he lived only to play music. He had long-term musical friendships with players like bassist George Mraz and saxman Lee Konitz. He told stories about rooming with Ornette Coleman and Don Cherry. Pat Metheny recognized him as one of his most inspiring teachers.

Attila played a cool yet emotive, beautiful, free-flowing, mellow jazz guitar. He recorded over 30 albums. He designed guitars and his patented guitar pickup was used by many prominent performers. There was a line of Zoller strings for guitar and bass.

"He wanted the sound to be just the way he wanted it," said his friend, trumpeter Howard Brofsky. "He had a sense of the international. 'I'm not a blues player,' he said. 'I didn't grow up in America. I'm not black, I don't come out of that tradition.' His sound was unique. He used to criticize students for playing licks that other people had played. He made a point of being original, his own person, totally independent and creative."

Attila never had great commercial success, but he won the New England Foundation for the Arts Lifetime Achievement in Jazz award in 1995, and in April, 1997, the American Guitar Museum on Long Island gave him a surprise birthday party and named the day Attila Zoller Day. The Hungarian government had just brought him over to play two concerts.

Attila pulled out a plastic bag filled with medicine and photographs from his Hungarian trip. He showed me pictures of his sister, his old elementary school friends, and the girl who had lived next door.

"They did the concert in my old home town, Visegrad. I hadn't been there for 40 years," he said. "My little daughter was shining. Everybody adored her."

From among the pill vials he chose a Zantac and passed on the morphine.

"I'm supposed to take it every five or six hours, but then I can't drive," he said.

He continued talking. He had fallen in love with Vermont the first time he came here, in 1972. And although he broke his leg skiing on that trip, by 1974 he had bought a house and started a summer jazz school. People played in every room of that house and under every tree, he said. He imported his friends to teach.

"I gave them room and board, and I cooked, too," Attila said. "I made Hungarian goulash and paprika chicken. It was hard times, but it was a nice way to start here a little scene."

There were never enough students, though, and Attila finally had to sell the house. After that, the Vermont Jazz Center, which was incorporated in 1985, moved from one space to another. But Attila's dream was to keep it going, and he was delighted when he met Eugene Uman, the current director.

"I thought that before I go to other hunting grounds, I should settle something so that the jazz keeps going," Attila said. "I devoted my life to that art form. I would like the spirit to stay going. We have a nice serious cat, Eugene, and his family is beautiful. It looks like we got it rolling in the right way."

The last thing Attila said to me was that dying had improved his playing.

"I play much better now," he said. "It's much more relaxed. You bring 100 percent more of yourself. I was always nervous. Now nothing bothers me. I'm free to improvise. I'm on the trip now."

Then he kissed me on both cheeks and hugged me again, and I could feel each of his ribs, sharp and close, under my fingers. He jumped into his little blue car, honked, waved, and took off like a flash. I left the parking lot right behind him and turned in the same direction, but he was long gone.

When the jazz center held its celebratory concert a month later, Attila wasn't there. He was in Grace Cottage Hospital, and although his doctor said he could play, he was afraid that his pain medication would affect the quality of his music. He died on January 25, 1998.

Since the lake at the Townshend dam was frozen, his friends scattered his ashes from a covered bridge just below the dam, where the water was still moving. Then they opened a bottle of champagne.

Every year, around Attila's June 13 birthday, the jazz center holds a concert in his honor. His dream and his music continues, and that was all he wanted — except to play more jazz, of course.

(Attila Zoller would be happy to know that the Vermont Jazz Center is still thriving in Brattleboro.)

~ ~ ~

November 7, 2002

THE DEATH OF THE PIANO FIGHTER

Warren Zevon is dying the way he lived: without tears.

Zevon, who is 55 and not going to see 56, has always been cynical, irreverent, funny and brutally honest. He's one of the great musicians and songwriters of our time, but since he never achieved widespread fame and big money, some might say he's had a cult following.

What a cult! He's collaborated with Neil Young, Bob Dylan (who recently added Zevon songs to his sets), Linda Ronstadt ("Poor Poor Pitiful Me," "Carmelita") Jackson Browne, R.E.M., Bonnie Raitt, Bobby Keys, Glenn Frey, David Lindley, Don Henley, Lindsey Buckingham and Stevie Nicks, Mick Fleetwood, Bruce Springsteen, Chick Corea, Jerry Garcia, Jack Casady and Jorma Kaukonen of Jefferson Airplane, George Clinton, Flea of the Red Hot Chili Peppers, Bruce Hornsby, Graham Nash... the list goes on forever.

And don't forget Igor Stravinsky. As a youngster, Zevon, a classically trained pianist, used to go to Stravinsky's Hollywood Hills home to play. Or the Everly Brothers. One of Zevon's first jobs was as their music director.

"My fondest memory of touring with Warren was the time we were staying in a hotel in Canada and we had to be brought to our rooms on the luggage carts," Don Everly said in the liner notes to one Zevon anthology. (Another one, "Genius," just came out on Rhino.) "We'd had a little too much to drink."

Zevon also has non-musical friends, like Hunter S. Thompson and Clint Eastwood. Carl Hiaasen collaborated with him on "Rottweiler Blues." I don't know which one of them penned the immortal line, "Don't knock on my door if you don't know my Rottweiler's name," but it should be a bumper sticker.

Back in the 1980s, Zevon was one of the first to openly admit he had addictions — a quart of vodka a day — and to conquer them. But when he later wrote "Detox Mansion," he approached the topic with his usual upbeat and cynical cheer: "Well, I'm gone to Detox Mansion, way down on Last Breath Farm. I've been rakin' leaves with Liza, helping Liz clean up the yard."

Zevon nailed it when he called himself "a heavy metal folksinger." While other singer-songwriters wrote ballads about ships lost at sea, train wrecks and loves lost at home, Zevon wrote about a Norwegian mercenary who gets his head shot off in Biafra and wanders around Africa looking for revenge. Damn if he doesn't get it, too.

Machismo was always one of Zevon's best subjects, but it was never the machismo of the swaggering bully or the I'm-on-top-screw-you fool. It was always the painful machismo (or machisma) of outsiders fighting to the death for what usually turns out to be a losing proposition.

His fans identified. Every time I saw him play, men cheered and waved their fists when he sang the opening line of "Lawyers, Guns and Money": "Well, I went home with the waitress, the way I always do." As if all those fans were going to do the same thing, instead of going home to an empty apartment or a wife demanding to know where they had been.

In his brilliant contribution to the minuscule category of folk boxing songs, "Boom Boom Mancini," Zevon succinctly captured this world view: "Some have the speed and the right combinations, but if you can't take the punches it don't mean a thing."

Zevon was what Billy Joel wanted to be. Joel was only a piano man, but Zevon rode his piano like a Harley. "I'm a holy roller, I'm a real lowrider, hold me tight honey, then hold me tighter," he wrote in "Piano Fighter."

Death always rode with Zevon. He called one of his songs "I'll Sleep When I'm Dead." They made a movie out of that. They also made a movie out of the title, "Things to Do in Denver When You're Dead." His last two albums were "Life'll Kill Ya" and — after he was diagnosed with inoperable lung cancer — "My Ride's Here." His prophetic logo is a grinning skull wearing his trademark sunglasses and smoking a cigarette.

You might think all this is posturing. After all, he wouldn't be the first musician to hide behind a swaggering image. But now, with the cancer spreading through his body, Zevon isn't singing "poor poor pitiful me."

He's going out bravely, and he's going out publicly.

In September he announced that he was dying. Last week, while he could still walk, a great-hearted and brave David Letterman devoted an entire "Late Night" show to him. It was television at its purest and finest. Zevon looked like hell. His neck had shrunk and his cheeks hung in dewlaps. When Letterman said he looked remarkably well for someone who would be dead in a few weeks, he said, deadpan, that it was the makeup.

Zevon's deep, sexy baritone was gone, and he was too weak to rock. So they backed him with flutes and strings and he sang three songs, including the tender "Mutineer," which always tears my heart out. It was so painful to watch that at one point I turned it off. But I quickly turned it back on, because, after all, if you can't take the punches it don't mean a thing.

According to the Los Angeles Times, a friend has set up a small recording studio next to Zevon's bed, and he's spending his last days hanging out with his children, reading a flood of admiring tributes just like this one, and writing and recording new songs.

"I have a little mischief in mind," he told the reporter.

Zevon's death will be a great loss. We'll never again hear him complain that Pearl Street in Northampton, Mass. is "a filthy pit," or threaten to kill anyone who asks him to play "Werewolves of London" again.

I'll always love Zevon and his music. He might mock that kind of affection, but he's the one who said about love, "You can't start it like a car, you can't stop it with a gun."

In "Boom Boom Mancini" Zevon wrote, "They make hypocrite judgments after the fact, but the name of the game is be hit and hit back."

Zevon took the punches and he's riding out on top. I admire his style.

(Randy turned me on to Warren Zevon, and it was true love from the first. When I started reviewing concerts for the Springfield Union-News, I covered every Zevon show, spending a lot of time in the "filthy pit" {he got that right!} downstairs at Pearl Street. When I wrote this piece, Zevon was still in the process of dying. This being Brattleboro, it turned out we had a connection. His ex-wife happened to live in town. She thoughtfully e-mailed me to say that she had sent Zevon a copy of my article, and that he'd liked it. What more can I say, except he died in 2003 and I still miss him? And that I recently saw a bumper sticker that said, "Don't knock on my door if you don't know my Rottwelier's name.")

~ ~ ~

July 10, 2003

A TRIBUTE TO THE LATE GREAT KATE

How did I love you, Katharine Hepburn? Let me count the ways.

When she died on June 29 at the age of 96, the first thing I thought of was the dress. It's the one — you know the one — she wears in the party scene in "Philadelphia Story," that filmy yet structured white gown with a design of silver geometrics that makes her shimmer and glow, a Diana in the moonlight, about to receive her comeuppance from champagne and Jimmy Stewart and her own thwarted sexual desire.

Last year I encountered that dress on display at the Costume Institute at the Metropolitan Museum of Art. The silver lamé was a little frayed, and on a dummy in a glass case it certainly didn't shimmer and glow. But it was beautiful, and there was one indisputable and astounding fact about it — the wearer couldn't have had more than an 17-inch waist, if that.

An impossible waistline tells a great deal about Hepburn's stamina, determination, athleticism and discipline. Most of us would love to shimmer and glow for an evening — isn't the wedding industry built upon that premise? But very few of us would starve ourselves for a lifetime to do it.

Hepburn has always been my idol. Her independence, her financial savvy, her intelligence, her great and eccentric beauty, the sheer force of her personality, the sense that she was, in many ways, in control of her life and career — all these things gave me courage at a time when I wanted to live my life on my own terms as a writer and the only career path that seemed open to me was marriage and motherhood.

Hepburn was a realist about the opposing forces of marriage and career. "I want to be a star, and I don't want to make my husband my victim," she once said. "And I certainly don't want to make my children my victims."

In the newest issue of The New Yorker, Claudia Roth Pierpont suggests that Hepburn's independence was less than true.

"We held her close... because of the insistent life that hummed through every taut and peremptory inch of her, and that we imaged to be as natural as breathing or winning for someone so easily, imperiously free," Pierpont said. "It was in making us believe in this that she may have been our greatest actress of all."

The "proof" that Hepburn's strength was an act is supposed to reside in her relationship with Spencer Tracy, on and off the screen.

This is how Hepburn herself described the formula for the great Tracy-Hepburn gender-role comedies: "She needles the man, a little like a mosquito. Then he slowly puts out his big paw and slaps the lady down, and the American public likes to see that. In the end, he's always the boss of the situation, but he's challenged by her. That — in simple terms — is what we do."

Garson Kanin, who co-wrote some of the best Tracy-Hepburn comedies and was a good friend of the couple, understood why the formula worked. In his 1971 book, "Tracy and Hepburn: An Intimate Memoir," he said: "The audience is drawn to her, yet wants reassurance that she is real— Nothing more endears a Queen to her subjects than a hiccup in public, a slip on the ice, a fall from a horse, or, best of all, a marriage to a commoner."

Off the screen, with no audience to play for, the queen and the commoner had their difficulties. After Tracy died it was revealed that he was a bully, an alcoholic who would sometimes disappear with a suitcase full of bottles and reappear only when they were empty, and an occasional abuser. He insisted that his name precede Hepburn's in every billing. And throughout their affair, he refused to divorce his wife, essentially keeping Hepburn an adulteress for the 27 years they were together. All in all, their relationship does not make a pretty picture, especially for feminists.

Hepburn did not care. In her 1991 autobiography, "Me: Stories From My Life," she said: "He didn't like this or that. I changed this and that. They might be qualities which I personally valued. It did not matter. I changed them... We did what he liked. We lived a life which he liked. This gave me great pleasure."

It was all worthwhile because, she said, he fascinated her. "He had the most wonderful sense of humor," she wrote. "He was funny. He was Irish to the fingertips. He could laugh and he could create laughter. He had a funny way of looking at things — at some things, I should say."

The director George Cukor, who often worked with Tracy and Hepburn, and on whose property they lived, said, "What I remember most is that they could bicker and argue and say dreadful things to one another, but always come out of it laughing and hugging like teenagers."

In the end, her feelings toward Tracy were what I came to admire most about Hepburn. She knew his faults, she loved him passionately and she was intensely loyal to him. She was a free woman, and she freely chose to devote herself to him.

"I really liked him — deep down — and I wanted him to be happy," she wrote. "We just passed twenty-seven years together in what was to me absolute bliss. It is called LOVE."

If you want to see that love captured on film, watch the otherwise saccharine "Guess Who's Coming to Dinner." Tracy was dying when they made it — he only lived for 15 days after the film wrapped. At the end of the picture, there is a close-up of Hepburn looking at Tracy with tears in her eyes — the sight of it will break your heart.

After Tracy died, Hepburn gave us the ultimate strong and independent woman, Eleanor of Aquitaine, in the great 1968 film "The Lion in Winter." This time she didn't have to bow to convention. Older, fiercer, and unable to use her sexual powers to win back the love of her king, Henry II, played by an equally fierce Peter O'Toole, she sharpened her claws and relied on her intelligence, wit and cunning. She won an Academy Award for her thrilling performance, one of four — an all-time record.

"Katharine Hepburn's popularity has never waned because people know (magically, intuitively) that she stands for something, even if many of them have no clear idea as to what that something is," Kanin said. "They recognize that in a time of dangerous conformity, and the fear of being different, here is one who stands up gallantly to the killing wave."

All movie stars are beautiful. Hepburn gave the world a model of a woman who is fierce, free, forceful, intelligent, unconventional, and yet able to love deeply, if not always wisely. She was never a perfect role model, but then, no one ever is. And I will always love her.

~ ~ ~

July 24, 2003

How We Pick Our Icons

How do we, personally, chose our icons?

After I wrote about my undying admiration for Katharine Hepburn, who died in June at the age of 96, I was surprised by the number of women who stopped me on the street to tell me that they felt the same way.

One of them tipped me off to a new book by Hepburn's close friend, the Pulitzer-prize winning biographer A. Scott Berg. Naturally, I bought "Kate Remembered" as soon as it hit the bookstores, and last weekend I read it all in one big gulp.

Berg met Hepburn in 1983 when she was 75. Perhaps because he is a biographer by profession, she openly discussed her life with him. The book is the story of their friendship and also a heart-rendering account of Hepburn's later years, when her spark and independence sank into the mists of a very old age.

When I finished the book I thought that perhaps I loved Hepburn because I am so much like her. And how could I have known that all those years ago when I first fell in love with her?

When I say I'm like her I don't mean that I have cheekbones to die for, a lithe and athletic body, a past littered with rich and famous lovers, a fan base that spans the world, and a history of making some of the greatest films of the 20th Century.

But in many ways, Hepburn looked at the world and lived her life in much the same way as I do.

For example, last month I wrote a piece about how I find God in nature. It's not an original thought — I believe the Transcendentalists devoted a considerable amount of their energy to the idea. But still, my piece caused a bit of a controversy, so I was surprised and delighted to find this quote from Hepburn in Berg's book. She's talking about her favorite flower, the humble Queen Anne's lace:

"Now how can anybody look at this and not believe there is some higher power, some divine force at work in the universe greater than Man, some god that created it, that created all this, that created us?" she said.

Although Hepburn loved Tracy for 27 years, she told Berg that she never wanted to marry him. She wanted to "live like a man," which meant living "by herself, paying her own bills, and ultimately, answering to nobody," Berg said.

I have always felt the same way; driven by the need for a career, for much of my life a happy marriage was the last thing on my mind. Like many women who came of age during the era of Second Wave Feminism in the late 1960s and early 1970s, I wanted to live as a free individual, not identified as a wife, mother, lover, or helpmate. Women like me wanted our own lives. Hell, we wanted our own wives.

Whether we were gay or straight, the big problem was finding a safe way through this unexplored and dangerous territory. We had few role models to guide us. Most of us weren't interested in the gorgeous sexual victimhood of Marilyn Monroe, or able to copy the wealthy grace and pliancy of Jacqueline Kennedy, or wanting to spend the time and money on the over-designed mysteriousness of Garbo and Deitrich. Thank God there was the forthright, strong, independent — unmarried! — slightly androgynous and yet beautiful and desirable Hepburn.

With her penchant for deep female friendships, her many lovers, her characters — all with careers or career aspirations of their own — and that glowing sense of life inside her, she became a valuable light in the cultural darkness of the time.

A considerable amount of that darkness remains in the culture today. Feminists are often scorned. Strong and successful women like Hillary Clinton and Martha Stewart often become targets. I have a friend who raised millions of dollars for an organization dedicated to helping disadvantaged girls become strong young women; she was forced to resign because her board found her "too aggressive."

Hepburn, on the other hand, surmounted every obstacle.

"The natural law is to settle," Hepburn told Berg. "I broke that law."

Hepburn's strength and independence made her anything but unapproachable. She had many lovers, Joel McCrea, Leland Hayward and Howard Hughes among them. But she told Berg that when she met Tracy it was like being "hit over the head with a cast-iron skillet." She stayed with him, she said, "because I truly learned that it was more important to love than to be loved."

That's the same lesson that many independent women learn if they are very lucky, somewhat accepting and a little bit wise; it is why I am — to my great surprise — happily married today.

When Hepburn was well into her 90s, Berg asked her what she thought the purpose of life might be.

"To work hard and to love someone," she said. "And to have some fun. And if you're lucky, you keep your health... and somebody loves you back." Can anyone put it better than that?

Hepburn was always wary of her fans. While she was happy to hear that she had pleased and entertained people, she was disturbed when they told her that they spent their nights at home watching her films.

"If they're really inspired by what I've done with my life," she told Berg, "why don't they do something with theirs?"

She — and her mother, Katharine Houghton Hepburn, a famous First Wave feminist — might be happy to know that so many women did exactly that.

I felt a deep sense of loss after I finished Berg's book, so I went into my yard and gathered some of the Queen Anne's lace that grows wild there. I'll keep some in a bowl beside my bed until the summer ends, to keep her memory fresh.

June 17, 2004

WORLD PEACE, ONE FRIENDSHIP AT A TIME

The death of John A. Wallace last Friday at the age of 88 brought back many memories. Not of him, because I didn't know him very well. He was a tall, reserved, dignified man, and that made him a tough interview on the few times I talked to him. But I knew him well because of the institution he founded, the School for International Training in Brattleboro, Vt., which changed my life.

When I got to the school in 1987 as a student in the Program for International Management (PIM 40), SIT was part of The Experiment in International Living, now called World Learning, Inc. The Experiment was founded by Donald Watt in 1932 to provide young, upper-middle-class WASPs with a few months of life with a family in another country. They would learn the language and culture and, hopefully, make a few lifelong friends. I don't know if Watt created the homestay, but he certainly was a pioneer in the movement.

His great idea was that world peace might come more quickly if we all recognized that the brotherhood of man is really a brotherhood or a sisterhood or a peoplehood — politically correct language sometimes gets in the way — but in any case, a family. World peace, he said, one friendship at a time.

It's a comforting if unrealistic idea, because war often manifests itself first in families and friends — look at Bosnia and Rwanda.

Watt's idea had its first tragic encounter with reality in 1939, when a group of Experimenters had to be evacuated from Europe just before Hitler declared war. But it sprung up again after the war, when "Never again" was a phrase on the lips of more than just the world's remaining Jews.

According to Wallace's obituary, in World War II he was one of the first soldiers to enter the concentration camp at Bergen Belsen. "What he saw there convinced him to do whatever he could to make sure nothing like that would ever happen again," said his obituary. He and Watt were kindred souls.

So Wallace founded The School for International Training.

People in my class came from all over the world: the U.S., of course, and Finland, Thailand, India, Indonesia, Tanzania, China, Pakistan, Bangladesh, Nepal, Italy, and Togo. We spoke French, Finnish, Swedish,

Spanish, Chinese, German, Portuguese, Cebuano Surigaonon, Japanese, Bengali, Hindi, Kiswahili, Malay, Urdu, Arabic, Tagalog, Bicol, Setswana, Punjabi, Thai, Sierra Leone Creole, Pulaar, Greek, Italian and English. All the Americans had considerable overseas experience, either as Peace Corps veterans or in jobs with international nonprofit organizations or as hard-bitten travelers looking for a soft landing.

Today, I'm told, PIM courses are rigorous and the students are hard-working and serious. When I was there, the courses were less than challenging. Watt called his autobiography "Intelligence is Not Enough," and we frequently muttered that a little intelligence might help.

SIT is "experiential," in that it tries to give you the emotional experiences necessary for cross-cultural learning. But most of us had spent years living with poor people in underdeveloped countries and we were way ahead of our teachers.

Irreverent, arrogant and rowdy, we specialized in having a good time. One of the first things we did as a class was build a float on Upton Pond. We created a new culture based on Rhinegold beer. The wife of one classmate was Polynesian; she taught us how to weave grass skirts from the rushes by the pond. In the yearbook, there's a picture of me in one dancing the hula.

My roommate, Andrea, was often our cruise director. She gave one of her best parties after she decided that Hussein, a dignified Pakistani bureaucrat, needed to hang out more. We broke into his room — about 30 of us, with a great amount of beer, and with Andrea in a rhinestone tiara for the occasion — and shouted "Surprise!" when he came back from class. Although the party started as a joke, he was so deeply touched that we — who moved so easily in foreign cultures — learned an important lesson about how difficult it might be to fit into our own. The experiential method worked.

I came to look at SIT as a railroad roundhouse. We were all trains coming in on one little track, getting turned around a bit, and leaving on another to save the world or, at the very least, ourselves.

I'm still in touch with many of my classmates. Anjali went on to create a non-profit organization in India that nurses the victims of AIDS. Andrea has raised millions of dollars to help disadvantaged American girls. Vilawan is a Buddhist monk. Yixun is a Shanghai entrepreneur.

While many SIT students go off to make the world a better place, some of us are still living and working in Windham Country. SIT may be responsible for the depth and richness of international understanding that you find here. Our children spend time living and traveling in other cultures. We support many international cuisines. We speak many languages and know many cultures and understand the dangers of demonizing entire populations for the sake of empire.

Because Americans are blessed with an enormous and bountiful country that extends from sea to shining sea, they frequently don't travel far. They are, for the most part, cross-culturally deaf, dumb and blind. They are oblivious to the enormous diversity of colors and cultures and countries that share the planet with us. Most of our schoolchildren cannot find Panama on a map, and for some strange reason, we're proud of that.

I've read somewhere that until he became president, George W. Bush never traveled overseas. And when former president Ronald Reagan came back from a trip to South America, he famously said, "Well, I learned a lot. . . . You'd be surprised. They're all individual countries."

It's easy to support right wing death squads in South America when you aren't sure where those countries are. It's easy to sell arms to Iran and biological weapons to Saddam Hussein, or to invade Panama, or to invade Iraq on a whim to depose Saddam Hussein, when you can't imagine that the people who live there are real people. Ever wonder why the American press doesn't tell us how many Panamanians, Afghans or Iraqis have died in our tragically silly impulse wars, or why the torture at Abu Ghriab happened so easily? It's because to most Americans, people from other countries are not real.

But it's hard to think of a person as a "gook" when you hang out with Yixun, or when Vilawan cooks you a special Thai dinner. You can't call a person a "wetback" when you know Gisella, or a "towelhead" when you know people as different as Hussain, Anjali, Mansur and Tridib. You can't call a person a "wop" when you've watched the ebullient Antonio struggling with his English, or a "fag" after George has flamed his way into your heart. Hopefully, you can't call a person a "kike" when you know me.

If Reagan and the Bushes had been given homestays when they were young, or at the very least some cross-cultural sensitivity training, we might not be in this mess today. World Learning and SIT are remarkable achievements, and Jack Wallace and Donald Watt are remarkable men.

January 27, 2005

JOHNNY CARSON AND OUR OWN MORTALITY

The death on Sunday of Johnny Carson raises thoughts about entertainment and mortality.

If only because death is so frightening, most of us seek some kind of immortality. We have children so our genes can sail down through the ages. For centuries painters, writers and composers have made art in the hope that their work would last longer than their mortal bodies.

Since the advent of film and recording devices, actors, musicians, singers and yes, even comedians, can also play the immortality game. Greta Garbo's looks and Maria Callas's voice are still available to us. Fred Astaire and Ginger Rogers will dance forever as the feathers escaping from her dresses float lightly around their faces.

"One of the pleasures of steady movie-going is that if a performer has lasting power, you can grow up and then older along with them," writes New York Times film critic Manohla Dargis. "That's true of stars you discover when they're young adults and even more so for those you follow from childhood, like Elizabeth Taylor and Winona Ryder. There is something satisfying about that first encounter... which becomes a marker by which to view the past, both theirs and yours."

Each generation chooses the stars with "staying power" who will be their "marker by which to view the past." My generation chose Bob Dylan and the Beatles; for many of us, the death of John Lennon was our first experience with the loss of a contemporary. But for close to 30 years, Carson was America's marker. His death is very much a death in the family. And every death teaches us a little more about our own mortality.

People call Carson the epitome of Middle America, but the truth is that he was one of the coolest people on television. He brought hip into America's living rooms without America knowing what it was. He was bawdy and politically incorrect in a way censors would never allow today — one skit had him talking about a girl he knew in high school, "Gina Statutory," wink, wink; he compared her to Lincoln because "everyone took a shot at her in the balcony."

Carson was unimpressed with authority. He took the charisma of Frank Sinatra's performing style — and life style — and translated it into something that would be comfortable in America's living rooms.

His was a dual personality — earnest, sincere and polite on the surface, and sharp and cynical beneath. When he retired, it took two to replace him, Jay Leno for niceness and David Letterman for irreverence.

Entertainment can be an ethereal business. Carson based a lot of his performing style — especially his timing — on the great comedian Jack Benny. When I was a child, Benny's television show could reduce me to fits of explosive laughter. But although his shows are still available on kinescope, they are rarely shown today.

Milton Berle, "Mr. Tuesday Night," introduced vaudeville comedy to television and was forgotten just a few months after he died. When Bob Hope died, he was eulogized to the skies, but I haven't heard his name mentioned since. Of all the great early television comedians, only Lucille Ball's shows still have cultural currency, and that may be because each tells a story of its own.

Carson is less likely to be forgotten. He mentored so many great talents that his shows will be raided for clips for the foreseeable future. Several of his "Best of" collections are available on video.

Also, by the time Carson retired, his work (which he inherited from Steve Allen and Jack Paar and refined) had been refracted by multiples. Anyone on television today with a desk and a chair for interviews — Letterman, Leno, Conan O'Brien, Jimmy Kimmel, Jon Stewart, a plethora of skits on "Saturday Night Live, a host of failed hosts, and even Ellen DeGeneres, in her way — is his descendant. He was also the inspiration for Garry Shandling's hilarious backstage comedy, "The Larry Sanders Show."

Carson's influence was international. On National Public Radio the other night, I heard an interview with a late-night talk show host from Tsibili, Georgia. The guy had copied Carson to the point of having his own "Heeeere's Johnny" introduction.

There was always a downside to Carson, too. He had Sinatra-like machismo and disdain for women; it came through clearly in the cleavage-heavy bimbos he chose for his skits. His move to show-taping signified the end of edgy live late-night television. Intellectual conversation disappeared over the years, to be replaced by celebrity shills. And he never had to make conversation with Ashlee Simpson or a gangsta rapper covered in bling, so we'll never know how well his storied good manners would have held up in the modern age.

But when I look at pictures of Carson now, I feel something like a deep and abiding love for the man. In spite of his well-known aloofness, he gave his audience some ineffable but precious part of himself. He was America's "marker with staying power" for 30 years. His death has shown us our own mortality.

Imagine what it will be like when Dylan dies.

~ ~ ~

June 9, 2005

SAYING GOOD-BYE TO MARTY JEZER

(This was the hardest piece I've ever had to write.)

I've never seen anyone more alive on his deathbed than Marty Jezer. When I visited him last week, his ever-expressive face was animated, his huge eyes were glowing, his thoughts were flowing as openly and fluidly as ever, and his speech — stuttering and all — was running witty, deep, and open-hearted. It was typical Marty except that most of his hair was gone and he was all bone, lying in a hospital bed in his home, on a day when making connections with hospice had already tired him out.

I told him that in my opinion, it's a shame we hold memorial services after people die, so they can't hear what their friends really think about them. To paraphrase an old Nitty Gritty Dirt Band song, "Memorials cheer the living, dear, they're no good to the dead." So I said I'd write an appreciation of him while he was still alive to read it, and he said "Go for it." So here goes.

When I first started writing my own column — about music, mostly — I got a letter from Marty telling me that my opinions were "really off the wall." Then, in two single-spaced, closely-typed pages, he instructed me on the fine art of listening to Billie Holiday, early Louis Armstrong, Ella Fitzgerald and Sarah Vaughn. His words remain wise and eloquent today — although I don't think we'll ever agree about Frank Sinatra.

I didn't know Marty then, although I knew about him — that he was a well-known left-wing writer, one of the hippest people of his generation, and one of those legendary early commune hippies who came to Vermont in the 1970s and stayed to make a life here.

Marty was no hippie caricature, though. He was a well-respected and much-loved contributor to the daily life of our community, an adept and knowledgeable political columnist, and the author of four books, one of which was made into a movie.

When I finally met him, it took a while to get through the stuttering. Then I realized that he was just about the funniest man I would ever have the pleasure of knowing. From the beginning, to me, Marty was a man of great humor, deep intelligence and strong opinions which he loved to exchange with others.

"One of the challenges (and pleasures) of writing for a local newspaper is that most readers do not share my politics," he wrote. "Truth is, I'd rather be read by people who don't hold my views. Sometimes I picture in my mind's eye a local conservative and write with the intention of changing his or her mind. Other times I write with the image of lefty friends in mind, trying to persuade them to think less ideologically and more pragmatically."

The goal, he said, is to find enough common ground for dialogue, but at the same time question authority and your own assumptions. Who can argue with that?

Marty has been fighting cancer for some time, and for a while he thought he had it licked. When it returned, there was nothing left for the doctors to do.

I asked him if he was scared. He said, "Only of the pain." Luckily, a medical miracle of a pump is keeping him pain-free so he remains a conscious participant in his own life.

Our conversation turned naturally to politics, and to the country's dangerous, right-wing ways. He was patriotic and optimistic at the same time. "It's my country and I'm not ashamed of it," he said. "Half of us haven't bought into Bush. The good fight is still being fought."

He had a CD player propped up against the bed, and he played for me Madeleine Peyroux's version of Leonard Cohen's beautiful love song, "Dance Me To The End of Love." The lyrics had special meaning: "Dance me to your beauty with a burning violin/Dance me through the panic till I'm gathered safely in/Lift me like an olive branch and be my homeward dove/Dance me to the end of love." As a singer Peyroux has always been compared to Billie Holiday, so in a way, music has come 'round full circle for Marty.

He was angry that his life was coming to an end, when he has enjoyed the living of it so much. But he recognizes, he said, that he has had a marvelous life. After talking about his love of his work, Brattleboro, his family and his friends, he added with awe, "And I heard Count Basie in his prime! I heard him!"

At least, we joked, he had lived long enough to learn the identity of Deep Throat. And we agreed that we may all die before we learn the greatest secret of our generation: Who shot Jack Kennedy, and why.

This has been a difficult column for me to write. As your extended family surrounds you and your many friends line up to talk politics and music one last time, all I can say, Marty Jezer, is that it's been an honor and a privilege to know you.

Go dancing all you can, my friend, but you will never come to the end of love.

∼

(I thought I would have more time with Marty, but to my dismay he died from metastasized testicular cancer two days after this piece appeared in print and on-line, on June 11.

Afterward, I was deluged with emails from people from all over the country who had known and loved Marty and his work.

The stuttering community, in which he was widely respected, expressed their grief and reproduced my piece in newsletters and on stuttering Web sites.

The National Writers Union — Marty was a founding member of the western Massachusetts chapter — also posted it.

A woman wrote to tell me that she had had a crush on Marty in high school.

People who knew Marty in New York during the Sixties wrote to share reminiscences.

One true lefty had to challenge my opening line — "How many people have you seen on their deathbeds, anyhow?" (Marty was my fourth.) And more than a few wrote to tell me that they knew who killed JFK.

Many people who read Marty's political books and his column, but didn't know him personally, wrote to share their shock at his dying. A professor from *Sydney University said he taught from Marty's book, "The Dark Ages," and "he has a fan Down Under." Another wrote, "Please tell Marty that this activist-journalist peer has always treasured him, in the Sixties and now in the Bush era, for his level-headed wisdom. He is a role model for us all."*

An old friend of Marty's wrote, "If only God were bribable, I would be glad to dedicate what seems most appropriate, say, a dozen jugs of real Vermont maple syrup given to a soup kitchen — in exchange for one more pain-free year of Marty's life."

I copied all the emails and letters and gave them to his long-time partner, Arlene Distler, at the memorial service — which, by the way, was attended by several hundred people.

But here's the kicker. I knew that Marty read the piece on the day before he died. But I didn't have the nerve to ask Arlene what he thought of it until early January of this year.

This is what she said, in an email: "I think he was feeling a bit embarrassed at the time, was not in a mood to hear about how wonderful he was. He was in a lot of discomfort, and was very impatient about everything. This dying thing was a big pain in the ass to him. We all thought he was pretty cute about it, though...said something like, "Well, that's how she sees it"...we all knew he was thrilled."

And I breathed such a big sigh of relief.)

September 8, 2005

STRONG WIND

"Strong wind, strong wind/Many dead tonight it could be you/ And we are homeless, homeless/Moonlight sleeping on a midnight lake."[1]

How do we comprehend the drowning of New Orleans, home of Bourbon Street and Rampart Street and the St. James Infirmary and the whorehouse of the Rising Sun and so much jazz and folk and blues and Rock 'n' Roll that the city has always been one of the most crucial touchstones of American culture?

The roots of American rhythm are in Africa, and their tore-off broken branches were forcibly brought here in slave ships and still, somehow, took deep, deep root. And in the 19th Century, in Congo Square in New Orleans, the harsh rules of inhuman bondage were temporarily loosened while a multitude of African descendants played African instruments and, as best they could remember, played African rhythms and danced African dances and sang African songs.

"Town's folk would gather around the square on Sunday afternoons to witness," wrote historian Thomas L. Morgan. "In 1819, a visitor to the city, Benjamin Latrobe wrote about the celebrations in his journal. He was amazed at the sight of five or six hundred unsupervised slaves that had assembled for dancing. He described them as ornamented with a number of tails of the smaller wild beasts, with fringes, ribbons, little bells, and shells and balls, jingling and flirting about the performers legs and arms... In addition to drums, gourds, banjo-like instruments and quillpipes made from reeds strung together like panpipes, marimbas and European instruments like the violin, tamborines and triangles were also used."

Out of these gatherings, these mixings of African music and culture and European culture and America and hard times, came the greatest music America would ever know. Ragtime and Stride led to Jazz led to Boogie-woogie led to Gospel and Rhythm & Blues and Rock 'n' Roll and Zydeco. Then there was Cajun, come from the bayous by way of Canada and France. It is safe to say that virtually no form of American music in the last 150 years has not been influenced by New Orleans. Musicians from other parts called it the Big Easy because the city had so much music that it was an easy place to get a job. Let the saints go marchin' in. Let the good times roll.

Louis Armstrong grew up in New Orleans; they named the airport after him. His trumpet is in a museum there — or at least it was, before Katrina hit. The Marsalis family. Three generations of Nevilles. The great and amazing New Orleans Jazz and Heritage Festival.

"Well, I'm walkin' to New Orleans" happily sang Rock and Roll Hall of Famer Fats Domino, one of the greatest boogie and stride piano players of our time. Lost in the floodwaters for almost four days, they finally pulled him out last Thursday. Another Hall of Famer, the legendary Allen Toussaint, who wrote "Java," "Whipped Cream," "Right Place Wrong Time" and "Mother-in-Law," among so many, many others, and who produced so many great artists, was also missing during the first days of the flood. Later they found him at the Superdome. Irma Thomas, officially named by the city the "Soul Queen of New Orleans," may still be missing.

What happened to your vaunted mojo, precious city?

"Superstition is all I own/I've got black eyes and black cat bones/ My demons won't feed me/They don't need me/I feel small... Just as tough as you can make it/I can take it all... If you teach me how to take it easy/I'll take it all."[2]

Maybe we should ask the rock & roll doctor? "Patients come from Mobile to Moline from miles around/ Nagdoches to New Orleans/ In beat up old cars or in limousines/To meet the doctor of soul."[3]

Doctor, O doctor, what do we do now for our rhythm and our blues?

We mourn, baby. Now it's all we can do. We mourn.

"Whippoorwill's singing/On a soft summer breeze/ Makes me think of my baby/ I left down in New Orleans."[4]

New Orleans has always been tied to its landscape.

"The stars can see Biloxi/The stars can find their faces in the sea/We are walking in the evening by the ocean/And the storms will blow from off towards New Orleans."[5]

That one storm, that Katrina, she blew down Biloxi, she blew down the Gulf Coast, she drowned New Orleans. She sure blew.

"What has happened down here is the wind have changed... Louisiana, Louisiana/They're tryin' to wash us away/They're tryin' to wash us away."[6]

Ten thousand may be dead. They are the weak, the sick, the old, the infirm, the many, many poor. They are the ancestors of the slaves of Congo Square. Bodies floating in the muck, and all of us, some way deep in our hearts, homeless, homeless, moonlight sleeping on a midnight lake.

"Roll out your old-time carriage/Roll out your rubber-tyre hack/ There's 12 men goin' to the graveyard/but 11 comin' back."[7]

New Orleans is the spiritual home of American music. Now it's a waning stew of rot, sewage, rats and poisonous snakes.

Strong wind/Strong wind/Many dead tonight/It could be you.

(Since this piece was written, New Orleans has made a mighty struggle to come back from close to total devastation. And Irma Thomas is not only alive and well, but hard at work staging the 2006 New Orleans Jazz and Heritage Festival.)

Footnotes:

1 "Homeless" by Paul Simon and Joseph Shabalala

2. "Take it All," Chris Smither.

3. "Rock 'n' Roll Doctor," Lowell George.

4. "Magnolia," J.J. Cale.

5. "Biloxi," Jesse Winchester.

6. "Louisiana 1927," Randy Newman.

7. "Frankie and Johnny," traditional.

Afterword

Afterword

January 19, 2006

I'm An Old Woman, Hear Me Roar

(This is the only column from 2006 in the book, and I thought I might need to explain why I'm putting it in. But after reading it again, perhaps no explanation is necessary.)

In medieval times, they called older women "hags" and taught children to be afraid of us. As civilization progressed, we were called "witches" and burned at the stake. When we started agitating for our rights, we were called "feminists" and put in jail. Then we were called "women of a certain age." We were ignored, and we disappeared from the culture.

Now we're the next big thing. We're the newest trend. We're powerful. We're hot. We're happening.

I'll be 64 in a few days, and believe me, I know this isn't "late middle age" and I don't have any illusions about living to be 128. But believe me, I'm not even halfway finished with my life yet. I exercise. I dance. I write. I have a healthy sex life. I hang out with my friends. Will you still need me, will you still feed me? Looks like the answer is a big resounding "Yes."

In a Parade Magazine cover story a few weeks ago by baby boomer chronicler Gail Sheehy, women like me are "the experienced woman — open to love, sex, new dreams and spirituality and committed to revitalizing marriage... Now is her time." We're called "seasoned." We're called "spicy." And what does Sheehy think we want? Same old thing — a man.

In this month's Town & Country, we're the "Woman of the Year." "She's the most powerful consumer in America," the magazine says. "And as she starts to turn sixty this month, the affluent baby boomer is doing what she's always done —redefining herself, reshaping society and making us all think again." And what does Town & Country think we want? More expensive consumer goods.

It's funny, all those magazines, movie studios, television networks and newspapers that have been eating their young in an effort to chase 18-to-35-year-olds? It turns out they've been barking up the wrong demographic. Older women are the ones with the time and money.

According to Town & Country, approximately 42 million women are aged 40 to 60. Women solely or jointly own 87 percent of homes. Women control or influence 80 percent of consumer purchases. Boomer women are six times more likely to share responsibility for savings and investment than their mothers were. Full-time college enrollment by older women has increased 31 percent in the past decade. By 2010, 60 percent of the wealth in this country will be controlled by women.

There is no precedent for this. Both my grandmothers, for example, were done with their lives by the time they were 50, even though one lived to be 89 and the other to 94. After their children married they had nothing left to do but care for their husbands, baby-sit their grandchildren and cook a few festive holiday meals. Maybe they played cards or mah jong. To my horrified eyes, they spent 40-odd years killing time.

Me? I don't know the meaning of the word "retire." Why would I stop writing? Why would I stop prodding the world to be a better place? Why, for that matter, would I want to stop paying my bills?

None of my friends talk about retiring. They're running corporations, starting new businesses, courting clients, doing art, planning their futures.

To tell the truth, I don't know what age is. When I was 35 people told me I looked 25 and I shrugged. When I was 50, people told me I looked 35, and I still shrugged. The other day someone told me I didn't look a day over 50 and I wanted to slug her.

Role models are hard to find. Town & Country points to Diane Keaton, and while I adore her, I didn't look like her when she was Annie Hall and I don't look like her now. New York Times columnist Maureen Dowd has best platform in the country for her opinions and what does she choose to write about? Finding a man. Wimp!

Give me Shirley McLaine. Or Katharine Hepburn in "Lion in Winter." Sharp-tongued, truth-telling, unafraid-to-be-unattractive, unafraid-to-be-wrong, don't-give-a-damn-if-people-like-me, raunchy, amused, bemused women — these are women you can sink your teeth into.

Let's remember that there's a huge down side here. As Martha Raye famously said, "Old age is not for sissies." Strange things happen to your body. My heart has a murmur. I have to do pelvic floor exercises. Who knew your knuckles could rise up like mountains and eat your fingernails? My knees? Let's not even go there.

I've been to too many funerals. Friends whom I love like I love my life are struggling with cancer. I've been through so many dramas with my mother that I count a day when she says, "Everything's fine" as a day when I am allowed to breathe.

Still, there are many benefits. Through painful trial and error, I know who I am. I know what I like, whether it's in music, food, clothing, hair color or bed.

True, I've never given that Academy Award acceptance speech. Or, come to think of it, the one I wrote for the Miss America pageant when I was a hopeless teen. I may have given up hope of a Nobel Prize for Literature or that damned elusive McArthur "genius" grant, or something even more elusive to freelance writers — discretionary income.

One truth you won't read about women like me? We can drop dead at any time. Heart disease and cancer hover over us. A stroke can stop us cold. We have to live our lives at full speed now, because in actuarial terms, we've just come on death's radar screen and he's starting to stalk us. And believe me, he's even scarier than that guy our mothers warned us about when we were little — the one with the lost dog and the candy.

So welcome, popular culture, welcome to my world! I'm having a great time. What took you so long?

"Wise Words"

"We give a hoot"

WILL WRITE FOR FOOD

The Owl Publishing Project